ADVANCE PRAISE FOR *THE EVAPORATION OF SOFI SNOW*

"A smart, intriguing adventure of high-tech futuristic gaming. Mary Weber takes readers on an intergalactic journey intertwined with complicated family issues, politics, loyalty, secrets, and betrayal."

—Wendy Higgins, *New York Times* bestselling author

"Mary Weber spins a compelling tale with lyrical beauty and devious twists. *The Evaporation of Sofi Snow* is the kind of book teens and adults will devour and talk about—endlessly."

—Jonathan Maberry, *New York Times* bestselling author of *Mars One* and *Rot & Ruin*

PRAISE FOR THE STORM SIREN TRILOGY

"A perfect conclusion to this delightfully brave trilogy, *Siren's Song* will leave you eager to read whatever falls from the pen of talented author Mary Weber next."

—*USA TODAY*

"There are few things more exciting to discover than a debut novel packed with powerful storytelling and beautiful language. *Storm Siren* is one of those rarities. I'll read anything Mary Weber writes. More, please!"

—Jay Asher, *New York Times* bestselling author of *Thirteen Reasons Why*

"*Storm Siren* is a riveting tale from start to finish. Between the simmering romance, the rich and inventive fantasy world, and one seriously jaw-dropping finale, readers will clamor for the next book—and I'll be at the front of the line!"

—MARISSA MEYER, *NEW YORK TIMES* BESTSELLING AUTHOR OF *CINDER* AND THE LUNAR CHRONICLES

"Intense and intriguing. Fans of high stakes fantasy won't be able to put it down."

—C. J. REDWINE, AUTHOR OF *DEFIANCE*, FOR *STORM SIREN*

"A riveting read! Mary Weber's rich world and heartbreaking heroine had me from page one. You're going to fall in love with this love story."

—JOSEPHINE ANGELINI, INTERNATIONALLY BESTSELLING AUTHOR OF THE STARCROSSED TRILOGY, FOR *STORM SIREN*

"Elegant prose and intricate world-building twist into a breathless cyclone of a story that will constantly keep you guessing. More, please!"

—SHANNON MESSENGER, AUTHOR OF THE SKY FALL SERIES, FOR *STORM SIREN*

"A touching and empowering testament to the power of true love and of knowing who you are, *Siren's Fury* is a solid, slightly steampunky follow-up to the fantasy-driven first book that will leave you with a sigh—and a craving for the next volume in the series."

—USATODAY.COM

"If you're looking for your next fantasy series, definitely pick up The Storm Siren Trilogy. The story, the characters, and the writing style impressed me so much, and I can't wait to see what the author has in store for her readers next!"

—*LOVE AT FIRST PAGE*

"[*Siren's Song*] has many battles and explores the costs that come from fighting evil, whether external powers or the evil within the human heart. This novel will be difficult to follow for those new to the series, but for readers who have cheered Nym and Faelen on, the conclusion will be both painful and satisfying."

—*Booklist*

"This series comes to a close with an intense pursuit of good by evil, with the fate of all in the hands of teenaged Nym. She is consistently inconsistent in her feelings and fears, truly human in her characterization, and a champion accessible to readers who can identify with her insecurities."

—*RT Book Review*, 4 stars, for *Siren's Song*

"Weber's debut novel is a tour de force! A story of guts, angst, bolcranes, sword fights, and storms beyond imagining. Her heroine, a lightning-wielding young woman of immense power and a soft, questioning heart, captures you from word one and holds tight until the final line. Unwilling to let the journey go, I eagerly await Weber's (and Nym's) next adventure."

—Katherine Reay, author of *Dear Mr. Knightley*, for *Storm Siren*

"Mary Weber has created a fascinating, twisted world. *Storm Siren* sucked me in from page one—I couldn't stop reading! This is a definite must-read, the kind of book that kept me up late into the night turning the pages!"

—Lindsay Cummings, author of *The Murder Complex*

"Don't miss this one!"

—Serena Chase, USATODAY.com, for *Storm Siren*

"Readers who enjoyed Marissa Meyer's Cinder series will enjoy this fast-paced fantasy which combines an intriguing storyline with as many twists and turns as a chapter of *Game of Thrones*!"

—Dodie Owens, Editor, *School Library Journal Teen*, for *Storm Siren*

"Readers will easily find themselves captivated. The breathtaking surprise ending is nothing short of horrific, promising even more dark and bizarre adventures to come in the Storm Siren trilogy."

—*RT Book Reviews*, 4 stars

"Fantasy readers will feel at home in Weber's first novel. . . . Detailed backdrop and large cast bring vividness to the story."

—*Publishers Weekly*, for *Storm Siren*

"Weber builds a fascinating and believable fantasy world."

—*Kirkus Reviews*, for *Storm Siren*

"This adventure, in the vein of 1980s fantasy films, has readers rooting for the heroes to smite the wicked baddies. Buy where fantasy flies."

—Danielle Serra, *School Library Journal*, for *Storm Siren*

"Mary Weber's debut novel reflects an author sensitive to her audience, a stellar imagination, and a killer ability with smart and savvy prose."

—Relz Reviewz, for *Storm Siren*

"Between the beautiful words used to create this fairy-tale world, to the amazing power of the Elementals, to the aspects of slavery and war, I'd say this book is a must-read for any fantasy lover. It's powerful and will keep you turning pages faster than you thought possible. I can't believe this is Mary Weber's debut novel. Congratulations!"

—Good Choice Reading blog, for *Storm Siren*

THE EVAPORATION OF SOFI SNOW

OTHER BOOKS BY MARY WEBER

THE STORM SIREN TRILOGY

Storm Siren

Siren's Fury

Siren's Song

THE EVAPORATION OF SOFI SNOW

MARY WEBER

THOMAS NELSON
Since 1798

The Evaporation of Sofi Snow

Published in Nashville, Tennessee, by Thomas Nelson. Thomas Nelson is a registered trademark of HarperCollins Christian Publishing, Inc.

Thomas Nelson titles may be purchased in bulk for educational, business, fund-raising, or sales promotional use. For information, please e-mail SpecialMarkets@ThomasNelson.com.

Publisher's Note: This novel is a work of fiction. Names, characters, places, and incidents are either products of the author's imagination or used fictitiously. All characters are fictional, and any similarity to people living or dead is purely coincidental.

Library of Congress Cataloging-in-Publication Data

Names: Weber, Mary (Mary Christine), author
Title: The evaporation of Sofi Snow / Mary Weber.
Description: Nashville, Tennessee: Thomas Nelson, 2017. | Summary: Seventeen-year-old Sofi battles behind the scenes of Earth's Fantasy Fighting arena helping her younger brother, Shilo, and when a bomb destroys part of the arena, she dreams Shilo survives on the forbidden ice-planet.
Identifiers: LCCN 2016058194 | ISBN 9780718080907 (hardback)
Subjects: | CYAC: Brothers and sisters--Fiction. | Virtual reality--Fiction. | Extraterrestrial beings--Fiction. | Science fiction.
Classification: LCC PZ7.1.W425 Ev 2017 | DDC [Fic]--dc23 LC record available at https://lccn.loc.gov/2016058194

Printed in the United States of America

17 18 19 20 21 LSC 5 4 3 2 1

For my siblings,
Whose individuality keeps life interesting,
and loyalty keeps it intimate.
(And who secretly know I'm always right
even if you won't admit it.)

And for Robert Perez,
Who impacts the world of teens & old-ish
people far more than he'll ever know

AUTHOR'S NOTE

Dear Reader,

These pages contain a cast of characters with diverse backgrounds, heritages, strengths, and motivations—all in honor of people in my own life. In Miguel, you'll see my husband's relatives and dear friends; in Sofi and her mom you'll find homage to my grandmothers, as well as my mama, and their unwavering power as women. And in Shilo you'll get a peek at my siblings. I hope you enjoy them, pull your own strength from them, and find yourself celebrating in the immense beauty that is community and, ultimately, our inimitable humanity.

THE PLANET

THE ICE-PLANET ARRIVED IN THE DUSKY HEAT OF SUMMER TWI-light during Earth's Fourth World War. Just when the moon's jeweled fingers were slipping through that one broken slat in the barn roof that Papa always said he'd fix but never did. The same slat through which he'd pointed out Ella's favorite star to Sofi and her brother, Shilo.

As if everything within Papa's wrecked heart was trying to keep their focus off Earth's brutality by reminding them of their half sister's spot in the heavenly skies. As if their forsaken little hearts needed any reminding of where her spot—or their mother's—should be.

"Shh." Papa put a finger to his lips and beckoned Sofi over to watch the planet settle in place. "I won't let anyone harm you. See how it's moving across the moon?"

Six-year-old Sofi mimicked him to her brother, putting her own finger to her lips. "Shh. They're coming, Shi, but we won't let them harm you." To which baby Shilo spit and giggled before swatting at a firefly.

Sofi pulled his tiny hand into hers as the sinister globe stopped a good distance beyond the moon—and uncomfortably too close to Earth. To them. To their little broken-slatted barn that sat planted like a patch of sumac right on the decimated border of Old North Carolina and the rest of the starving, war-ravaged world.

"Planet Delon" the broadcasters had called it.

"The Delonese Death" was what her expatriate neighbor, Mr. Watte, was calling it.

"The blasted planet from the pit of you know where" was what Sofi had decided to call it . . .

That had been years ago.

Eleven to be exact.

But now here she was . . .

Standing in the same place, same barn—just missing a few walls—with Shilo.

Still calling it that.

A sudden rustling emerged from the overgrown bushes, causing Sofi to glance around.

"You think it's the tech buyer?" Shilo's twelve-year-old voice cracked mid whisper.

She peered into the dark. "I don't know, but if I tell you to run for the hover, you run."

He looked insulted. "And ditch? More like I'll kick whoever's sorry bu—"

A boy emerged. Two boys in fact, each barely older than she was. Clearly drugged up. Skin and bones. Like many in the populations being "overseen" by the United World Corporations.

The bigger kid held out a broken-tipped knife and Shilo slid in front of Sofi—never mind she was half-a-head taller than her brother.

Sofi scowled. She shouldn't have let him coerce her into

bringing him. Especially for the thrill of earning a few extra bucks off her old tech devices.

"We only want food," the boy said. "Just give it to us and we'll leave." He brandished his half knife again, wider, before doubling over in a coughing fit.

Sofi nudged around Shilo and reached down into her pack to pull out a sandwich. Then tossed it to them and watched the taller boy fall on it like a starved animal. The shorter boy took one bite, then slumped down and stared up at the sky. Sofi's gaze softened. Food wasn't going to fix them.

"Are you guys from out here or from the child black markets?" she asked gently, but the boy's hacking up of phlegm cut her off as he squatted by his friend, and Sofi's handheld buzzed.

"And there she is," Shilo groaned. "Tell her we're getting tattoos."

Sofi snorted and swiped the screen to see their mother's face looming.

"Sofi, where are you? What have you two done? FanFight III starts tom—"

Sofi clicked her off. *As if the woman will even be at the Games.* "Time to go," she said to Shilo, then turned toward the impoverished boys, only to find the shorter one's foggy breath had stopped and his gaze fallen still. It was fixed in a frozen stare on the ice-planet.

She tossed the bigger one the few tradable coins she had in her pocket. He took them and turned without a word.

The next moment Shilo slid his oversize hand into hers, his voice quiet. "Sofi, sometimes I hate all the death. It makes my soul tired."

1

SOFI

HER FIRST TIME AT THE FANFIGHT GAMES, SOFI LOST PART OF herself to a boy the rest of the world hailed as a god.

The second time she'd nearly lost her brother, Shilo.

The third time . . . *This time . . .*

Sofi pursed her lips and slipped her fingers over the threaded owl necklace at her throat. Then dropped it and reached back to retuck loosened strands of hair into her long, dark ponytail. The hair band snapped hard against her thumb.

This time they wouldn't lose.

She inhaled the ready room's quiet, surrounded by its bare gray walls, gray floor, and the single door, beyond which stood her team at their stations in the bare gray gaming room with its giant window overlooking the live arena. Waiting for her.

She wet her hands at the sink beside the commode, then quickly wiped away the tiny sweat beads assembled on her forehead, earned by helping Shilo defeat the arena's catacombs amid the other players fighting for the same.

She hardly glanced in the mirror. *On to the next round, girl.*

Stepping to the door, she pulled out her phone and swiped a finger over the handscreen. It brought up a pic of her and Shilo and Papa back on the same farm she'd made an unapproved visit to last night. It sat a few hundred miles away and what felt like as many years gone. She enlarged Papa's face. *Try seven years gone.*

After tapping her finger over his dead heart for good luck, she straightened her shoulders and reached for the door just as a news feed scrolled across the top of the picture.

> FanFight Games see biggest turnout in their 18-month, 3-time history. Over 10,000 in the stands & a million more watching across Earth.

The screen blinked and the news spread out to display shots of online spectators around the world. All with intent faces and hands on their teleconsoles, ready to weigh in on upcoming votes and arena changes. But what Sofi most noticed were the backgrounds behind the faces. Some elegant, some in dirt hovels or hostel rooms, and even more in tech dorms with geek equipment lining the walls. At least three-quarters were accompanied by friends or family members who'd likely taken the week off to hover over the four-day event of thirty players and their teams competing in five levels of elimination.

The news clip was trailed by a reminder. The United World Corporations cordially invite you, Sofi Snow, to attend their party this coming Saturday in celebration of the winning FanFight team.

Attend or Decline? Sofi snorted as a knock on the door brought her focus up.

"Sofi, you're about to be back on."

She tapped *Decline*, then yanked the door open. "Let's do it," she muttered to Heller as the crowd's roar blasted into her.

"FanFight! FanFight! FanFight!" Their screams rocketed through the room's acoustics.

Sliding her phone into her pocket, she nodded to Luca and the triplets at their stations. "You guys good?" Then she strode to her black gaming platform facing the window.

"Nothing to report yet," Luca said. "They just released the players into the round's final segment."

Her stomach squeezed. "And Shilo?"

"Three players ran ahead of him, but he's leading the rest."

Of course he is. Her breath eased.

Sofi pulled on her tech gloves and reopened her holoscreens from the flat computer-desk. Shilo's blip was there. *Good.* Then she peered up through the floor-to-ceiling window in front of her to the massive outdoor Colinade just as the stadium's background music took over. Big. Expansive. Thrumming waves of epic splendor to drown out the noisy crowd seated in what looked like a Roman coliseum.

It almost too perfectly matched the music—with the stadium's cascade of red sun-drenched banners rippling on the steamy breeze. Like bloody tendrils reaching from the railings of all thirteen stories in the sloped amphitheater that had been set as a symbol of glory in the middle of Old America's Manhattan electric metropolis. Sofi's bones shuddered with the rhythm, and life, and soundtrack pouring off the levels.

"Like the open mouth of a parasite," she'd once described the white marble event center. To which her brother had laughed and suggested that, if her assessment were true, what did that make her, seeing as she worked at the bottom of it?

She'd given him the glare.

But it *was* true. As true as her brother's goodness and her own icy heart. It was like some creepy nod to what the audience represented. With their glittery couches and cabana-lined levels leading upward to enormous telescreens slanted over the entire place. And beyond those, the rich blue sky. Wealthy human leeches soaking in their organic money, kissing up to the Delonese, and always suckling for more amid a resounding musical opus.

It didn't matter that today's games marked eleven years since the aliens had shown up. Sofi's mouth still turned sour at the thought of them. All human-looking and freakishly tall, with their endless secrets and expansive technology that ended Earth's Fourth War.

She sniffed.

And yet . . .

She laughed sharply—and yet here she was like all the rest of them, in her geek room glancing up through floor-to-ceiling windows to study the Delonese's private placement on level two. She inspected the curtain that covered most of their cabana, but the only glimpse she got was the hem of a sheer green dress above neat black boots.

After a second, she returned her gaze to the rest of the famous audience, only to squirm at how many faces she knew, before drifting on to where the Corp 30 entourage was seated. Looking for the umpteenth time today for one person in particular.

Her mother.

As expected, the woman's stately employees were there in her stead. Just like Papa had been when it came to raising her and Shilo. Until he wasn't, because he was dead.

Sofi felt the cool disdain creep up as the FanFight's glorious soundtrack faded and the crowd's yells reemerged to rival the entire vibrant scene surrounding them. That sky. Those fluttering banners. The 3-D scrolling advertisements mounted between each of the thirteen floors, spouting the latest tech and drugs from the thirty Corporate Nations. Because apparently sport-fighting with their finest was the perfect way to sell luxury droids and cancer creams and prepaid flights to Delon. When said flights became available.

The crowd was growing louder again, shouting down from their GMO-free custom couches and juicing cafés docked along every level within. Even with so many thousands of spectators yelling, one couldn't miss the requested specifics. The acoustics and those giant audio-fed telescreens singled out comments and attached them to zoomed-in shots of the live action in the arena below. Giving Sofi an earful of what they wanted.

"More power! More blood!"

"More *drama*."

She smirked and pulled her focus back to her vid-gamer room and the holographic screen floating between her and the giant windows overlooking the interactive arena.

"What's up with the other gamers this round?" Heller murmured. "It's like they're lazy."

Sofi didn't turn in the dark-eyed guy's direction—just nodded as both on the screen and through the glass she settled in on Shilo. Still making his way through the virtual desert in there, at the heart of where all thirteen coliseum levels were focused.

Her fingers tightened. *Keep going, bud.* He was now a good quarter klick in front of the majority and headed toward the final obstacle of this round: a metal poison wall that the three faster players had just reached.

Except—

What in heck? Before Sofi could react aloud, two of the three players had jumped onto the twenty-foot-tall wall and attempted to climb its long, needle-thin spikes. The next moment, electrical currents snaked out, throwing them to the ground just as the spikes bristled like a sea urchin and doused them with poison.

"Ah, those guys are toast." Luca swore.

The players' screams filled Sofi's headphones while the acid ate holes in their suits and skin, and their faces morphed into masks of paralyzed pain.

"Bad play, dudes," Heller said.

Two seconds later the poison hit the third kid's back as the girl tried to scramble away. *Fast. But not fast enough.* Sofi swiped up the vid on her screen and zoomed back to rewatch what precisely they'd touched on the spikes and metal.

"Okay, Shi, when you reach the wall," she said after a pause into her com, "the spikes bend and there's a current that runs through them at ten-second intervals as soon as human contact is made."

"You got all that from one replay?" Luca said.

"Soooo . . . you're saying my body is literally electrifying." Shilo shook his hip in a dorky-sexy dance move that was actually impressive, considering he was running.

"Very funny. Focus," Sofi growled as two of the triplets snickered.

"Will you listen to that crowd?" The announcer's voice suddenly came over the room's speakers. "Corp 30's player, twelve-year-old Shilo, has now taken the lead and there's nothing being done about it! Only the second day in and the audience might just be headed for boredom! With two days left, is it too early to call the winner?"

"Nice, man," Luca groaned. "Way to rile them up."

"He's right, though," one of the tech triplets said. "The other gamers are making this section too easy." She mirrored an image of aborted game-code onto Sofi's screen. "Annnd here we go." She promptly followed it with a refreshed page showing the others immediately responding to the announcer's challenge. "Now they're in a panic."

Sofi snorted and typed in a search on her virtual dashboard. "Of course they are." She knew the gamers who were playing them: Tor, Celine, and Daja, along with a host of others. She could feel them looking out from their glass windows, calculating the next few moves just like her—monitoring their players who were high-tailing it through the half-virtual, half-real desert sandscape of dunes, catacombs, and heated atmosphere in a circular game field so vast, it could only be seen in its entirety from the audience above.

Sofi swallowed and checked on Shi again. Still fine. Still safe. "Heller." She paused. Debating. Before she nodded and turned. "Strengthen the firewall."

"Oh girl, you *know* it," Heller whooped.

Biting back a smile, Sofi flipped a switch and yanked her headphones on. Turning up her scrapp music in one ear and her team's breathing in the other.

More drama, my loves?

"Shi, I'm putting codes in play."

"About time," he panted.

She cracked her middle knuckles as her gloved fingers tensed with the music's off-key voice and pulsing build.

In this enclosure of side-by-side game rooms, high enough to jut out over the arena but low enough to encircle it beneath the stadium seats, they were the maestros. Sure, the skill and energy might be the live players, just like the tech belonged to the Corporations and Delonese. But the coaching, suit abilities—minus the cloaking capacity that had been banned from the Games—and defensive maneuvering? That was the gamers.

That was Sofi.

And at age seventeen, she was the best.

She had to be. For Shilo's sake.

A few seconds later the music bass dropped and her hands vibrated to the thumping rhythm, moving the screen aside and enlarging the one next to it with her gloves. Zeroing in on the arena and players who were now 160 feet behind Shilo.

What drama *would you like, pray tell?*

"Sofi . . . ," Luca cautioned from his station beside Heller.

She grinned and typed in coding for a gust of acid wind. Followed by the calling up of the sandworms she'd created. "How about we release the beasts?"

2

MIGUEL

UP ON LEVEL THREE, MIGUEL WAS LOOKING DOWN ON THE ARENA from his lounging couch when Nadine, as she simply went by on her i-reality show, walked into his already-packed cabaña. She was wearing a yellow variation of this year's Poverty Threads—a disturbing look Corp 12's FashionBaby had come up with to show solidarity with the world's enormous homeless population. Never mind that the homeless couldn't afford them.

He'd meant to move before she arrived, blast-it. Now she was homing in on him like a meat-wasp in summer, stinger out and ready to pounce.

Getting slow, Miguel.

He chewed his lip. Served him right for having led her on at last May's Corp 24 skin-renovation premiere. As their goodwill spokesperson to the public, she possessed a gift for beautiful words as well as a penchant for prying. Something he knew a little about. And with long silky legs, gorgeous eyes, and a colorfully inked full-body tat so delicately painted, she could confidently work it. Except so could he—even down to the tattoos that stretched from midcalf up to his neck with swirls and pictographs and inked poetic words that all the ladies loved.

Miguel glanced around to summon help, but in true form

the others were busy screaming at the arena players or making handscreen vids to humblebrag about the Games to their online followers. He smiled and stuck out his tongue for one vid being made by a kid, to which the boy squealed and waved a thank-you.

Ignoring the chuckle drawing close behind him, Miguel shifted his attention to drift a dark, carefully practiced lazy eye down to the arena where the fourth of the players was about to make it to that poison wall, far ahead of the others. Hopefully he wasn't about to get acid-burned like the three before him. The announcer on the overhead television was already talking about getting in final bets and votes for FanFight favorites before tomorrow.

"Yesterday we started the Games with thirty players!" the guy shouted. "One from each of Earth's thirty Corporate Nations—and we ended with seventeen! Today, four more have already been eliminated—which begs the question, *who* will be left by this evening? Because remember this, whoever wins tomorrow goes on to the *Fantasy Five.* To fight four challengers from around the world—challengers of *your* choosing, from professional sport-stars to i-reality victors—in the *ultimate match*!"

Miguel narrowed his thick brows, pursed his mouth, and peered upward past those telescreens overhead to the rich blue sky, and to the planet just beyond the barely noticeable day-lit moon. Amazing how some things stayed the same.

The Fantasy Fighting Games had been the result of Earth's unquenchable thirst for virtual fun, violent sports, and citizen-elected superstars. Created eighteen months ago, the biannual Corporate Nations–produced FanFights had brought the world together in a way not quite seen before. And they'd emerged to the tune of heavy technology, a whole lot of Delonese influence on players' suits and arena materials, and the legal testing of any Corp-produced enhancement drugs.

Not to mention the bucketloads of blood spilled. Despite the fact no one actually died, the FanFights could be brutal—the gamers and Corporations saw to that. As if the Fourth War hadn't satiated the people enough.

Except for the kids who played and won. To them, the Games were far more than entertainment. They meant life. Relief from poverty, barely affordable medications, and a severe lack of jobs. Something Miguel was reminded of every time the tele showed the star players who'd made unbelievable *dinero* off the wallets of those cheering right now. As well as every time they squandered those millions and ended up sold in the black-market alleys.

His stomach squeezed.

The cabaña sides fluttered in the breeze just as a finger trilled down his neck, sliding to his linen-shirted chest and belly. Miguel shifted away but kept that easy smile on his face. "Eh, Nadine. What a surprise."

"Miguel." She bobbed her red curls in his face as she deftly made room for herself on the cushions beside him. The rare smell of natural almonds wafted off her tattooed skin in a fog and mixed with the cinnamon scent, thanks to the air coolers overhead. Its smell, let alone the edible nut from which it was made, was a luxury barely enjoyed anymore, even at his status.

He sniffed. "Been traveling, I see."

The strawberry hair bounced again. "Corp 24's new i-realities are set in Old Europe. The food there is so wholesome and unfettered, and"—her voice tinkled—"far more available than the teles would have one think."

Miguel pursed his lips. Corp 24's show being "reality" was

about as true as the hair color of every person on the dais. And Nadine's assessment of the natural food availability even more so. "So is that what you're in town for, then? To advertise the show?"

"I'm here for their latest unveiling." She nodded to one of the screens directly across the stadium, displaying Corp 24's logo. The large telescreen was showing an ad of a tiny, square hand device being waved over a row of six actors. It blinked green on all but the sixth—at which point it flashed *Altered* in bright red. "Our first public use takes place tomorrow. It's a prototype that tests for other-than-human genetic influences."

Miguel batted away a gnat. He'd heard rumor of the device—and assumed that by "other than human" she meant Delonese, who, aside from their generous technology and environmental assistance, kept most other aspects of their culture and race religiously to their own planet. Earth's thirty Corporate Nations had long ago taken to issuing continued reassurances of the visitors' limited human contact, but the doubt and unease of enough people had still urged the testing of such claims.

Huh. He wondered how that'd go over. He may only be a second-year ambassador, but even he knew any DNA mixing was extremely unlikely, mainly due to the immense arrogance the Delonese held regarding their genetic superiority. But what *if* any anomalies came up?

That'd be *interesante*, as his mother used to say.

The telescreen blanked, then moved on to advertise an energy invention of Corp 13's, the first new product they'd put out in years. Rumor had it they'd been too busy making back-room investments into another Corporation.

Nadine bumped a thin arm against his chest. "And you?

From the news-port pics, you've been traveling yourself." She tipped her head toward the amphitheater's section reserved for the Delonese attendees one story below. All of whom, as a delegate, he'd already schmoozed with over the past two days.

He loosened his smile and caught the eye of the girl seated on the velvet couch across from him on Claudius's left. His friend either didn't notice or didn't care she'd been flirting with Miguel all day.

Instead, Claudius just blasted Nadine with his grin. "Oh, we most definitely have."

"And?" Nadine looked from him to Miguel. "How is it?" Her tone turned breathless. "I've simply been dying to know. Are you like a god up there?"

Miguel waved nonchalantly. "Ambassadors."

"Same thing. I bet they adore you." She examined his white mid-buttoned collar with her nails. "I'd imagine they'd adore anyone close to their height—probably makes them feel more normal."

He almost smirked. It was true that the Delonese were notoriously tall—averaging close to six feet five—even the women. He suspected his own sizable frame had helped gain their respect in some weird way. Either that or his age. At nineteen he was Earth's youngest delegate, and the Delonese had their super-weird fascination with youth.

"Is it true they're hiding something?"

Miguel slipped his brown manicured hand over her fingers and turned his tone playful. "In my experience, *mi amor*, everyone's always hiding something."

The stadium vibrated with the abrupt roar of the crowd. The overhead screens focused in on two of the competitors, broadcasting the plans they were making while they ran. They were going to catch up to the Corp 30 player, who'd finally arrived at that metal wall, and crush him.

"So, have you taken anyone with you? Surely they'd allow you a friend?" Nadine moved her hand to his arm. "I mean, can you imagine the i-realities we could make? We'd be showing people what they want—the truth in the common way I can give them. Not just what the visitors want us to see." She lifted a brow at Miguel and leveled her voice. "You should take me."

He left her hand on his arm, aware that they'd suddenly gained the attention of the entire lofty cabaña—even as the flickering ads and arena drama continued in the background. He flashed the group his compelling smile and winked. "My dear lady, I think we both know I'd never get *anything* done if I took you. Am I correct, *compañeros*?"

Her laugh rang out loud against the crowd's yells and was promptly joined by the laughs of his acquaintances as the wind flapped the curtained sides harder, pushing heat up from the arena. She flipped her hair. "Always the player these days, but never the lover." She pouted. "Tell me." The electric air breezed her almond breath over him. "Who is she?"

Three seatings down, the female music-artisan Bex let loose a smooth laugh. "Who says it's a she, Nadine?"

"Ah! Ratting me out already." Miguel laughed. "I see how it is."

"Who says it's human?" muttered another, lounging on a periwinkle mat with two sisters in front of him. "Miguel's tastes are ever expanding, from what I hear."

One of the sisters let out a loud *shush* at the group, and Miguel pushed away the recollection of waking up beside her some years ago. "Did you guys see that?" she said. "There, in the arena! Look at the sand darkening behind the winning player. Something's morphing."

Miguel glanced down at the kid now kneeling in front of the wall. He was trying to figure a way through it rather than climbing over the thing from what Miguel could tell. Except headed his way was something beneath the sand, turning it an uncomfortable shade of red.

Miguel stiffened. *Ándele, kid.*

3

SOFI

THE SANDWORMS WERE ALMOST IN PLACE WHEN THE ALERT went off on Sofi's screen.

The thing blinked, then promptly spit up reactions from the gamers hiding behind the other tech-room windows surrounding the entire arena. Game-heads, as the team leaders like her were called, began sending their own codes scrolling down the side of her hologram. The ones from Corporations 2, 10, and 27 were already blocking and counterattacking her.

"Ns?" she said to the triplets.

"On it."

She watched the assailing streams of code erase her acid wind with ease.

"Winds gone," Heller announced. "And Shilo's stuck at the metal wall trying to figure a way through it."

Crud. "Okay. Watch the worms, Heller."

"Sofi—" Shilo's voice crackled.

"All we need is to get one through. And, Shi, what do *you* need, buddy?" she said into her earcom. "See if there's a way for you to touch the wall using a tool, without hitting the spikes. Luca, can you help him? I'll assist in a sec."

Her fingers typed at the holoscreen faster than she could

think. Listening to her music in one ear while pushing more code—looking for a door to wiggle the virtual worms through. The armored images she'd inflicted on the other Corp players in the catacombs had been excellent.

But these? These Heller had helped design, and they were genius. Their coding was small enough nobody had caught one sitting dormant beneath the sandscape at the arena's edge in front of her.

The announcer's voice emerged through the room speakers. "I hope you're seeing what I'm seeing! Corp 30's player is *stuck* at the final obstacle of this round. Is this the end for him?"

Sofi forced back the twitch of fear. *Focus, Sof. He'll be fine.*

"Because, let me tell you," he continued, "in the three biannual games hosted over the last eighteen months, Shilo and his sister are one of only six teams to have been with us from Game One. Is it because their mother is the CEO of Corp 30, ensuring they're always given a second chance to enter? Or because they really are *that* good? Well, friends, guess we're about to find out!"

"They're rewriting the code." Heller's voice tensed. "They're going after us."

"Almost got it."

There.

A sliver of space opened. "We're in."

Three seconds later Sofi's screen lit up with a giant blue worm erupting beneath two players in the desert sand a fair distance behind Shilo.

The crowd above exploded in pleasure. Followed by screams from the arena as the cyberworm engulfed Corp players 8 and 3. Their suits buzzed out and shut down faster than the kids' gamers could recover.

"You's my girl," Heller hollered. "Only eleven Corps left, including us."

"Well hold it, preciouses, it might just be they *are* that good!" yelled the FanFight announcer.

"No, no, no! What's he doing?" Luca said. "Your brother's using his laser on the fencing!"

Sofi shoved the worm codes to Heller's screen and enlarged Shilo's hologram to see what the tech was talking about. Shilo was indeed using his laser on the metal wall.

"Oh gad, Shi. Careful," she said into his headpiece.

His little twelve-year-old voice sputtered through. "Sof, please. I could do this in my sleep."

"Dude," Luca interrupted. "Three players are lying unconscious—so don't be dissing no caution, Shilo."

"Just keep the laser from the bases of those spikes."

She glanced at the three kids a few feet from Shilo. She'd known they'd fail from the moment they strolled into the arena yesterday amid lofty cheers at the FanFight's opening round. No matter how effective their Corp's enhancement pills were for swiftness and sharp eyesight, or how shiny their suits, something in their swagger had been too hasty. *Sloppy.* It'd said they were more enamored with the fame and financial winnings than making it to the end—and that was their mistake. Now they were stuck, waiting to be rescued—or resuscitated.

Their Corp leaders wouldn't be happy.

She shook her head and checked Shilo's desert surroundings again, confirming what the suit and cameras said—the other players were still far behind.

As if he was sensing her tension, her brother whispered, "You seen Mom?"

"No. You?"

"I think she just showed up." Shilo didn't turn his head. "First level, in the corner at my six, but can't be sure."

Sofi acknowledged him in silence. The biggest game in the second half of Corp 30's year—you'd think she'd come see her kids in it. For a moment Sofi imagined she could feel her mother through that window watching Shilo from the stands. In pride? In expectation? Ha. Did the woman have any feeling at all for her son? For either of them?

Her shoulders stiffened. Sofi had practically made it an art form to try to provoke feelings in the woman, of the negative variety mostly. The fact that she had left right after Shilo's birth for an opportunity to advance her pharmaceutical company—no matter that it was "So no other mother would lose her child in the way we lost Ella"—was barely tolerable. Shilo'd been so small. So sad. So *sick*. And Sofi terrified.

That Shilo'd been supposedly cured of his bone disease four years later, thanks to a fluke, didn't matter. What if he hadn't? What if it eventually reflared? The reality was, eighteen months ago Shilo'd been dragged into fighting in these Games by their CEO mother for the financial benefit to her Corporation. And in Sofi's mind, that risked his health each time. Not to mention his freedom and a life he wanted. The whole thing was unforgivable. And Sofi would never forget it.

Her mouth went sour. Blind irony was a bleeding witch.

She scanned the sand before her cold lungs gave in to the ache that never left no matter how many distractions she employed. "Let's just finish this round, okay, bud?"

Heller let out a shout at the same moment the audience in the stands roared fresh approval. The announcer came on. "Corp 30's worm has downed another player! This has gotta be their biggest foil of the day!"

"Ah, they killed it," Heller howled, and a second later the worm shattered into virtual blocks across Sofi's screen.

"Doesn't matter. I think we're about to have company." Sofi kept her gaze glued on Shilo. She tilted her head closer. Then frowned. The sand beneath him was changing into an odd color. She traced her finger in rhythm with her music along the ground between the remaining players and Shilo.

Her frown deepened. The dirt was now dark red and rippling. "Luca, pull power from Shilo's weapons to strengthen the body shield. Triplets, run a scan on—"

"What the heck?" Heller yelled.

Sofi choked on her spit as a decayed hand thrust up through the sand just behind her brother. "Shi?"

"I'm close, Sof."

Another hand. Then another. They were coming up everywhere.

Oh gad. "Shi, you gotta move now, buddy."

"I'm trying."

"Not good enough. Move."

"Not helping."

Sofi clenched her jaw and shoved back the fear that'd almost gotten him killed in the last FanFight Games. *Breathe and let him do it.*

"Wait a minute!" the announcer shouted. "What's with the ground beneath Corp 30? Heads, shoulders, and decayed torsos are *crawling up* through the sand!"

It was a field of freaking zombies. Sofi ignited Shilo's boots. "Okay, move now, Shi."

"A hand has him by the ankle, but *oh*, they've ignited his low-hover boots!" the announcer yelled. "And he's almost done cutting through the metal wall. It looks like it's working. Now if he can just— Oh, he's done it! He made it through to the other side!"

Shilo's face appeared beyond the wall. He scrambled forward, cutting the parawire and the power to his boots before he stopped and peered around with the realization he'd just completed the round. He was safe.

Sofi exhaled so hard she almost threw up her lungs. *Good going, Shi.*

"Dude, move!" Luca yelled.

Sofi frowned and looked back, only to realize he was barking at Corp 17's player who'd just come over a hot dune. The fans on all thirteen levels were shouting the same as one of the zombs went for him. The kid's mask and boots were torn off within seconds as the mouths and hands of more undead moved in to claw at his flesh. Sofi looked away, ill.

"Who's that guy's trainer?" Heller mumbled. "Remind me to buy him a drink and pee in it."

Suddenly the metal wall shook and the attached needles on the zomb side began spraying their poison, dissolving the undead as soon as it hit them. The announcer's voice barked again. "Not only did Corp 30 make it, but it looks like they've just cleared the path for the rest of the players. That leaves one more round to go today before the final extended level tomorrow!"

Sofi shook her head just as her screen filled with a silver flag planted in the ground. Then Shilo's sweaty face bent down and kissed the thing.

"Show-off," Sofi muttered.

"So how many players are out?"

"Twenty-one. Good work, grub."

Shilo nodded and scrambled for the arena's camouflaged wall and the tiny yellow circle painted on a section of doors.

Two seconds later Sofi's screen blinked black and the room lights flickered on. "Sofi," a male voice purred. "Your team has earned a nineteen-minute reprieve. You are no longer online to interact with the arena. Please do not interfere with the other players, nor be late, or you will be forced to forfeit."

"Yeah, yeah, yeah." Sofi yanked off the headphones, shoved the holoscreens away, and stepped off the six-inch-high black gaming platform that, aside from the other three just like it, were the only items in the gray room.

Behind her, Heller and Luca let out sighs and high fives before turning to N and N and N—the triplets who, for as long as Sofi'd known them, preferred to go by the same letter, same pink clothing, same short purple hair and wild makeup. Even Sofi couldn't tell them apart most of the time. She figured it had something to do with maintaining their autonomy in a world ruled by skycams, security cards, and every detail of one's life uploaded to the net every hour of every day.

Whatever the case, they were grinning like the online characters they gamed with in their 3:00 a.m. free time. She smiled.

"Drinks," Luca said, crushing an empty can of Rush between his hands.

Sofi shook her head. "After we check Shi's virtual supplies, let's run simulations and restock his weapons. And, N?" She glanced at the middle sister. "Run a security scan again. It felt like Shilo's suit might've been glitching. Make sure we don't have a hacker."

The girl looked amused. "Not possible." But moved to obey as Sofi turned and, letting her shoulders droop, stretched her neck beneath her thick, dark ponytail and stared out through the wide window at the arena. The last of the players was almost home.

"Nice gaming, Sof. We did good and he survived," Heller murmured over Sofi's shoulder.

She nodded, knowing what he meant. This time six months ago, at the last FanFights, they'd almost lost Shilo in a gamer's avalanche that neither had noticed until almost too late. She'd gotten too anxious—too emotional—watching Shilo almost get creamed by Corp 5's team. She hadn't caught the cracking ice above him. It would've been the Games' first-ever fatality. A reality that had only hit Sofi a few days after. At which point she'd blown up at herself, and then at her mom for placing Shilo in the games in the first place and Sofi in the position to protect or fail him. Yeah, it had been a freak occurrence, but still . . .

Sofi had cussed out her mother for it. Because unlike the other gamers and players "who competed in the sport for prestige and hope of money," she'd reminded her mom, "Shilo and I never had the choice."

Her mom cut off that phone call just like she had all the others.

"This time he'll win, Sofi. You'll see," one of the Ns said quietly.

Sofi gave her a slight smile and tucked a stray hair behind her ear as she watched the privacy wall slide down over their window, blocking their arena view.

Yes. We will win. And as winners, we'll give and then demand everything. And leave all this social drama behind.

4

MIGUEL

WOULD THE ANNOUNCER NEVER STOP? THE MAN JUST KEPT droning on.

Miguel stood and ran a hand through his rainbow-colored hair even as he kept his answers to Nadine steady. Her questioning was relentless about which celebrity was dating whom and what latest pills the Corps would be showcasing at the Fantasy Five Fights next week. Not that he'd given accurate info on that last one. Far be it for anyone to think he couldn't keep secrets.

He flourished a hand to grab the group's attention. "Well? What say you all? The *señorita* is asking who you're currently dating. Any confessors?" To which the lot of them laughed and began ratting out the others.

Perfect. He strode to the cabaña's tap station for something icy to soothe the dry itching in his throat just as the audience sent up a cheer. The last of the nine players had made it through the wall thanks to Corp 30 cleaning out the zombs in one fell swoop with that spray of poison.

The announcer spent half a second congratulating them before moving on to talk about the arena changes the audience would be voting on for the final event of the day. "Get your obstacle suggestions in before it's too late! Remember, *you* create the environment—*you* create the entertainment."

Audience-determined playing fields—they'd been a smart idea and translated into high-priced ticket sales and scenarios like that last round's catacombs and zombies.

"All right, guys," Nadine exclaimed. "This time let's vote for a nighttime safari. Or a horror theme park."

"Or a mock-up of the ice-planet," Claudius offered.

Delon? Miguel's brow shot up. Now that'd be interesting. "Or a reenactment of Dante's Inferno," he added, provoking fresh hooting.

More suggestions flew, but Miguel tuned them out, preferring to sip his drink while the curtain flaps fluttered around them. The electric-cooling air gushed over him with the scents and sounds and excitement-induced sweat nearly suffocating the space.

Which was how he missed the change in presence behind him.

The hand was in and out of his pocket before he realized, and by the time he'd swung around to look, the person was gone, and the sea of bodies typing in arena votes were those who'd been with him all day.

Miguel uttered a polite *perdón* to the group before he jumped a set of cushions and, drink in hand, strode through to the back where he stepped out to the walking aisle.

He nodded at the bodyguard. "Did anyone walk in or out of here just now?"

"I'm sorry, sir, you've a full booth today. Could you be more specific?"

No. No, he couldn't. Besides, something told him the intruder was already gone.

He glanced around a few times, then strolled back into the

cabaña. Moving to the front, he peered down at the people and levels and other crowded stalls. The audience was too thick and too focused on the scene below. And the crowd with him was too . . . normal. The person had been a ghost.

He pushed a hand through his thick, colorful hair and, frowning, reclaimed his spot just as Claudius shot him a look.

Miguel shook his head and smiled, then nodded toward the arena where three black platforms were being lowered by metal cords to hang over the empty field. Each one was six and a half feet wide by thirteen feet long, like mini landings the players would soon be dropped onto from the stadium's beams using cables attached to their suits. The metal ropes stopped and the platforms came to a halt midair to hover sixty feet above the arena's bottom.

Miguel waited for Claudius to follow his gaze before he slid his hand to his back pocket and deftly removed the scrap of paper. With two fingers he flicked it open, then closed and tucked it away inside the fold of his hand. His heart died. His breath died.

The tiny photos on the page. The words.

"Make sure the blame sits on Corp 24."

¿Qué?

He narrowed his gaze and refused to glance toward the Delonese across the stadium from him. How the individual got hold of the images, he'd no idea. But the fact that they had—the fact they existed at all—and that they showed the faces . . .

His stomach turned and his face grew warm. He peered over at Nadine. Crud, those pics were in someone's *hands*. His stomach turned and his face grew warm as he put the paper away.

The next moment the crowd around him erupted, and Miguel glanced up to the screen spanning over the white marble stadium.

"Individuals!" the announcer said. He fluttered his arms like a bird as his silver suit and white hair fluttered right along too.

The audience's chatter faded.

"A player has taken ill *off* the arena." The man waited for the booing to subside. "As you know, since his illness was not during play, his corporation is allowed a replacement. A rare occurrence indeed!"

Rare? "Not really," Miguel announced jovially on behalf of his cabaña mates, who promptly agreed. Hopefully it was something more entertaining than the last time it happened—when the poor sap who'd somehow electronically hacked his name onto the list got taken out within the first five minutes. When would they learn that mental acuity was only half the play? Good genetics, the best gamers, and a kick-tail suit of tech armor were the other.

"Corp 24's replacement will be a new entry from their Antarctix region."

His mouth went dry as the crowd jumped to their feet. Now they had his attention. He peered over at the Delonese and then at Nadine, who was looking as surprised as the rest. *Corp 24?*

"How long you think he'll last?" Claudius asked.

"Ten minutes, tops."

"Honestly? Twenty." Nadine slipped her hand onto Miguel's arm. "Poor thing."

The bets flew around him and he could practically taste the oily anticipation wafting off their skin. Miguel just studied the weight and measure of the new player the telescreens were displaying. *Why Corp 24? And who is ordering it?* The FanFight's theme music blared across the arena again, calling the rowdy stadium to silence.

"Corp leaders and highly respected Delonese friends," the

announcer said, his deep voice echoing through the Colinade's levels. "As well as friends of friends, friends of mine, and friends with *benefits*!"

The audience laughed with an intoxicated edge, and Miguel joined right in.

"We're pleased to bring you Round Number Four, with our *nine* remaining contestants. Before we lower them onto their platforms, we'll ogle them on-screen. As their vids hit the teles *above you*, please welcome back Corps 1, 13, 19, 25—"

The moving pics flashed overhead and the spectators went wild. Other than Corp 24, the players were all familiar and favorites, thanks to the media promo frenzy during the past half year. Especially the ones returning from the previous Games.

"Last but not least, Corp 30! Winner of the last round!"

Corp 30 . . .

A pic of Shilo without his face mask flicked onto the screen for the second time that day. *Man, Shilo looks like his sister.*

Miguel glanced away before anyone could notice his jaw tighten, but not soon enough to avoid his guilt flaring.

She was down there in a tech room. Black leggings, hoodie, and, if he had to guess, her beloved headphones on to tune out the world, and a quirk around her lips that could suck the breath from a person's chest and claim it as her own.

Miguel went from feeling ill about the photos in his pocket to being aware of her all over again, in his lungs, in his head, at his fingertips. The brush of excitement on those lips. The innocence in her whispers—and the kindness extended that had broken something within him he'd never been able to recover.

He swallowed and shoved a hand through his hair. *Stop, Miguel.* The feelings and remorse only got worse the longer he acknowledged them. The soft bloom of a love barely formed and the permanent reminder he'd plucked it and tossed it aside like a cad.

He pursed his lips and, shoving the memories down, forced a wide smile as the announcer finished to the hungry roar of the audience. They were ready. They wanted what the arena and Corps had to offer. They wanted the blood fights.

"Fantastic!" Nadine exclaimed.

Miguel dropped his gaze to where she was pointing in the arena, with its shifting green-screen topography beneath the floating platforms. The sides were slowly opening along the walls. The next second torrents of water were released, gushing into the giant arena and covering the already-morphing landscape.

The players' pics flashed one more time on the screen above him to the audience's now deafening cheers. Corp 24's appeared last.

"Make sure the blame sits on Corp 24."

Miguel reached for the slip of paper in his back pocket.

5

SOFI

"SOFI, I'M FINE." SHILO SMOOTHED HIS REPLACEMENT SKIN-suit around his ankles before yanking back on the fresh pair of boots. "It's just a bruise."

She scoffed. "Yeah, well, that thing almost broke your bone. So appease me and show me you can walk on it, because I'll need to recalibrate your suit if there's any issue."

He leaned on the bruised leg and spun an old-skool hip-hop move. "See? The medics got it."

She stood. And tightened her ponytail. "Okay, thank you. Now you can go."

"About time. You're going to make me look like a wimp on the vids up there if you keep analyzing."

She laughed and dropped her hands. "Um, that's kinda my job."

"Although, since I'm fine—you gotta admit those zombs were pretty cool. Did you see the way they tore through the sand?"

He'd obviously not seen the way they also tore into player 17.

"Corp teams," a smooth female voice came on. "I'm pleased to remind you the event will commence in six minutes."

Shi rapped his knuckles across her head. "Gotta go. Tell the Ns I say hi."

She whacked his arm. "Stay focused." Then left him and listened to the announcer's voice echoing down the long, roundabout hall. He was saying something about bringing in a replacement player for Corp 24.

"That guy is huge." Luca pointed him out on the vidscreen a minute later when Sofi strode into her team's room. "Where've they been keeping him?"

"That guy is hot," crooned a triplet.

Sofi smirked and eyed the telescreen's 360-degree shot of Corp 24's player. The announcer was still waxing eloquent on the guy. He was indeed hot and probably her age, seeing as he looked like a man but couldn't legally be older than seventeen to play. She bit her lip and continued assessing him. Unless someone was gaming the system.

Huh. Good for them.

"Welp, I predict another Sofi conquest. Time to hide."

"Not funny, Luca. Personal life's off-limits."

"Uh-huh." Luca lifted a brow. "Except we actually have to look at your boy toys while you're dating them. And do you see the miniscule mole on that guy's perfect face?"

Sofi snickered.

"Hey, I'm just defending our right not to be around perfection. Makes the rest of us look bad."

She shook her head and turned to see the Ns each flash her a thumbs-up as the door slid open and Heller strode in. He punched a button on the wall and plopped a round of Rushes down on a side table that shot out, his cheek piercing changing colors to match the room's lighting. "So, is Sof planning on sleeping with the new guy yet?"

"Seriously?" Sofi laughed. "I hate you all." She grabbed a

drink before their comments could gouge her lungs. She didn't need their approval.

Heller winked. "You know I'm just playin', girl."

"Corp teams," the smooth female voice came on. "I'm pleased to remind you the event will commence in 123 seconds. Please return . . ."

"Annnnd saved by the robot." Sofi swigged her drink. "Let's go." She turned to her station as the lights flickered dim and the holoscreens blinked ready for use. Sofi typed in her Corp code as they each took their places. "What've we got this round?"

The hologram popped up, and ten seconds later the wall concealing the windows slid open to reveal the arena in front of them. "Hello, Corp 30. Welcome back. You are officially relogged in."

Every one of them let out a gasp at the sight, except for Sofi. She felt her spine shift.

Are they kidding?

A freaking ocean covered the entire arena. Blue, crystal-clear water lapping from one side of the stadium basin to the other.

The floor beneath Sofi's feet shuddered, and a second later her stomach lurched as the entire level of gamer rooms began to descend. Waves rocked against the giant windows, slapping them with foam while they sank down, until all but the top three feet of glass was submerged beneath the oceanscape. She was staring into an enormous pool of water reaching higher than her head and deeper than she could swim. And so lucid she could almost see the other side.

She glanced through the three-foot slit of dry window to gauge the reaction of the crowd. They were ecstatic.

"Well, this is new," Heller breathed.

Sofi analyzed her limited view of the ocean layout. Most of it would stay hidden until the players entered each section. What she wouldn't give to study it from above.

She looked over at the Ns. "What are you seeing?"

"Most of the coding is behind firewalls, but we're making out Tasers, spearguns, and basic stuff. Although . . ." The one nearest Sofi flipped her screen around. "It looks like there might be a few animorphs being written."

Sofi's pulse quickened. That could be interesting. And fun.

"Okay, let's adjust Shi's suit to compensate for underwater electropulses and static." She peered through the patch of dry window at the nine players settling onto the black platforms hanging in midair above the water.

Every one of them was dressed in gray with only their height and weight and Corp-colored vests to differentiate them. The new Corp 24 player was wearing the telltale black and was flexing his arms before tapping a box of bioweapons attached to his thigh.

"You there, Sof?" Shilo's voice came on.

She flipped her holo onto him. He was in a yellow vest, standing on the farthest platform, already kicking off his boots in exchange for the waterproof stockings underneath. Same with the other players. *Smart.* Except unlike the others, he'd drawn a cougar head on the side of his mask in honor of their heritage.

Sofi's throat swelled. "You look imposing for a twelve-year-old chump," she whispered in his com. She couldn't be certain, but it looked like he raised his fingers in an old-skool "rock on" sign.

Nice, Shi.

Music shook the coliseum and Sofi braced. She tightened her gloves, then turned her scrapp song mix on as the countdown across the holoscreen began. *Four, three, two . . .*

"Jump," she said.

He hurtled off the platform, and Sofi's holoscreen morphed in front of her to show the players plummeting into an ocean cavern. At the same time, her entire room shifted, as if on tracks, thirty feet to the left. Shilo's winning of the last round meant her team got a choice, up-close and center window view of the cavern and—

Sharks. A whole flipping lot of them.

"N."

"Coding repellent into his suit," they responded.

"Daaaaaaang," Heller said.

The players hadn't even flinched from what she could tell. They were all heading down toward the bottom where a brass box signaled their first find. "Get there. Open it. Find what you need. Get out," she wanted to tell her brother.

But he knew what he was doing. She watched him dodge the drone sharks already homing in on the players and pretended her stomach wasn't twisting. "Add another two pounds of weight to his suit, Luca." *C'mon, bud, go quicker.*

Players 1 and 19 reached the box and yanked it open just as a spear materialized ten feet behind.

"Shi, move!"

Her brother jerked back, and the lance flew past and pierced Corp 19's leg as the others swarmed. Sofi leaned forward. "Watch the knives appearing."

Shilo ducked down to the box, then emerged from the fray just as Corp 19's blood was filling the water, drawing in the sharks. The girl pulled away, but one of the beasts grabbed her leg and yanked violently. Within seconds the player's suit ripped and more blood flooded the pool.

Sofi's stomach lurched. They'd have to drag her out fast. She could already hear an underwater portal opening for security to reach her, poor girl.

"Guess where that kid's headed," Heller muttered. "Black-market death fights in a wheelchair. She'll last a week."

Sofi's chest clenched. *Focus on Shilo.*

Heller pointed through her screen to a blinking override on Corp 24's player.

She frowned. The guy was along the underwater wall where Shi was sliding away from the frenzy. "Hey, N? Run the aud-scanner on 24." She waited, glancing up at the crowd with its new faces and different section of stands, thanks to the room having shifted over to provide her another view.

The flashing caution kept blinking on her screen. The guy was now following Shilo.

"Hey, Shi," she said into the com. "Keep an eye on the guy behind you." She typed in an extra layer of shield around him, then pulled up the Corp 24 player's specs. Nothing unusual. Perhaps he just knew staying near Shilo was his safest bet.

Something suddenly felt wrong, though. Eerie almost. Her gaze flicked up at the audience again. As if from this shifted position her perspective had shifted as well. She went to look away—until her eyes caught on *him.*

In his sassy hemp-woven cabana on level three. Rainbow hair, tattooed body, and a slight bit taller than the media preferred their celebrities lately. But what his body lacked in societal perfection, his charisma, manipulation, and fetishes made him a god where they were concerned. *Miguel.*

Even after a year and a half, she wanted to rip the smile from his beautiful brown skin and let him see how far she'd come.

That she didn't need him. Heck, how she'd ever been attracted to him was ridiculous.

"Sof," one of the triplets said. "I think we found something."

She frowned and peered back at Shilo, who suddenly let loose from the wall and swam toward the edge of her window. He was heading for a small cleft in the rock. Corps 1 and 24 followed.

"It appears someone's interfering with Corp 24's gamer."

Sofi zoomed in on the guy. "What do you mean?"

"I mean they're not in control of him or his systems at all anymore. They've been overridden."

What? She scrolled through the override code while keeping her voice steady in her brother's com. "Hey, Shilo, I need—"

The player was already on top of him. "Blasted heck, Shilo, move!"

The guy's forearm came down and swiped an electronic pulse that sent Shilo flying ten feet through the water into Sofi's window. His body slumped with a sickening thud in the earcom.

"Shilo!" She set off an EMP charge on his arm to keep the player back. *What the—? What is he doing?* The crowds were going feral with their screams.

"N! Luca!"

"On it."

Sofi pushed and pulled code across the screen, rewriting aspects of Shilo's suit to check for damage and inflict its own on the other player coming at him again. "Shilo, wake up."

His sensors blipped just as the Corp 24 player reached him. She sent off a Taser wave but the guy merely ducked. She snapped Shilo's suit with an electronic pulse, but the player twisted out of range. What the heck? Why weren't her maneuvers working? It was like the guy was expecting them.

"Heller, stop him."

A laser emerged from Shilo's wrist and shot at the guy, forcing him to dodge away as it ricocheted off the rock wall.

"Get up, Shilo," Luca grunted.

Shilo's eyes fluttered open through the televisor. *Good boy.*

As if he could sense her thoughts, her brother looked over, straight into the window.

The next second Corp 24 launched into him, wrapping his arms and legs around Shilo and dragging him until he was pressing him against the window in front of Sofi's face. The guy held Shilo in place even as Sofi caught a flash of fear in the dude's expression. It quickly morphed into determination.

Sofi punched the spikes on her brother's suit, but something jammed them.

Luca's fingers stabbed through her holo. "He's not even reacting to my sting-eels."

"Guys, we've got a bigger problem," Heller said. "He's got something on him."

Sofi's throat went numb. *The bioweapons.*

"Those biocartridges aren't just for immobilizing Shi's body . . ."

"Shield's up," N yelled. "Shilo, pull off!"

Shilo's suit rippled as Sofi launched another electronic pulse. He promptly shoved against the Corp 24 player—hard enough to gain leverage and put his feet on the guy's chest to push off. He began to swim for the water's surface.

Corp 24 grabbed Shilo's leg and pulled him back down.

"Sofi, move back from the window," Heller said.

"No! Shilo!" Luca yelled. "Sofi, that bioweapon is a type of—"

"Sofi, I said *move now*!"

6

MIGUEL

HIS MIND WAS FIXED ON THOSE PHOTOS IN HIS POCKET.

Tiny pictures moving about the paper—photos of him. With them.

Miguel locked his jaw.

Nadine peered over to catch his eye. She smiled and he automatically returned it before his gaze strayed to one of the overhead stadium telescreens that kept showing the crowd's faces. *Think, Miguel. What are they planning that would require these lengths?*

It was another few seconds before he noticed the commotion going on around him. The audience screaming down at the arena where two of the players appeared to be struggling beneath the water.

He furrowed his brow and glanced at the closest tele giving an intimate view of the Corp 24 kid attempting to drown another.

What in—? What was the guy doing?

These FanFight levels were about blood, sure. But not murder. At least not yet, and certainly not from the players.

He frowned. Was this what they wanted him to blame Corp 24 for? If it was evidence the blackmailer wanted, the Corp was clearly doing fine indicting itself on its own. The small kid being pressed against the tech station glass suddenly shoved the larger guy away. It was Sofi's brother.

He was fighting for the surface.

Miguel stepped forward—

Boom!

The entire Colinade shuddered as seawater exploded up a quarter of the stadium.

Miguel was at the railing along with Claudius and Nadine and half the others in his group who weren't tearing for the cabaña's exit. He stared down at the waves and screaming people mobbing the aisles of the Colinade. Surf crashed and gushed as the water was sucked into the chasm created by the bomb. All those tech teams and gamers . . .

Es la muerte.

Someone was smart enough to trigger the arena's giant drains as the green-screens appeared, and the crowds turned to utter chaos with people trying to get out before the whole place went down.

Except something told Miguel the Colinade wasn't going down.

The bomb hadn't been for the audience. How he knew, he couldn't say, but the explosion had been specific. Timely. It'd been intended for the players.

It had been meant for Shilo.

Sofi.

7

SOFI

SHE WAS DROWNING. DYING. SOFI KNEW THIS.

Her body groaned, pinned against a wall by the ocean crushing in while the explosive, glass-shattering, stone-breaking roar still pounded her head.

It wouldn't stop. The freezing, violent shoving of flooring and wall beams bouncing through the rooms and around her, tearing this way and that into spaces ripped open in one giant hole.

Her chest was burning. Her mouth, her throat, her arms.

She gasped and more water came in to fill her lungs. She heaved. *Oh, please, no, not this way.* Every cell in her body was alive and on fire, in heightened awareness that there was no air no air no air. Only death.

Her chest convulsed again, her body shuddered, and any thoughts or fears or consciousness faded to nothing.

Until something hit her.

Hard. Her chest and lungs were shoved down and suctioned out, and the stabbing in her neck became electricity in her veins.

Sofi rolled onto her side and choked and gagged, then threw up an ocean on the wet floor, her body practically hacking up her insides onto the boots of a med worker.

"Miss, can you hear me? Nod if you can."

She nodded. "Where's Shilo?" she tried to say, but the fire in her throat wouldn't let her.

"We'll get you out of here."

She was lifted onto a free-floating med cot, and a blanket and straps promptly zipped over her limbs, pinning her down.

With it came panic. *Where are they taking me? Where is Shilo?*

Sofi blinked at the fuzzy lights overhead. They were moving. Or she was moving. Being taken toward a med transport made for the injured and dying.

"My brother," she mouthed.

"Don't talk, miss. We've got you." The man was breathing heavy beside her cot.

"Shilo." She forced the whisper through the flames in her throat and rolled her head to the side to search through the haze and jumble of medics and wet bodies for her brother. She needed a glimpse of his face.

There were a lot of faces. Some alive. Some not so much.

Her eyes strained. Her body strained. Her elbows strained against those straps, her mind beating a refrain that something didn't make sense. She had to get away from them. Get away from this place.

"Miss, you need to calm down. You'll be fine."

No, I won't be fine! Something is wrong, fool. She jerked against the belts. "My brother, Shilo," she gasped. But no one heard.

They slowed as more med workers filled the space, and she began to lose focus again. The mental fog crept in to cloud her vision and make her wonder if any of this was real. Her body relaxed.

Which was when she spotted him.

He was on a similar med cot, hair matted down in short, damp black curls. His face turned away. His chest moved beneath the blanket. He was breathing, but it wasn't until his hand twitched that tears of relief attacked her eyes, blurring her vision.

Shilo is there. He's okay.

How he had survived she had no idea.

"Miss, I need you to lie back."

Sofi blinked and glanced up at the man. What? Then she was looking at Shilo again and the unusually tall medic adjusting the straps over his thin body, Shilo's legs sticking out past the blanket where his suit had been cut away. She frowned.

Something felt wrong again. Who was with Shilo? He didn't look like a normal medic.

In fact, he didn't look normal . . .

The man shifted Shilo's hoverbed and, in doing so, moved to face her. Sofi's lungs deflated. She jerked and tried to scream, but an ache in her neck suddenly flared, and her med cot buzzer sounded.

A mask was shoved over her nose and mouth, and then the gas turned on.

8

MIGUEL

MIGUEL AND CLAUDIUS EXITED THE COLINADE WITH THE OTHER United World Corporation delegates despite attempts to stay and provide whatever assistance the two could offer. Even with security moving them "quickly," though, it took an hour to get outside to the street—where things were just as chaotic with the blue low-floating med vehicles and high-flying enforcer hovercrafts swarming beside old civilian cars and crowds who'd come to snap vids.

"What'd you see?" voices yelled. "Is it true a bomb took out the arena?" "Were any of the Delonese hurt?"

The lights and cameras wielded by glossy-lipped reporters and titanium assistant droids lit up the late-afternoon shade, all hungry for firsthand reactions from the world's most influential. They were like piranhas attacking beneath the Manhattan skyrises and the security drones buzzing over the city.

Miguel pursed his mouth, aware that any other time he would've played to the attention, enjoyed it even and the power it yielded.

Just . . .

Not today.

Clenching his jaw, he braced against the ache that had

erupted the moment the bomb went off in front of Sofi's window, taking her out along with her brother and the others. Then he swallowed and looked away. *Focus, Miguel. Just stay alert. Stay aware.*

Pasting on a broad grin of white teeth against his dark skin for their pics, he waved *adiós* to Claudius and beckoned his men as a flash went off in his face, then another and another. Let his staff deal with the frenzy. In a few minutes the gossip mags would have an entire audience pouring outside who'd be thrilled to give their stories.

He took a visual sweep of the Corp heads and delegates being tucked into their custom hovercars and searched for signs they knew more than they should. They always did, and his talent at finding out served to keep the elite indebted or in check and him in the positions he needed.

Unfortunately, their features showed nothing more than fear or fascination as his earcom blipped. "Sir, your car's here."

Miguel flattened his lips and tapped it. "Actually, I think I'm going to walk."

Clearing his expression, he turned from the crowds and faces of the heat-stricken workers and, patting the note in his pocket, ducked for a side street just as a row of picketers flashed their bright-yellow signs with slashed-out alien heads. "Delonese mean death!" "They're going to destroy us!" "Get rid of the aliens now!" they shouted.

Until the expected posse of peacekeepers surrounded them. He shook his head. Didn't matter how many times they were arrested or silenced over the past eleven years, new ones always popped up wherever the Delonese did.

He took off toward his house—jogging quickly, then harder,

pounding the ground beneath his feet—as if doing so could ease the horror over what had just been done. Over losing her. He needed to watch the news—sift through the faces and physical tells. He needed answers as to what had happened. His chest burned. He could feel the cold pressure against his neck, like a clock's hands slipping into place, moved by loss and threat before the toll of revelation sounded.

"Make sure the blame sits on Corp 24."

A wadded-up piece of trash skittered down the shadowed street as a group of twentysomethings strode toward him, loudly chattering about the scene they were headed to, until one glanced over and saw Miguel. The man paused, mouth open, then nudged his friends. "You *guys*. Miguel."

"Get a selfie," his friend said in hushed excitement.

"Buenas noches." Miguel nodded and kept jogging as the sound of their cameras clicking followed him—forcing his thoughts away from Sofi and onto the fact that this whole thing would make a lot more sense if Corp 24 hadn't already sealed their own guilt.

Which clearly meant it hadn't been Corp 24.

His mind flashed to the Delonese. The ones who'd left through their private exit moments after the explosion. What was their part in this? Or anyone's, for that matter—the anarchists, terrorists, or Corp leaders even, let alone every other official he could imagine hatching such a plan. He sped through suggestions of the disenfranchised and extremists he knew while enforcer hovercrafts whizzed by far overhead.

The question wasn't just who could've done it or who'd want to.

But *why*?

The scent of lilacs welcomed him to his street where the

trees effectively covered the sterile smell Manhattan had become known for. The housing rows shimmered in the afternoon light—silver doors, glossy windows, giant brick steps covering weapon detectors and ID sensors and cameras at every single angle.

For the short time between World War III and the Fourth War, most people had understood such measures. Some even welcomed the idea of being "living" cameras and had taken to wearing virtual contacts enabling interweb access at the blink of an eye. Until the Fourth War hit the horizon and realization dawned of how easily such devices were hacked—and overnight they became a threat rather than protection. Now such things were eyed with suspicion by both the average Earth citizen and the Corporations who utilized them.

Miguel's street had exactly 257 of those kinds of cameras.

One of his security details was swarming the place, and the second he got within view, their hands went to their earcoms, reporting him safe. When he reached his gate, they ushered him up the steps and watched the ID sensor silently scan him to ensure Miguel was, in fact, himself.

Then they followed him in.

He left the team on the first floor and took the elevator to the sixth. And promptly flicked the tele on before rolling up his sleeves and clicking a security button beneath the oversize cherrywood desk. It would run interference with vids, bugs, or other devices because he despised being watched. And yes, he knew the irony in that.

Retrieving the note from his pocket, he spread it out on the table to study the font, the letters, the smell. He studied how it had been folded and the pictures. What angle they'd been taken from. What dates. And from how far away.

He scowled.

At least the individual had been merciful and used paper rather than the web. Although such care only meant they were more serious.

It meant they knew he'd comply.

"Today's attacks seemed to target only a few of the players—"

Miguel looked up. The news tele was flashing pics of the gamers and techs. They showed the Corp 24 murderer, then one of the gamers—Tor—he thought, then Shilo . . .

"Investigations are under way, but it's believed whoever did this had motives other than simply disrupting the Games."

His shoulders tightened, and he turned to the windows to gaze out at the Colinade seven blocks away where the smoke was dispersing.

A second later he pressed his earcom. "Call Vicero."

9

SOFI

SOFI SHIFTED IN HER SLEEP AS HER MIND FLICKERED THROUGH **the blackness before locking down inside a dream of her brother.**

"Sofi?"

"Shh, fool," a boy mumbled.

Shilo frowned and tried to retort but couldn't concentrate due to the icy rod stabbing his side in the dim. He shifted against the cargo wall that was freezing and vibrating with the low thrum of a huge engine. It felt like they were flying. And there was the cold . . . His teeth chattered as the condensation collecting on his skin stung him with the memory of what happened.

The noise.

The medic traders. They'd taken him.

His spine shivered. Taken him where?

Shilo peered through the pitch black and visualized the huddle of bodies crowded around. "Hey," he whispered at the boy who'd shushed him. "Where we at?"

"Told you to hush, didn't I? You wanna get us killed? Besides, you already asked earlier and I still don't know anything."

Earlier?

Shilo sucked in his aching tummy and tried to listen to

those engines. To whatever was going on beyond the cargo space. After a minute he gave up—maybe he didn't want to know where they were going.

Or what would happen once they got there.

Sofi drifted and fought through the dark. Struggling to surface from the nightmare that had settled in. Something about Shilo, cold in a cargo hold and wondering where he was being taken.

The images were like a fog now, curling and dancing, reaching from the recesses to send wispy tendrils down to her lungs. She gasped and tried to open her eyes. *A dream.*

It's just another nightmare, Sofi.

She slid her hand to her throat. Her necklace was still there, knotted tight, its owl loops and feathers bringing the comfort it always did from Shilo. Catching the remnants of her nighttime fears.

She frowned.

Shilo. She'd heard him in her dream—heard his voice and fragility. She'd seen what he'd seen and felt what he'd felt—the cold and metal and condensation—so distinct it was real.

It was beyond real.

Moving her cheek against a pillow, Sofi noticed the voices in the hall. They'd started up a few minutes ago—or maybe forever—she couldn't remember. Talking. Arguing. One was her mother's corporate vice president, Ms. Gaines, aka a company shark.

What was she doing here? Sofi waited as the woman's tone grew clear enough to form words that formed sentences that Sofi's thoughts could latch onto.

"I don't care. Ms. Snow's health is not the concern, our company is. Wake her and question her."

"I'm merely suggesting a bit of time might render her more useful. The girl impossibly survived and her brother is . . ."

Sofi's chest caught and her eyes flew open to the overhead halogen lights blasting down on her. They were in Corp 30's headquarters—in the med sector with its distinct chemical smell. She waited for the man in the hall to finish, but he left his statement hanging in a phantom answer. *Finish the sentence, dude. My brother is what?*

Silence.

She glanced at the slightly ajar door where a sliver of corridor was showing, but the only thing visible was the back of Ms. Gaines's silver head. *Breathe, Sofi. Think.* She'd seen Shilo at the Colinade. He'd been injured but alive. He'd even moved—and with technology nowadays, the only way a person of their status usually stayed dead was if they were found that way. So why was the man hesitant to wake her? What was it that would upset her?

The Delonese medic's face flashed through her mind.

The Delonese.

Her stomach twisted. *What if?*

"We've not found him yet," the man's voice murmured. "We're still looking."

Oh gad, was Shilo *missing*? Had he been taken by that Delonese medic? What if it was something like in her dream just now?

She needed a handscreen to search for him. Her gaze narrowed as she peered around the room at the windowless paisley-papered walls, door, and a med machine a few feet away with an IV tube running to her neck. And not a computer or tele in sight.

"What of the others?" Ms. Gaines's voice emerged again.

"Ms. Snow's team, along with gamers 2, 24, and 10 and a couple of their techs—all dead."

Sofi blinked and felt her skin ice over. *Heller? Luca? The Ns?*

"And our Corp team's bodies? The gear and equipment?"

"Destroyed. All of it."

"But what of Shilo's items—his suit and . . . *tech* he'd been using?"

The male voice hesitated. "They were with Shilo."

"All the more reason to begin questioning Sofi immediately," Ms. Gaines said. "I want to know everything she knows, saw, and anyone she could've told."

"And the girl's mother?"

"CEO Inola is not to be bothered. You report directly to me, or I will see to it you are removed for good. And, Eli? The moment I say you're finished with that girl, you delete every trace. Is that clear? Every. Trace."

"If her mother asks?"

"If her mother asks, her daughter is already dead."

Sofi choked. *What?*

The door started to open. She clamped her eyes shut. She had to get out of here. She had to save herself and then go find her brother.

Footsteps.

The faint scent of musky hair cream signaled a man was walking toward the bed. He detached the IV from her neck, then yanked the sheet off her body before walking out.

"Get the sterile room ready," he said to someone in the hall. "Then prep her."

10

MIGUEL

"I NEED NAMES, VIC." MIGUEL TAPPED THE BLACKMAIL NOTE while he spoke to the female face looming through his handscreen. "Who's alive, who's dead, and who knew about the bomb? Also, I need all the info on the Corp 24 kid—his past and who had access to him in the last year. Plus, the bomb's design and who could've made it."

The girl's face laughed. "Whoa, *man*, you know I always get your stuff, but it's gonna take time."

Miguel snorted. "Seriously? I could ask five others for the same stats and have it by seven tonight."

The auburn-haired, blue-eyed image lifted her hands as if hurt. "Yeah, but would they be as charming as me? No. Besides, you know I'm good for it."

Miguel stared at her. She was jittery today. Probably still annoyed at the dude who'd tried to hack her last week. But she was right—she was more than good for it. She was the best. A virtual wealth of resources. "Okay, just see what you can get me. I'll pay double."

"Double? Wow. In that case, give me an hour."

Miguel waved as if to say, "Yeah, fine." "Oh, and, Vic? I'm

going to need all the pertinent vids that were taken in the arena today."

"Audience vids? Easy-peasy. Want me to shoot them to the regular box?"

"That'd be great, actually. And, Vic? *Gracias.* I owe you."

"Yeah, you do." She pretended to take a swig of coffee. "Sayonara."

Miguel clicked off the com and ran his hands over his face. Rubbing the strain from his eyes and skin. What a freaking mess.

The door chimed. "Ambassador Claudius, sir," a robo-voice said.

"Let him up." Miguel left the note on the table and turned to face the room's large tele just as his handscreen buzzed again with a text encoded from the UWC.

He swiped his thumbprint and waited for the cipher to unravel.

United World Corp meeting 9pm. Level four. Your attendance mandatory.

A World Corp meeting tonight? He raised a brow and scrolled over to source the address.

The fact it was happening was a given. They needed to deal with the situation as a united group, or at least appear to do so. That they were calling for it this evening rather than tomorrow, though—before everything was accounted for and safety measures taken—was more than a little odd. People were still in reaction, especially those most affected.

A few seconds of digging brought up the text's origin. He paused.

Corp 30 was calling it.

He frowned and shut the screen down before other messages

could erupt from news releases and friends who'd been flooding his in-box for the scoop.

"Well, you look ready for a snooze fest."

Miguel turned to find Claudius standing in the living room, wearing what appeared to be a cougar-print bodysuit and a fake dolphin coat from next season's "Save the Mammals" line.

Miguel raised a brow.

"I mean your face—" Claudius waved a hand at his cheeks. "It's all tense and pale. Well, tan really, but pale compared to your usual. You look stressed or in need of food."

"Gracias. I think." Miguel eyed the bodysuit. "I assume you didn't get the text about tonight's meeting."

"Just got it on your elevator. I went home to feed the parrot real fast and change so you and I could go out, but . . ." The twenty-four-year-old, Euro-born, three-year ambassador looked down at his clothes and shrugged before he walked over to the wall drink dispenser and helped himself to a glass of manufactured club ice. "You know *why* they're calling the meeting tonight?"

"Corp 30 requested it."

Claudius spun around, his blond hair hardly moving from its gelled peak. "Oh." He stared. "Man, I'm sorry." His loss for words about mimicked Miguel's. He opened his mouth. Shut it. Finally. "Good gad, that'll be a disaster. That woman will be out for blood. Who in their right mind agreed?"

"The other Corporations, from what I can tell. It'd be worse if they didn't. It'd look insensitive at best. At worst, suspicious."

His friend groaned and wandered to the desk beneath the giant window. "Such a shame, seeing as I was coming by to drag you out. Figured you'd need some fun in light of the whole . . .

thing." His gaze extended sympathy to Miguel. "And clearly I— *Hello*."

He halted in mid-lift of his drink and leaned over the note the blackmailer had given Miguel. Claudius's expression widened, then darkened, and he let out a low whistle before looking up. "That's not pretty."

Miguel snorted. "Agreed."

"Any idea who it's from?"

Miguel shook his head. "They slipped it to me right before the explosion."

"So, what are we going to do? I mean, besides find the fool."

Miguel cracked his neck. "I've got Vic running traces."

"But if they leak it? Miguel, you'll be finished." Claudius's voice lowered. "As will the rest of us."

"I know."

Claudius took a sip of his drink and stared at him. "I've no idea what they've got against Corp 24, but if it comes down to one or the other, you'll need to pin Corp 24 to the wall for all our sakes."

"Except that doesn't stop them from using it in the future."

"Okay, but what about tonight? You think they'll bring it up at the meeting?"

Miguel rubbed his forehead. "I think they're playing a bigger game."

His friend coughed and set down his drink. "A game in which they're trying to make you their pawn."

Miguel looked away and locked eyes on the tele, staring at the screen without seeing it—until at some point he became aware the news was plastering up pics of Sofi and her brother along with their childhood home, school, dead half sister, and everything else the interweb had pulled up in the past hour.

"Shilo and Sofi's father, a Professor Snow from Old Canada, married CEO Inola just before her corporation took off," the tele narrator said. "With the birth of their two children, followed by the loss of her firstborn from a previous relationship, some say CEO Inola disappeared more into her work—leaving her husband to manage the farm and kids. And once the professor died of a heart attack, she never pulled back out of it—leaving ten-year-old Sofi to raise her young brother. Tragically, those lives ended all too soon today."

Miguel's gaze hardened and his lungs burned. The next moment his handscreen buzzed. He looked over. "Open."

Vicero's face appeared. "Okay—the audience vids I'm still filtering, but the names, I got. You ready?"

"Vicero, my *lady*. Hello, you beautiful being."

Vic furrowed her virtual brow and turned until she saw Claudius. Her gaze narrowed. "Um, nice man-suit. Your mom know you're out like that?"

"Whatever. My mom would've *begged* me to wear this suit. I mean, you know—if she hadn't died in a fiery car accident when I was nine."

"Looking at it makes *me* want to die in a fiery car accident."

Miguel waved a hand between them, his mood prickling. "Okay, enough flirting with the AI. What do you have, Vic?"

"Hey, just cuz I'm Artificial Intelligence doesn't mean I don't enjoy some attention." The AI patted her auburn hair self-conscious-like and smiled at Claudius.

"It's because of the suit, isn't it?" Claudius mouthed at her. "You think it's hot." Then aloud, "See, Miguel? She thinks it's hot."

The AI rolled her virtual eyes, but the blush that lit up her cheeks looked exceptionally real.

Miguel glared. "Vicero, focus."

"He hasn't eaten recently," Claudius said by way of explanation.

"Ah, explains it." Vic nodded. "Right. So I, uh, got some stuff for you. Still running scans, but here's the initial gist. Corp players 1 and 24, gamers 2, 24, and 10 and their techs are all dead. My sources are also saying techs from Corp 30 are goners as well, although there seems to be some confusion, especially the three Ns—which may have to do with the fact they're identical."

"And Corp 30's head gamer?"

The AI pretended to shuffle virtual notes. "Oh, right. Her. She's alive. Well, at least for now."

The air left the room. Left his lungs. Left any aspect of its natural state, sending Miguel's chest imploding. His gaze flickered. *¿Qué?* He leaned in. "Did you just say Sofi's alive?"

"Yep, suave man, she is."

The inhale he'd been holding came out in a rush of relief and unreasonable ache. He blinked and refused to acknowledge the heat tightening his throat. "*How?* Where? Is she hurt? Wait, what do you mean 'for now'?"

"I mean someone's taken a vested interest in the fact that, for all intents and purposes, the explosion should've killed her. But super weird—it didn't. And from what I can tell, they might be planning to fix that or something. And the only way I know this is because I"—she smiled proud-like at both of them—"tapped into Corp 30's sound system and ran word patterns over the voices until I found people talking about Sofi. At least until they found my bugs and kicked me out."

Miguel whistled. Even he was impressed.

"Also, another bizarro thing—the firewalls surrounding all online info regarding Sofi, Shilo, and a few others are tight." Vic paused and fastened her stare meaningfully on him. "Like tighter than they should be, if you get me. My comp-worms are on it, and I'll let you know. But in the meantime, there seem to be some weird vibes coming off the Corp's systems."

"Which systems?"

"Still tracing 'em."

"Okay, and what about Shilo?"

"Again with the firewalls being hindering or glitchy. Because it's like all trace of him after four thirty this afternoon went missing. And the only vocal convos I heard regarding him were that there seems to be a lot of confusion as to what happened to him."

Miguel raised his brow. Missing?

"Oh, and your Corp 24 player who was actually a murderer and bombed half the arena? His file's been faked, although only a few like me could recognize it." Vic batted an eye at Claudius, which looked weird but Miguel didn't have the patience to tell her people usually bat both lids when flirting. "And even fewer could've pulled it off."

"So was the player even a legitimate replacement?"

"No."

No surprise there. "Then who put him in the FanFight?"

Vic's mouth went still even as her hands fidgeted. "That's the other thing. The, uh, initial code points to your girl as having set him up."

Miguel froze. "*¿Qué?*"

"You know. The gamer chick, Sofi? It looks like she was the person controlling the bomber dude right before he went *boom*."

11

SOFI

SOFI WAITED FOR THE DOOR TO CLOSE BEFORE KICKING THE sheet off her ankles. She coughed and brushed the dark hair that'd loosened from its ponytail from her eyes. *Fool.* If the man had known anything of her med history and drug tolerance, he never would've unplugged that IV. Rather, he would've checked to ensure the fluid bag hadn't run out five minutes ago.

Sliding hands beneath the barely there medical gown, she felt down her smooth arms, torso, and legs. From the sensitivity in a few ribs and a shin, those had likely been broken and would've been repaired in the hover. *Thank you, medics.*

Now for Shilo.

Climbing off the tall bed, she strode to the IV machine, yanked the tube from its box, and coiled it loosely around both hands, then popped open the machine's lid and snapped off the thin metal prong used to transmit fluid before she spun toward the exit.

The door handle turned with ease. She edged the thick titanium open and held her breath so as not to alert the guard. *Cripe.* He was standing right there, his back to her, looking at his handscreen.

Sofi flattened her lips. *Sorry, pal.*

In one swift motion she slipped the IV tubing over the man's head and pulled it across his neck like a garrote, then yanked him backward into the room.

His noises were soft, muted—full of awkward choking and feet flailing as his hands attempted to shred the brown skin from her arms. She kept her face passive and pulled the tube tighter. She'd watched the Corp trainers coach Shilo often enough to know how it went—she'd even let him practice on her wrist until he got it right.

The guard's body writhed and twisted, his fingers drawing blood before grasping and nearly tearing off her gown, until . . .

He slowed.

Then slumped at her feet.

Sofi calmed her thick breathing and checked his pulse—not dead, but he'd be out for a while. Tucking her stray hair behind her ears, she re-coiled the tubing around one arm and moved to the door to peer down the hall. More doors. Red. Numbered. All sterile looking against white walls, white floors, and white ceilings. All shut.

She closed hers and headed toward the end of the hall where a lone elevator faced a tiny window through which shafts of nighttime city lights were splaying out across the tile, giving the eerie sense of warmth.

"Hey! You! Stop!"

Crud. Sofi tore for the elevator as a female guard rounded the hall from the opposite end.

"Patient Snow is in the hall," the lady yelled. "I repeat, in the hall headed for the elevator on floor fourteen." From the sound of the heavy boots, the woman was plowing full speed for her.

Sofi dropped to her knees in front of the elevator's card-swipe box and pried the base open using the metal prong. The footsteps were pounding closer. It took two seconds to find the wires and pull them to shove one against the card reader's wiring, igniting sparks that flew up in Sofi's face as the door slid open. Sofi jumped in, then shoved her foot against the sealant button just as the guard reached her. The woman's hands nearly got crunched as the heavy metal shut and clicked.

Sofi exhaled. *So far so good. At least I'm in the elevator.*

Now for the hard part. She glanced up at where the cameras should be—and five seconds later hoisted her body to balance on the elevator's silver handrails to reach them while the guard pounded on the door from the outside.

Using the prong again, she pried away the metal around the first camera and yanked it out, wires still attached.

"Patient Snow," the elevator speaker said. "You are in violation of your clearance. Please return to your room."

Not likely.

She tore the head off the camera's lens and smashed its glass face against the ceiling before proceeding to do the same with the others. Once finished, she knelt at the elevator's control panel and went to work accessing the simple computer behind it. It wasn't much, but it was connected.

Using the internal drive, she rewired the thing to give her control, then pressed level three. The elevator shifted and began its descent. Rather slowly, compared to most modern lifts—giving Sofi the chance to exhale and rock back on her heels. Until a moment later when an old-timey saxophone song clicked on over the speakers and began playing what Shilo liked to refer to as "old people's lovemaking music."

Sofi winced. *Good grief, Mother, get with the century.*

While the eternity of crooning sax continued, Sofi uncoiled

the plastic tube from her wrist and tied it around her waist to keep the black med gown she was wearing in place. At least without gaping holes. She hoped.

Mercifully, eventually, the elevator arrived at the third floor. With a soft ding its door opened and Sofi stepped out into the unnaturally bright, familiar hall and ignored the startled faces suddenly looking down the corridor at her.

She strode past two rooms to the "lab," a patchouli-scented office nicknamed by Shilo and her years ago, when Mom had forced them to start "visiting" a Corp 30 therapist. Whether to tame Sofi's behavior or convince them their mother's actions were in Shilo's best interest, Sofi'd never been sure. But they'd had one too many extended visits here—to "monitor her level of crazy," the doctor had actually stated. Although in truth, they felt less like "monitored therapy" and more like a study of her tech skills and physical health. Like a small rat under a microscope.

Usually in the wake of her rebelling about something.

She despised it.

After tugging open the door, she walked in to find Dr. Yate not there. *Thank heck.* Sofi dead-bolted the door behind her before heading for the inner glass office just as the startled voices in the hall turned to angry tones and running feet. "Which way?" she heard a guard say.

"Room 33."

"Sofi," Ms. Gaines called. "Open up, dear. We want to talk with you."

Dr. Yate's inner office was locked. Sofi grabbed the metal chair from behind a desk and threw it against the glass, only to have it bounce off and nearly smack her in the arm as the door to the hall behind her shrieked from something hitting it.

Come on, Sof.

She tried the chair again. Nothing.

Feeling around the doorjamb, she searched for a way to pry open the locking mechanism. Nothing. The next moment a sound crinkled close to her ear. She twitched a finger to brush the noise away and proceeded to pick up the chair again. Maybe if she held it while hitting the glass rather than throwing it . . .

"Sofi," a voice said loud and clear beside her.

She jumped and spun around just as a gunshot rang out. Were they seriously shooting at the door?

Cripe. Not just shooting. They'd put a hole in it.

You've got to be kidding. She ducked, then waited a half second before shaking her hair away from her ear and turning to hit the glass again. If only her doctor kept a computer out here, she could open the room with their systems. Which was exactly why he didn't keep one, he'd once cheerily informed her.

It now made sense why all the Corp's main doors were still in the Dark Ages with old-fashioned lock-and-key systems—hence the shooting out of the dead bolt behind her. Advancements in technology like the door in front of her had forced them to re-embrace the old security for a reason. She'd have to remember to thank her mother's paranoia and Sofi's own helpful motivation in that area. Ahem.

"Sofi, you there?"

She slowed. Frowned. The air next to her ear crackled again.

"Sofi, *psst.*"

She looked around. *Heller?*

"Please say yes if you are."

She reached for her ear. Her com from the arena was still in. How in—? "Heller," she breathed. "You're alive? Where are you?"

"Mom's Basement. You?"

"What? I'm in Corp 30. I—"

"I know. Are you still in the elevator?"

"No, third floor in the office that leads to the fire escape. The door's locked and the idiots are shooting through the one behind me."

"Two seconds."

She could hear tapping in her ear as another bullet pierced the lock. She dropped to her knees and kept her head low. "Heller, they're through—I gotta go *now*."

"Okay, got it. Go, go, go!" Dr. Yate's glass office door in front of her clicked and slid open.

"Heller, remind me to hug you." She rolled through the doorway and scrambled toward the dark window. Vaguely aware that behind her the glass door slid shut again even as the outer metal one exploded all over the room.

Heller cleared his throat in Sofi's earcom as the men entered through the smoke. "You've got about seventy seconds. I shut down the cameras on the outside of the building and sealed all the ground-floor doors, but it's going to last maybe a minute before they reactivate them."

"Got it." She was already climbing out the window and onto the sleek emergency ladder. The thing shuddered with her weight. With a single inhale, she kicked it and hung on as the ladder shot down through the dim night air to the ground, then jerked to a stop just before she hit the damp pavement.

Without glancing up, she ran for the yellow-lit parking lot across the street, clenching and unclenching her hands to ease the shocking pain from the ladder. "I'm out," she breathed to Heller. "Heading into the parking garage."

"I'll find you a ride."

"No need, I got it." She eyed one of the pay-by-mileage public transport hovers three rows down. "But do you have any credits on you?"

"Yeah, why?"

Sofi opened the car door, ducked into the seat, and promptly looked at the vehicle's computer interface before tapping the screen and swiping through options. Twenty seconds later she'd accessed the Darknet via a backdoor hub and typed in the first free code she found. The car started as she disengaged the autopilot.

Heller's tone tightened. "I don't know what the heck you're doing, but they're out of the building and headed straight for you. Move."

"I'm searching for the— Hold on, got it." She disengaged the hover's tracking device just as shouting echoed through the car lot. "Never mind about the credits. Stay put, and I'll find you."

Slumping in the seat, she flipped on a funk-pop music stream Shilo would've approved of and pressed the *Drive* button to back out of the parking space while the Corp's private soldiers ran for her car. One grabbed the rear hood and pounded the metal with his hand while lifting a gun in the other. He yelled something.

Sofi shoved the hover into Forward, then jerked her head down as a gunshot took out her back window along with a portion of the front. *Crud.* She bobbed and punched in the accelerator and left the soldier behind in a rush to the far exit, where she veered out onto the busy nighttime street.

With one last look in the mirror at the men running for their vehicles, Sofi merged her way into the center of downtown traffic and let the zooming cars overtake her. Until the *beat, beat,*

beat of her pulse gradually slowed as the false sense of anonymity surrounded her. And eventually, her gut climbed down from her throat—the city lights and hovercars and buildings engulfing her into their arms.

Twenty seconds later she blinked and refocused. They'd be coming for her. The hovertracking might be disabled, but the shattered windows would be all over the soldiers' screens within minutes and they'd return her to whatever interrogation they'd planned, to extract information she didn't have.

Then they'd cause her to disappear, with no one but Heller the wiser. And a brother who needed her now more than ever.

She swallowed.

"Heya, Sof. You still alive?"

"I'm here. Just need a minute."

"Cool."

Ignoring his relief, she used one hand to pull up the hover's camera and centered it on herself. "Okay, I'm sending you a vid to upload on the public wave. It'll come through in a few moments."

Tapping the *Record* button, Sofi cleared her throat and enlarged the camera's time stamp, then dialed a backdoor addy she and her team kept for private contact and synced it to the screen.

She swallowed and looked at the lens. "Good evening, folks." She smiled and peered up at the traffic slowing ahead. "This is Sofi Snow, daughter of CEO Inola from Corp 30. It's 8:59 on the second night of the FanFight Games, and this recording is following the terrible explosion today in the arena." She paused. *So far so good.*

"I just wanted to tell y'all I'm alive and currently searching for my brother, whom I believe to also be alive."

She could say that without endangering him, right? She had

no proof, but it might make whoever had him think twice. *If* they had him.

"So here's the thing . . ." She stared at the camera again. "If anyone listening was involved in the attack or with our attempted murder, you should know I will find you. I'm already aware of who you are. And for the rest of you"—she winked—"well, enjoy."

Leaving the vid rolling, she swerved the lens to focus for a brief second on the smashed window behind her, then shifted it to focus on the empty brown passenger seat. And turned her funk-pop music up to blaring, in honor of Shilo and her gaming team.

12

MIGUEL

BY THE TIME EARTH'S WORLD WAR III HAD ERUPTED, EVERYONE knew it was coming. Controlled oil shortages and energy crises, a declining environment, and corruption at the highest levels had already set them on a collision course. That, along with twenty-four-hour hate-speech spewed by one offended online group or another, and a new breed of terrorism exploded. As did opinions on whom to blame among a vicious and disheartened population of 7.3 billion people.

The war lasted just over three years.

The resulting meltdown, however, took out one-half of Earth's inhabitants and even more of its resources—until what survived was far more broken and barren than it had been even at the war's end. With the nuclear holocaust's radiation and chemicals infecting the devastated environment, Earth had effectively settled on a course for a dystopian society as individuals and governments fell victim to isolation and disease.

Which was when the private Corporations emerged.

One by one they scrambled to scrape up the last of the brightest scientists and best tech, and re–set up shop, even while the original governments mounted a weak stand against them.

Thus, the Fourth War.

In comparison, it was a blip on the radar due to the emergence of the Delonese planet and the offer of help from their race of rather tall humanoids who'd wormholed from light-years away in search of similar beings. How they'd done it—shot their planet through a wrinkle in time into a perfect orbiting position beyond the moon—no one understood. And the Delonese weren't interested in explaining, especially once the questions turned to demands.

Unfortunately for Old Earth's regime, the introduction of Delon's technology was sufficient confirmation that a new system was indeed needed. The people of Earth wanted healers instead of politicians. Social business systems instead of governments. Within two years, new country lines were drawn, new statespeople set in play, and a new world emerged, united by those who owned the cities and products that people needed for survival.

And overnight, the thirty strongest Corporations—which produced the medicine, technology, media, and food necessary for continued existence—became the new ruling powers. All while the Delonese interacted behind the scenes, providing assistance far beyond Earth's means. Taking the world from a ravaged state to a synthetically recovered wonder.

That was the reality a little less than a decade ago.

Now, seven years later, at the age of nineteen, Miguel was entering his third year as a commissioned ambassador, and the Delonese were trusted allies. Or supposed allies. As were the United World Corp members whom Miguel was currently surrounded by as he stood inside a windowless, wood-paneled room at the International UWC Building.

He cleared his throat and took a breath before he turned to

scan the Session Hall and his fellow political players. Including Claudius, who was striding through the refreshment doorway.

"Miguel! How are you?" His earcom translated Ambassador Danya's greeting as a woman matching his six-feet-six height approached and extended a graceful hand.

"Danya." He grinned and leaned in to kiss her cheek, ignoring her offered gesture before adding loudly, "How are Salim and the kids? How's the South Middle East region?"

Ambassador Danya laughed and pulled back with a look that said Miguel's lack of decorum was only allowed because it was him. "It's the East—busy as always." She dropped her voice. "Two of the five Corps just finished a bidding war over a start-up that's got a new growth hormone. Very messy. The UW even sent in their peacekeepers over it. Although I hear that's nothing to the ten European Corps constantly encroaching on each other's citizens and territory."

Without a pause she seamlessly switched to Miguel's earlier loud volume. "But enough of that, because the kids are growing! Little girl just turned three and boy is five, and the adoption for both was just finalized. And Salim is brilliant as ever."

"Of course he is. I expect nothing less." Miguel's smile broadened in genuine warmth for this lady who'd become a beacon of honor to him ever since he'd first been elected by the Corporate CEOs. Even in his days when he'd been less than, she reached out to him. It was something he'd quickly come to admire in a place that often duplicated the very governments they'd sought to do away with.

He patted her hand before he nodded at two friends sidling over. "Alis, Finn. You know Danya."

Ambassador Alis and Senator Finn from the Icelands region,

both in their late twenties and sipping sparkling water, tipped their shaved heads. "Lovely to see you again, Danya," Alis said.

"Same to you, friends." She offered a slight bow. Then smiled and glanced, unblinking, at Miguel. "Peace, dear boy. I'll speak with you again." She strolled off toward the Hall's cushy, red front-row seats, adjusting her blue head covering around her face as she went.

The warm ceiling lights glinted off Finn's smooth scalp while he cleared his throat. "All right, Miguel, tell the truth. Did you make money off today's game yet?"

Miguel quirked a brow. "Finn, you know I *never* talk moolah." He winked at the three Corp CEOs walking by who nodded him a greeting. "Unless, of course, you're selling something," he added, earning a hearty laugh from the duo.

"Actually, on that note, I've been meaning to ask—"

"Leaders and statespeople, please take your seats," a robotic voice translated into their earpieces. "We will now get started."

Miguel waved at Finn. "Later, because I'd love to hear it." He patted Alis's shoulder and whispered, "Chat soon, love." Then strode over through the maze of political-businessmen as they whispered "Hello" and "Good to see you, Miguel" until he reached where Claudius was settling into a chair along the back wall.

His friend held drinks for them, old-skool Bloody Mary for himself and spicy-sweet tea for Miguel. "Got your fancy drink, amigo."

"Says the *cuate* sipping his through a hemp straw." Miguel swiped his cup from Claudius's hand. "Next you'll be insulting anything fried," he grumbled. "Speaking of which . . ." He glanced at the cherrywood door through which the drink station was located. "How hard is it to get a vote passed for food cafés that'll carry more than synthesized fruit?"

"Statespeople and Corp heads, we are grateful for your attendance," the robo-voice said. "On behalf of all of us, and particularly Corps 24 and 30 and the North East–Americana region, we thank you for attending."

"Heard back from Vic yet?" Claudius whispered.

Miguel shook his head as an ambassador on the left babbled to her seatmate, "Ever seen all of them together like this?"

Miguel glanced around the warmly lit, expensive wood room with its high ceilings and plush seats, packed full with a few hundred people.

"Nope," came the neighboring reply. "Kind of makes you wonder how many of them are here just for the entertainment."

Claudius looked at Miguel and tipped his head toward the two conversing.

Miguel took a casual sip of his drink and nodded, then paused as the *té de manzanilla* hit his tongue. Even fake, it evoked a sense of childhood from his California home—despite the fact that most of California no longer existed, thanks to one too many nuclear-induced earthquakes during World War III.

He and his family had barely escaped them for the Old Colorado region—where his citizenship changed to Corp 19, which produced patent-owned artificial wood and steel for everything from buildings to housing to hovercars. It was there at the ripe age of eight he'd begun to learn politics and media sway while other kids clung to their mamas' apron strings.

Claudius leaned over to Miguel. "I was thinking that guy has a point about some of the senators being here more for entertainment. If someone wanted to expose those . . . photos . . . this would be an ideal audience."

The blackmail photos Miguel had placed last minute in his

breast pocket took on a few pounds. He glanced at Claudius. Yes, he'd caught the undercurrent and knew what he might be in for, and he was about to say as much when a prick of awareness stalled him. For as casual as they appeared, the senators closest to them had their heads tilted too near, too taut. Too invested.

He presented an innocent smile. "Exactly. Meaning this ought to be interesting, eh? For instance, shall we bet on whose faux leather pants will get in a bunch first? Because *how* is Corp 24 looking so calm when we *know* it'll be them?" Miguel tipped forward and got louder. "Good gad, these are the questions I need answered. This is why I'm here!" He lightly lifted his drink in the air. "We want enlightenment, dangit!"

Claudius offered him a sardonic eyeful even as he laughed quietly along with the two rows curved in front of Miguel. One of the delegates, an old woman senator from Corp 11's Asiatic region, turned and patted Miguel's knee. "Me too, sweetie. Me too." She took on a confidential tone. "Only thing better would be if our dress code wasn't so strict. All these men's shoulders and legs are so dang covered, there's not enough skin. Makes it hard for a woman to get a date from these meetings."

Miguel chuckled and swept up her hand for a kiss. "Kosame, you are my goddess."

The eighty-year-old winked. "Ain't that the truth. And better not forget it, boy." Then she went back to looking toward the platform situated in the circular room's center as the robo-voice began naming off each individual in the room as introduction.

Miguel eased back and studied faces as they were called upon. His skin prickled. He had to agree with Claudius—it was the perfect environment. The place was packed with every governing member from all thirty Corp Nations, either in person or via telescreens along the walls. Senators, VPs, CEOs, and Earth's ambassadors—their skin color and cultural style and hushed chatter of translated languages made the energy all the more electric.

"Wonder how our Delonese friends feel about being left out?" murmured a senator to Miguel's right.

Claudius raised a brow and peered at the empty seats that the alien guests only rarely received an invitation to occupy.

"Probably the same as we would if this had occurred on their planet while we were visiting," Miguel answered. "They'd want to discuss it before inviting our opinion."

"Statespeople and Corp leaders," the overhead voice interrupted. "We are now set to continue with tonight's order of business. Please welcome CEO 30 from region North Americanada to the podium."

Across the room the attendees froze as Sofi's mother, Inola, stepped to the platform. The telescreens circling the top of the room provided the audience with her professional photo and stats.

Not that any were needed. The woman was a legend. A phenomenon looking as young and foreboding as ever.

In fact, she looked like Sofi.

Her thick, long black hair hung loose around her shoulders and back, setting off her professional blue suit and jacket. More than the long hair, though, it was the cheekbones and eyes that matched her daughter's—the eyes wide and dark and darting around to read the audience without giving her own soul away.

"My friends, I thank you for attending on such short notice," the woman began. "Also for the care many have reached out with—to me, my company, and the beloved others who lost people in today's attack." Despite her words, Inola's tone and expression were stoic. Calculated. As if she were reciting a medical chart.

"As you know, at 4:03 p.m. during our third united and highly successful Fantasy Fighting Games, an explosion went off and killed eleven members, players 1 and 24, gamers 2, 24, and 10, and Corp 30's team, including my children. We are all still in shock."

Miguel studied her emotionless face through lazy eyelids. From what he could tell, she was speaking the truth. *Interesante.* More than interesting, it was strange. The woman apparently had no idea her daughter was alive.

An uncomfortable pressure formed on the back of his neck.

He frowned. Vic said it was CEO Inola's own Corp who had Sofi. He checked his handscreen—still no messages from the AI.

"With that in mind," the woman continued, "I've asked you here to waste no time in getting to the bottom of this—both as a committee and as allies. I request you speak frankly, and if not . . ." Inola lifted her head and swept the room with her fierce gaze, although it avoided reaching Corp 24, Miguel noticed. *Astuta.* She'd let the others crucify them for her.

"Our joint UW attorney general has already begun a formal investigation," she finished. "So, with that said, I now open the floor for conversation."

Except . . . the room didn't open up to conversation.

It didn't open up to any talking whatsoever.

He glanced to Corp 24's section for their reaction—only to have his gaze alight on the shiny, bald head of his friend Ambassador Alis, who was looking rather cozy with the group.

Claudius nudged Miguel. The individuals assembled were about as likely to be first at jumping in to discuss the woman's dead kids as to mention Corp 24 was to blame for it. Because if that wasn't sensitive enough, the very presence of the woman herself was—particularly for those senators who'd only recently joined the UW.

Above her, her life-history profile had returned to scrolling on the tele.

Raised in her native nation, Inola was one of the world's foremost medical researchers, and everyone knew it. She'd married early and put herself through three of the top scientific universities before World War III broke.

Unfortunately, as the photos depicted, the war not only took her husband but left her a radiation-ridden baby girl—and a small venture in a company focused on the genetic targeting and dissolving of cancer at a cellular level. It was a breakthrough that changed the course of every person's life on Earth, even in the midst of tragedy.

Miguel took a sip of his tea and assessed the expressions of the UW's members. Because, seriously, how do you not acknowledge *that* in figuring out how to address the woman before you?

The photos continued, showing that, shortly before the vaccine's discovery, Inola had remarried—this time to a college professor from upper Old Canada. But somewhere between the births of her second and third children, her daughter died—the girl's body too far gone for the cure her mother had created.

Now here was that same woman once again talking about the deaths of her other children.

No one under the age of twenty-five, besides Claudius and Miguel, was looking at anything but their hands.

"Inola, if I may." A man in his sixties finally stood. Hart, the CEO from Corp 13, had helped harness cold-fusion power with Delonese assistance—and since then had been rumored to be investing in another Corp. Which one and what for, Miguel had yet to determine. But the man was seated beside Corp 30's VP, Ms. Gaines. "Since your team has been investigating closely," he said, “would you please apprise us of the basic details beyond what we’ve seen on the news?”

Inola nodded. “At 3:35 this afternoon, Corp 24’s player took ill and was replaced by another.” As Inola spoke, the vids around the room switched to display the Colinade’s explosion and aftermath. “At 4:03, that new player, a Kyle Wickman from the Antarctix region, attacked Corp 30’s Shilo Snow and held him underwater.”

The faces staring at the teles were enamored. Miguel searched for any flickering eyelids or flinching lips, his gaze roving faster as he took note of who was watching the CEO, who was watching their own handscreens, and who was watching him.

Because oddly enough, there were a few. And not just in a flirtatious way.

Senator Finn. Ambassador Danya. And, curiously, CEO Hart himself.

Inola’s voice grew louder. “What followed was the explosion from a device that took out one fraction of the Colinade.”

A senator stood. “Do we know how security was breached?”

Miguel caught Hart glance his way again, but the look was gone before he could read anything in it.

“What about Corp 24?” demanded an ambassador, turning in Corp 24’s direction. “Are your people going to take full responsibility for this?”

A different awareness grabbed Miguel’s attention—another gaze directed at him. A woman observing him for the fourth time beneath her heavily made-up lids. Ms. Gaines.

He stared right back at her as Corp 24’s VP stood. “As of an hour ago, we have fired CEO Kim. And we categorically deny having anything to do with this tragedy.”

A low buzz rippled through the room.

Interesante. Miguel moved his gaze and leaned back to sip his *té de manzanilla.*

And let Ms. Gaines continue to study him.

13

SOFI

THE IMAGES WERE EVERYWHERE THROUGHOUT THE FLUORESCENT-colored city. Sofi weaved among the Thursday-night traffic while keeping an eye on the news pics moving across the boulevard's giant billboards and tall glass buildings.

They reminded Sofi of the one outdoor movie Papa took Shilo and her to when they were little and their small, broken town was trying to resurrect itself. Except these vids were of the FanFight explosion plastered alongside enormous, barely clothed 3-D models selling sex and cars and every recreational experience under the moon.

As usual, half the mannequins looked human; the others mimicked the taller, leaner Delonese with their wider noses and tan skin.

Sofi pursed her lips and glanced away as something shuddered in her chest. They gave her the creeps. The next moment she rolled her eyes as Corp 24's ad for Altered flashed on—their new DNA detection device. Rumor had it they'd been planning to unveil and demonstrate it on the players at tomorrow's games for the audience's amusement. It'd been a joke around the halls for days. "So much for that," she muttered.

A gust of air billowed through the shot-out window, ruffling her hair with the opposing scents of soy sauce and curry. Her stomach growled as the hovercar's music eerily thumped in time to the varied news shots on the screens—mostly of the damaged Colinade and panicked crowd, followed by faces and texts describing each of those lost or injured.

"*Please mourn with us*," the scrolling messages near the top read. And just below: "*Reward for any info leading to those responsible.*"

Sofi bent forward to study them amid the flashing lights and colors, grasping for the details she'd missed after the explosion. Until her throat caught at the sudden oversize photo of Shilo's face on-screen. *I'm coming, bud.*

A scuffle came through her earcom, making her jolt. "Hey, Sof—"

"Heller," she cut in. "Have you heard from any of the others?"

He cleared his throat. "From our team? No, it took every hack I had just to find you. I figured Corp 30'd be holding you in the same area they did before. When you were—you know . . ."

When she'd gone crazy numerous times. Yes. Thank you. Her mind flashed back to the nightmares that had originally sent her to the therapist. Usually of herself pinned to a cot with bright lights burning down on her, a butterfly specimen pinned to a board. When her brother found out, he'd made the owl necklace. "To chase away bad thoughts," he'd said.

She shook off the memory. "Okay, but what about Shilo? You didn't find anything on him?"

The club's music pulsed in the background, conflicting with her own and enhancing his hesitation. "I don't know what you mean. Sofi . . . Didn't you hear? He's—"

"Dead, yeah. Except from what Corp 30 said in the hall an

hour ago, they don't even seem to believe that." She moved her gaze to the accelerating traffic in front of her. "I saw him alive today when they were wheeling me out."

"Alive? Wait—you sure?"

"Positive."

"Then where is he?"

"No idea. But you *did* try to find him, right?"

"Shilo? Yeah, totally, I looked for him. Just like the others. But I'm telling you, Sof, we're the only ones who made it. We were the lucky two."

She gnawed her lip. Was he serious? How were they lucky?

"Hey, Sof, I swear I checked for him." His tone grew intense. "Like I said, you were the only one I could find. And not cuz I couldn't hack them, but like, cuz all his records just disappeared. I figured it was the Corp's way of cleaning up."

She frowned. Since when did any of them believe half of what the Corp did tech-wise? "And you didn't find it weird they'd erase files?" she started to say but stopped. He'd had a crappy day too. "Okay, I'll look at it when I get a comp."

Clenching her jaw, Sofi refocused on the sea of red tail beams suddenly slowing in front of her. They bobbed like the fireflies she'd chased as a kid when their house still stood beside the old barn. Back before her dad passed and everyone moved into tightly centered cities to be near Corp resources. A thing she'd hated—the lack of space and freedom from UW-sanctioned peacekeepers—up until now. Because it could only work to her benefit in finding Shilo. He had to be in the city, or at least someone in the city had to know where he was. "Destination in 1640 feet," the car's auto-tone said.

Good. She veered into the left lane just as a giant picture of her face from back at the Colinade slid across five boulevard screens.

It was promptly chased by a discreet video of covered bodies being wheeled out on stretchers. She ignored the chill that spread across her skin as the large printed words declared her dead. *Yeah, that's not creepy.*

"Hey, how close are you?" Her earcom crackled with Heller's voice. "People here've been asking ever since I showed them your vid. It's all over. They want the scoop. It's about to hit the newsreels."

"Almost there. And hey." She paused just as the street hoverlight changed to green and a group of protesters ran in front of her with their signs declaring "Aliens Will Kill Us All." She'd actually joined them once, to her mom's horror—especially when the woman had to send someone down to bail Sofi out of jail. She waited for the protesters to pass her car. "Thanks for your help back there at the Corp."

"No prob. You know me." His voice softened. "I'm always here for you."

She nodded. All of them were. The seven of them had been there for each other constantly over the past two years. *Until today.* Her throat squeezed.

"By the way." She frowned. "How'd you get out of the explosion and away from the Colinade? And do they know you're alive?" A twitch of panic seeped in. What if they knew? What if they were tracking Heller?

"Nope. They've no clue. At least besides the fact they're still searching for my body. Like I said, lucky."

She nodded. "Well, I'm glad you made it." The next moment she fell silent and accelerated through an intersection, only to swerve at the end before jetting into a lane of oncoming traffic. Three seconds later she slammed her brakes and right-turned it into an alley, then stopped the hover, killed the lights, and sat a full minute before she shut off the fusion engine. Just in case she had a tail.

She'd left the first guy following her back on 8th, and the other two were probably heading for her apartment—but no harm in being extra safe.

She smashed the camera lens she'd recorded her speech on, then double-checked the comp on the car's dashboard in case she'd missed something. Once done, she opened the door in the thin alleyway just as a drone flew by half a block over. She tugged her hair over the side of her face, yanked the black med gown tighter around her body, and swallowed before looking toward the underground parking garage two blocks away.

"Hey, Heller, I'll see you in two." Sofi shoved the hover door closed and took off at a jog in her bare feet.

When she reached the garage, she avoided the usual camera placements and snuck down two floors before stopping at a door with a sign written in black lights: "Mom's Basement."

"I'm here," she whispered and tapped out five measures from the song "We Drink in the Night" on the metal.

The door opened before she finished, and Heller charged into her with as much force as the blaring red entry glow. Short dark hair, dark eyes, and a strobe-light cheek piercing were complemented by a muscled physique that the old-skool gamer geeks would've killed for, even though nowadays it was the norm among the top techs. He grinned and released her to straighten his black jacket and jeans. Then scooped her forward and flashed the bouncer a high five, as if to assure him she was allowed.

The female bouncer ignored him and tipped her chin. "Hey, girl, what's up? Good game today. Sorry about your bro."

"Thanks, Raj. Nice to see you." With a steadying inhale, she followed Heller through the long hall toward the lounge as the door closed behind them.

The place was colder than normal, prompting the overhead vents to buzz like the yellow bulbs and make it all a bit misty. She sucked the frigid air into her lungs and aimed for the pulsing colors and metronic music growing brighter and louder as they approached the main room.

Heller leaned in and yelled something about her outfit in her ear, his scruffy chin scratching her skin, but she couldn't hear him.

Not that it mattered. She was focused on absorbing the noise and cold as it wrapped around her like her headphones usually did. She shivered. These days she craved it—to the point she often dreamt her veins were icing over and breaking her brittle heart.

She smirked. The last time she'd had that particular dream, a guy named Drafe had come to her room and fallen asleep after their time together. She'd woken up frozen and reached for the inhaler she hadn't needed since the age of ten and totally freaked him out. He never said anything about it afterward, but then, she'd never spoken to him again.

Her face warmed in the flashing rainbow strobe lights as she shoved the memory aside and entered the lounge that was pumping loud from telescreens and gaming teams and music.

Heller aimed them for a set of neon wall seats amid an onslaught of comments and catcalls from the other gamers, including a group of techs crowing their butts off while eyeing Sofi with varied levels of lust or hatred. Or a mix of both.

She put a smirk on and winked for the haters.

"Hey, Sof, you're alive!" someone yelled. "Dig the outfit."

"Saw your vid you just made," said another.

On the back wall above the oxygen bar a telescreen was replaying the actual games rather than the news assessments. Sofi's shoulders eased as she dropped into a seat and watched. She needed info and answers and a phone, and yet the idea that life was proceeding here just like normal was inherently comforting. In its own sketchy, pulsing way.

"Drinks." A guy wearing an animated-skull apron handed over two cups of green buzz—a mixture of hot green tea and foaming iced Popsicles. The moment he strode away, Heller pulled out a handscreen and slid it to Sofi. "Grabbed this from your locker back by the chat rooms. Figured you'd want it."

She nodded and took a sip of the buzz. And promptly flagged the animated-skull guy with two fingers—for a number two on the menu. Then sent him a thumbs-up and swiped the screen with her thumb pass code.

"I pulled the vids I thought you'd want." Heller leaned in, brushing her chest as he went to tap an icon. An image from a news feed popped up—one Sofi'd seen on the boulevard screens during her drive over. She moved it aside and flicked through the others, but a quick perusal showed more of the same. She closed it out and accessed the Darknet.

"Are there close-ups of Corp 24's guy or his gamers in the final moments?" she asked.

"Gone. And his file? Faked. Even his name is fake. He's literally a nobody."

"Of course. Can we do a money trace?"

"Already did. Nada."

Sofi flipped to her mother's Corp 30 database and after a moment pulled up the back door to hack it. Only to realize she'd need more bandwidth—and even then, curiously, their firewalls were brand new.

The animated-skull guy brought over her order. "Ran you a tab," he said with a sorry-about-your-day wink before walking off.

She nodded and grabbed a synthetic fry, then looked at Heller. "So, what's the Anonymous group saying?"

"Nothing yet. Though I'm sure they will."

She nodded and reattacked the comp screen—this time logging in to the UW's site and bypassing their security with hack codes one of the Ns had given her last week. She flipped through item after item and scanned for anything involving Shilo's name. Nothing emerged.

She ran a search for his first name, last name, and physical specs. A flood of boxes opened up, but the latest was the morning's log saying all players were cleared for the day's challenges. After that—nothing.

"Told ya," Heller said around a mouthful.

Switching over to the FanFight's private server, she ran the same search there. "You've got to be kidding," she murmured. It was spotless. As if Shilo failed to exist other than as a general player. "Who could've wiped it this clean?"

"Other than you and maybe Ranger? I know of one entity."

She didn't want to hear that. Didn't want to think about that. No, there were others. There had to be. Hackers erased files all the time.

"At least who could've done it that fast and thorough. Because if it'd been anyone we know, there'd be residue. Which leaves—"

"The Delonese."

He shrugged as she shoved a fistful of fries in her mouth.

"Sofiiiiiii!" The squeal came from behind her.

She turned to see what the commotion was, only to find her face on the giant screen at the bar. It was the vid from the hovercar, declaring she was still alive and kicking.

"Shh," someone at the oxygen counter yelled.

She started to watch but her gaze drifted to the smaller news vid set in the corner of the screen. It was displaying updated pics of the quarter-time break in the FanFights today, just before the water world and shark tank took over. The vid flickered through the players—including Corp 24's and Shilo—following them around behind the scenes in the med rooms and rest areas before and after she'd left Shilo.

She squinted and moved closer. *What the—?*

Sofi paused, blinked, and grabbed Heller's elbow.

Heller frowned. "You okay?"

Both vids abruptly ended to the tune of the room cheering and one of the guys calling out, "Suckaaaas!" at the tele while another pointed, shouting, "Who's in charge now, scabs? Sofi! Sofi! Sofi!"

"I'm fine." She swallowed. "I just need to hit up the chat rooms."

"Okay." His expression was leery. "Anything going on?"

She didn't answer. Just stared hard at the hall ahead and stepped forward with a sick sensation emerging in her gut. And tried to make sense of the fact that in the background of every one of those pics of Shilo, the Delonese medical personnel had been there, standing, watching him.

14

MIGUEL

IF MIGUEL HAD THOUGHT TO PUT A FIGHT-PIT IN THE SESSION Hall, he could've handed out spandex suits and mud buckets and charged money to see the CEOs take one another on. Alas, he had to be satisfied with the underhanded comments from the safety of politician seats. But still . . . the idea had merit.

In fact, he'd have to jot it down for future vote.

He slid Claudius the napkin sketch he'd made of the scheme and was promptly rewarded with a quiet laugh, followed by his friend surreptitiously pointing out a few he'd elect to go first.

Miguel nodded just as the VP from Corp 24 stood again to readdress the room. "As CEO Inola noted, the Antarctix player not only hacked us but a portion of *your* Corps' security and firewalls. And, in fact, the FanFight Games' entire defense system. Making this a global issue, not just ours."

"Good way to shift the blame," Claudius whispered.

Miguel snorted and continued to study their faces as he sketched. A habit developed years ago by way of analyzing them. "You study them," his father once told him, "if you want to work with them." Miguel had been seven at the time.

Except Miguel had studied so well that by fifteen he was

traveling the world with VPs. And soon after, earned enough Delonese interest that the UW had invited him to take an ambassador role—which, unlike the senators who needed election by individual Corporation-taxed constituents, was voted in by the CEOs themselves. Thirty ambassadors filled ten-year terms to represent the good citizens of Earth to Delon. It'd been a ride.

He dropped his pencil and pulled out his handheld again. Still nothing from Vic. *¿Cómo?* Where was she? He adjusted his shoulders and tuned back in to the VP who was saying, "Two of our own team died today, and we want to get to the bottom of it as much as everyone here."

Good gad, give it a rest. Considering they'd not even had twenty-four hours to investigate, Corp 24's posturing was rhetorical. Perhaps it was time to move the meeting beyond what they didn't know and probe into at least what *somebody* knew. Whose drama was this? What were they attempting to achieve?

Especially since the UW's behind-the-scene scans of these meetings made to analyze everyone's stress secretions and lies would be analyzed throughout the night and then the UW investigators would probe deeper in the morning. At which point he could have Vic access their files.

Meaning . . . if he wanted answers, it was time to stir the wasps' nest.

He lifted his hand to flag the speaker.

"Ambassador Miguel?"

He rose to his feet. "I believe I speak for all of us that not only are we committed to finding the who and why of this brutal attack, we refuse to allow this to start a war between us."

The audience's reaction was swift. They rose to their feet in unified applause.

"Thank you, Miguel," Inola said once the members were reseated.

"With that in mind"—Miguel stayed standing—"I propose we lay down our defensiveness and do what we came for. I propose we push past the decorum to the hard questions."

"Yes, thank you!" a senator from up front said.

"Agreed!" multiple of the assembly added.

Inola furrowed her brow. "What exactly did you have in mind?"

Miguel shrugged. "*Fácil.* Let's talk about if there's anything the thirty Corps or their players have that would warrant such an attack." He looked around. "Espionage perhaps? Stolen property? Anything worth attempting a cover-up?"

The gasp that rocked the room was the exact response he'd hoped for as he turned back to Inola on the platform and smiled. Then sat down.

Five CEOs, along with multiple leaders, promptly shot up in protest. "Madame Inola, I find this highly insulting." "This is irregular to say the least. Suggesting we dig into personal business, let alone assuming such things."

Miguel watched the strikingly tall Ambassador Danya turn and look back over the sea of heads at him, an expression of amusement on her tan face, the same look, he noted, on Alis and Finn and a few others, along with old Kosame in the row ahead of him.

"You have guts—I'll hand you that," Claudius said.

Miguel eyed the individuals standing. Ms. Gaines. Corp 13's Hart. A few senators. "You know we're all thinking it."

A hand went up and an ambassador asked, "Or could it have been solely the gamers or players? Is there a general unrest we're unaware of?"

All of the Corp CEOs shook their heads. No. The players

and gaming groupies knew the risk and wanted the money and fame that went with it. "If anything," said a VP, "outside gamers could've sabotaged it for a chance at becoming replacements. But that's very unlikely."

"What about basic terrorism then? Just because none of the usuals have taken responsibility doesn't mean they won't. What of Calentine? Or Swara's men?"

"That's a possibility," a few agreed.

"Or what about the rumors surrounding Corp 16 attempting to steal tech-suit designs?" a male senator by the name of Denzel asked. "Or Corp 13's backroom deals to branch out into human genomes instead of just cold fusion?"

The assembly gasped even louder than before, and Miguel actually laughed.

Clearly he needed to meet Denzel in person. He watched CEO 16's face turn so red and bulbous the poor man looked as if he might have a heart attack. Good thing his company had created the cure for that years ago. Nearby, Corp 13's Hart wasn't looking much better.

The voices rose and the accusations began flying, but before Miguel could make out a clear response, a message buzzed on his handscreen in a pattern that wasn't Vic's. Something told him he didn't have to look to know what it would be, but he peered down anyway. And suddenly felt the eerie sensation of nameless eyes watching him.

Blame Corp 24.

He glanced up. At Inola. At the vice presidents and CEOs in the room. Even as the ceiling teles flashed a red ribbon across the screens, alerting an impending bulletin update. His stomach twisted.

Two seconds later Senator Finn spoke up. His voice hesitant. Uncomfortable. "Or what about whether Ms. Snow herself was involved?"

The room turned to stare at him.

"Forgive my insensitivity here," Finn clarified. "But I'm asking about the possibility that Corp 30, and specifically the girl, Sofi, was behind the attack."

"I hope for your sake you're not suggesting my company and dead daughter were in any way responsible for the bomb that took her and her brother's life," CEO Inola said.

"Not me. But there is some evidence that supposedly suggests . . ."

Miguel frowned. *What is Finn doing?* Too late—he could already see it dawning on others' faces. His suggestion taking root. It'd be easier to blame the "dead" girl and knock her mother down a notch in the same swoop than dig too deep. He glared.

Sofi's mother lowered her tone. "In that case, Senator Finn, I suggest you get me the evidence. Until then, the idea is off the table. Because as it stands now, my children are dead."

As if in unison with her words, the televids from earlier panned over the Colinade's empty wreckage that'd since been cleaned up—while that impending message banner on the tele kept blinking.

"I'm truly unsure," Inola continued, "how by any stretch of the imagination it can be assumed Sofi had a hand in it or chose to commit murder-suicide for the purpose of—what?" Her tone had stretched to the brink of patience.

Not that Miguel blamed her. The reasoning was ludicrous. There was no productive purpose behind such an act. And yet . . .

And yet . . .

Her company was clearly hiding something.

"Or perhaps it's exactly as we all saw," Ambassador Alis said from beside Finn. "That along with the girl, Corp 24 really is to blame. Clearly—"

"Again, we'd invite proof," Corp 24's VP jumped in.

Miguel frowned. Not quite the accusation he'd expected from Alis's normally bipartisan mind. He shifted and ignored them. What was Corp 30's interest in maintaining the ruse of Sofi's death—even from her own mother?

He lifted his hand and flagged the forum. *Let's push the issue.*

"Miguel, you can't be serious," Claudius groaned.

"*Perdón*, Madame Inola, but—"

That red banner flashed brighter across the overhead news screen. *Blink, blink, blink.*

Corp 13's CEO Hart stood and interrupted. "In fact, I do have it on solid authority your daughter is alive, ma'am. That's not to say she's responsible—"

Cripe.

Inola's face went pale. She peered at Hart, and in that second Miguel could read her soul as plain as day. The look was one of unbearable hope that wished by some stretch of insanity he might be right.

The next moment her expression melted into disgust.

Before she could reply, the impending news bulletin turned the entire roomful of telescreens red—in effect saving Hart from her wrath as it inspired a hush through the audience.

Sofi's tired face suddenly appeared on the screen. Black eyes, brown skin, full lips, a cheek scuffed up and a cut above one eye. Miguel froze. *Sofi?* It looked like she was in a hovercar.

A vortex opened within his chest as the assembly let out a collective yelp. He searched her eyes, her expression, her furrowed brow—and shoved down the ache and hunger they evoked in him. She was clearing her throat as the camera jiggled slightly. Miguel narrowed his gaze. Was the hover's back window blown out?

She enlarged the camera's time stamp to show it was either a very good fake or else was made an hour ago.

"Good evening, folks." She smiled and peered up at the traffic slowing ahead. "This is Sofi Snow, daughter of CEO Inola from Corp 30. It's 8:59 on the second night of the FanFight Games, and this recording is following the terrible explosion today in the arena." She paused and gave time for Miguel's lungs to find air.

"I just wanted to tell y'all I'm alive and currently searching for my brother, whom I believe to also be alive. So, here's the thing . . ." Sofi stared down at the camera again. "If anyone listening was involved in the attack or with our attempted murder, you should know I will find you. I'm already aware of who you are. And for the rest of you"—she winked—"well, enjoy."

Leaving the vid rolling, she swerved the lens to focus for a brief second on the smashed window behind her, then shifted it to focus on the empty brown passenger seat. Her funk-pop music took over all sound as the city lights strobed across the lens.

CEO Inola's face had blanched. Even from Miguel's position, an expression of merciful relief and reddening, tear-glittered eyes was noticeable. Only to be followed by dawning horror.

Fortunately, no one had the gall to suggest what half the room was thinking. That Sofi's being alive could negate everything her mother had just said.

"Actually, CEO Inola—"

"Actually, what a wonderful surprise," Ms. Gaines exclaimed

from her seat. Her hands were on her cheeks. "Oh, Inola, on behalf of the room, we are so relieved. And we as your Corp 30 team and UW community"—she turned to the senators behind her and then the crowd—"will take full responsibility to see she's recovered safely."

Miguel's handscreen clicked and a pic popped up right as he turned it over. It was one of the damning photos from the paper in his pocket. His gut dropped. He pursed his lips and looked up.

A senator from South Americana had raised a hand. "I think it's clear we not only need further investigation as we've all agreed, but we need to find your daughter, Madame, and hear her side of things. I move to request she be brought in as soon as possible."

"I second that motion," said another voice.

"Agreed. Although I, for one, would also like the Delonese's assistance in this," Ms. Gaines added. "I believe it wise to take advantage of their skills in rooting out the truth from within the individual Corps."

"Yes," voices buzzed.

"They've been a balanced resource in the past. I second that motion as well," Ambassador Danya added, and over half the room raised their voices in agreement.

"Do we have a majority then?" Inola said. "Yes? Good. Correct me if I'm wrong, but I believe we already have a UW team set to meet up with them day after tomorrow. Ambassadors Miguel, Claudius, Lee, and Danya, I propose we tack our request onto their previously scheduled agenda. All in favor?" Inola peered around the room. "Excellent."

Miguel's handheld purred and another pic came through. *Crud.*

It purred again. Another pic.

Sí, sí, he got the message. He looked across the audience. The meeting was winding down. What did they want him to do—stand up and accuse Corp 24 right now? It'd be seen as a stall.

A moment later it was followed by vid streams flooding his in-box from Vic and the note: *Corp 24 kid, Alis, and Delonese coding.*

Ambassador Alis? What about her and Delon?

He stared at the message while the photos practically burned a hole in his spine. After peering over at Alis, Inola, and Ms. Gaines amid an atmosphere growing more palpable—like static in the air—he rose to his feet and squared his jaw. Let them think what they wanted. To heck with whoever was sending their manipulations.

He was the player, and he refused to be played.

"Miguel," Claudius hinted.

"*Perdón*, but since that's settled," he said loudly, "I request permission to take leave of this meeting as I believe I may be sitting on new info regarding Corp 24 and their player."

Both true and hinting at an accusation. Which will hopefully buy time.

"I'll do my part to substantiate before I bring it to the committee, of course. And in the meantime, I'll be hosting an informal fiesta tomorrow night. Something to celebrate our unity and get our minds off today's tragedy for a few hours." He flashed the smile he'd used to seduce many of them over the years. "Consider yourselves invited. 8:00 p.m. My rooftop." His hand waved elaborately. "And please—dress for *fun*."

With that he strode out amid voices coated in relief and interest after so much tension.

"Want to tell me what that was?" Claudius hissed as soon as they'd reached the hall.

"That was me buying us time."

"Yes, but you just baited them on both sides. Good heavens, Miguel."

The Session Hall doors shut as Miguel stepped into the elevator and swiped for the ground floor.

The music started up.

"So what was that *really*?"

"That was me stirring up the wasps' nest."

15

SOFI

"TO ANSWER YOUR QUESTION, WE'RE ON A TRAFficker ship." The boy's thin breath stuck to the skin on Shilo's arm, making it clammy.

Shilo opened his eyes and peered through the dark, only to see the kid's outline blend with the others. "Headed where?" someone whispered.

No one answered.

Shilo sniffed. Stories of Earth kids taken by traffickers were more commonplace than anyone would admit, even he knew that. None reported by the news, of course—but on the net, and on sleepovers when kids told scary tales, or as hearsay surrounding black-market sales.

None of those versions turned out nice.

Rumor was, those taken either were never seen again or occasionally escaped and were found naked and witless in some dirt patch. Although they couldn't remember where they'd been or how long they'd been missing.

"I'm scared," a kid whispered. The voice was fragile and shaken by sobs. A lot of them were by the sounds. All scared just as much as he was. All probably sensing what the older ones were trying not to admit: that while they were alive right now, when they got to where they were headed, they'd all wish they weren't.

Shilo gulped and tried to blink real fast so his eyes wouldn't cloud up, even though the dark would hide the tears anyway.

He swallowed. "It'll be okay," he said to the crying kid. "We won't let anything happen to you." He rested his head against his knees with his nose tucked into his elbows. Shilo inhaled, and even through his suit the scent of wheat fields and dirt and sunshine dragged images of the farm into his head. Home.

The swishing noise started up again and the gas returned for no reason, and Shilo retreated into oblivion.

"Sofi?"

Sofi's stomach clenched and her eyes cleared. She looked around. She was still in Mom's Basement, amid the gamers and bodies jostling to the music around her. What the—?

"You sure you're okay?"

She blinked and looked at Heller, her fingers going to her necklace. *What just happened?*

It was like the dream she'd had of Shilo earlier at the Corp building. Except this time she'd been wide awake and about to walk into a chat room. She shook her head. One moment she'd been talking to Heller—and the next she'd been in a trafficking airship with Shilo, seeing the kids he saw, hearing the whimpers and questions he heard. Feeling his fragility.

Warm vomit rushed her throat. She blinked again.

"Well, now you're weirding me out."

"Sorry. It was nothing. Just a dizzy spell." Just a fluke. An emotional reaction to seeing her brother on-screen yet again. To seeing him being watched by Delonese med personnel. She shivered as her hatred of the aliens flared.

Deep breath.

Except . . .

Except if it was nothing, then why was her head screaming the visions were so freaking real? Why was she suddenly recalling rumors about Delonese telepathy, or the obscure, random questions Corp 30's therapist used to ask about whether she and Shilo ever shared thoughts? Sofi straightened her spine and tucked her hair behind her. It was crazy. She knew that.

But she also knew what she'd seen at the Colinade.

And Heller was right—the Delonese were the only ones who could've erased Shi's online existence like she'd just seen.

Clearing her throat, she clamped her lips and resumed her trek down the hall while replaying the vision and those pics of the Delonese watching Shilo at the FanFight. If she let her mind roam with the idea that he was with the aliens, then it led to the obvious question of why. Why would they want her brother? What would they even *do* with him?

The immediate answer made her sick. She shoved aside the rumors, and gossip, and comments made at black-market dealings and on anarchist net sites. They'd only served to fuel her disgust and heighten her fear for her brother.

"Sofi!" A bearded guy in a red beanie waved them into a chat room crammed wall to wall with Luca and Heller's tech friends. From the look of it, a few were battling the newest net-war game while the rest watched the tele where a slide display had just appeared, flashing pics of the players who'd failed out of the FanFights in the past two days. It was the Basement's tribute—a rebellion of sorts against the media's recapping each day only in honor of the victors.

"What's up?" Heller high-fived bearded boy.

Ranger, as his friends called him. Sofi had known him all three years she'd known Heller. The twenty-five-year-old pointed to the screen, his expression solemn. "I'm betting half these players are headed for the market." He nudged Sofi's shoulder. "Hey, friend, glad you're alive."

She nudged back. "Hey to *you*. I'm really sorry about N."

He nodded and kept his suddenly misty eyes on the tele. She wasn't actually sure which of the three he'd been dating for the past year but knew enough to realize they'd been serious. More serious than she'd ever been. And while he clearly wasn't interested in elaborating just now, his pat on her hand said he appreciated her heart.

She stayed beside him and watched the screen flicker with the family and details of the twenty-one players who'd survived but still lost. Not that everyone here didn't already know, but honor was honor. As was a moment of silence for what would come next. Sofi swallowed.

Either the players and their teams would have to convince a Corp or a celebrity of their value and be claimed as a commodity or product seller, becoming rich beyond their dreams. *Or* they'd be sent to the black market to join kids and war vets in money fights, drug testing, and sex trafficking. All of which the Corps may have ruled illegal, but considering their own employees and officials frequented those spaces for entertainment, the rhetoric was a joke.

The slide show finished to palpable silence. Followed by murmured agreement with the vid's ending message: "We wish you the best, Fan players," as the screen returned to the news and Ranger spun round. "So, what can I do for you, eh? I presume looking into who set off the nasty boom."

Sofi nodded. "I need to borrow one of your servers." She passed him her handscreen, at which he grinned and beckoned them toward a trio of chairs before he pulled out his own handheld, connected it virtually to Sofi's, then handed hers back.

"Which sites we looking for?"

"Corp 24, the FanFights, and Corp 30." She logged in and went straight for her mom's company firewall, hitting it with a program the Ns had helped her create that ran through Ranger's setup.

He grunted surprise. "You're gutting your own Corp?"

"Specifically any involvement with the Delonese." She was already scanning for anything out of place. Any chink in the armored code.

There.

Her fingers dove for it, hacking through the backdoor pass codes.

Ranger continued to stare at her as his own fingers tapped away and Heller attempted to break deeper into the FanFights' system core. "For curiosity's sake," Ranger said after a moment, "can I ask what you're thinking?"

"She needs to find her bro," Heller answered.

"His body? That'd be interest—"

"No, alive." Sofi looked at Heller. How to explain her intuition, let alone the visions, she'd no clue. So she wouldn't. She tapped in a final stream—and Corp 30's data suddenly splayed out in front of her. She pinched her lip and ran a search for Shilo before glancing up. "I believe the Delonese might have him."

Their expressions turned dubious.

Right. Swiping her screen, she pulled up the behind-the-scenes news vid she'd just seen in the main room and played one after the other of what the station had displayed minutes before. "Okay, see that? In every scene." She swiped to another and froze the vid on Shilo, pointing behind him to the Delonese medic. "Why are they watching him? And why when we're looking for him is there suddenly no info?"

And why am I having dreams of him being on one of their flight-ships?

Ranger whistled.

Even Heller's gaze widened. He grabbed her device to flip through the scenes again for himself. When finished, he and Ranger both peered at Sofi.

"Ever seen the Delonese do that before?" she asked solemnly.

"They don't even interact with the CEOs or ambassadors that way," Ranger said. "For that matter, I've never even seen them interact on this level with *any* human. So yeah, I get that that's weird."

"Exactly." Sofi nodded. "And after the explosion when we were all being wheeled out? Shilo was alive, but a Delonese med worker had him. After that . . ."

Ranger nodded and looked at his hand-comp. "So what specifics do you need?"

She flipped her handscreen around to show them the section she'd just broken through of Corp 30's firewall, surrounding what appeared to be scrubbed data regarding Shilo and Corp 24's player. Except unlike the near-perfect deletions from the FanFights' docs, Corp 30's was a mess. It was like they'd written over Shilo's info so he was just a jumble of varied stories.

Ranger scanned it three times before handing it back. "Um, wow. That's ugly."

She snorted. "So who would've done it?"

"Someone brilliant enough to access what less than 1 percent of gamers are capable of," Ranger said. "But hurried enough not to value their own craft apparently."

She slid aside data streams, trying to organize the mess into some form of sanity. A moment later a flag popped up—her scanner siphoning to the top what it saw as the most formulated guess.

Corp 24.

She frowned and sent the notation over to Heller's handscreen in case he'd want to peek at it too. *But give me something I don't already suspect.* Sofi dragged up more code—until she abruptly found a set of documents opening like a filing cabinet. She flipped through them, faster and faster, as her chest simultaneously imploded because—oh gad. The Delonese didn't just have an observant curiosity in her brother.

They were *stalking* him.

Analyzing his blood, his abilities, his mental prowess.

Sofi's lungs dissolved. The notes on him from Corp 30, with Delonese oversight, went back years. What were they doing—why were they *monitoring* him?

And why did their mother allow it?

"I think I just found something," Ranger murmured.

"Me too," Sofi choked. She turned to check out the vid he was holding up. He tapped the screen to replay it in slow motion as she and Heller bent forward to focus. "What the—?" Sofi stared at the guys.

"Somebody didn't just rig Corp 24's player," Ranger said. "They rigged the entire last two rounds of the Games today.

The landscapes, the security, the layout of the ocean level." He pursed his lips. "And, Sofi—they set it up to look like *you* did it."

"What? That's ridiculous." Heller took the device from Ranger.

Ranger tapped up the backlog to show him.

Sofi ignored them both. If the Corp and Ms. Gaines were up to something, of course they'd put the blame on her. Better to keep Sofi preoccupied with deflecting accusations than let her seek out what they'd been doing to her brother—what they'd let the *Delonese* do *for all these years* to her brother. Or what the Delonese were doing to him now.

Better to bring her back in and get whatever answers Gaines wanted from her—under the guise of blame—than let her endanger their strategy.

It's what she'd have done in their position.

"Can we get vid from any of the internal rooms?" she asked Heller. "The gamer areas, med spaces, et cetera?"

Two seconds later he'd pulled up a grid on Ranger's screen.

She clicked and played each one. They showed the same thing they'd seen before, until she flipped to the final one—of the med hovers and VIP crafts taking off from around the stadium after the explosion. She pressed *Play* again and rewatched it. And shifted in her chair.

Something felt off.

She replayed it again while Heller asked, "What are we looking for here, cuz I don't see any—"

"There." Sofi pointed at the glitch. "Go back real fast."

There was a second Delonese aircraft.

It'd been hidden among the med hovers on the pads—the

fast-forwarded images showed it taking off a full half hour after the official Delonese transport had already left with the level-two guests aboard.

Which begged the question, who was on board *this* one? And why was it there to begin with?

Ranger clucked his tongue over her shoulder. "You may be right after all, girl."

"Dude, this just got a bit freaky-teaky." Heller ran a hand across his cheek and rocked back in his chair. "Like, WTF."

"Guys." Sofi looked at them both.

She took a breath. "I think I might need to get on Delon's planet."

Heller coughed and shook his head. "Impossible."

"Why? If anyone's capable, it's us. We can hack me onto a transport."

Ranger cleared his throat. "I think what he means is, you actually need someone who'd be willing to take you *once* we hack you on. And the list is pretty short."

"So we'll hack the list."

Heller grabbed Sofi's arm. "Hold on. Let's slow down and let the dust settle. Especially if they're saying you had anything to do with the bomb." He leaned in. "Let's clear your name and find who's responsible. Then, if necessary, talk about getting you to the planet in the safest way possible. So the Delonese don't literally shoot you down for invading their space."

"Slow down? Heller, this isn't about me, it's about Shilo. And if he *were* here, *we*, of all people, would be able to find him." She waved a hand at their three screens. "Or at least find some trace of him. But it's like he's literally disappeared—even according to my own Corp—and the only leads we have say he was last with the Delonese, who've been monitoring him for *years*." She slid him her hand device with the Corp 30 documents. "I'm not trying to be insane. I'm saying my gut is off the charts on this one."

She inhaled to steady her shaking stomach. "And my gut is what's kept him alive in the Games and kept our team near the top. And seeing as the Delonese prefer to stay on their precious planet away from the rest of us—if Shilo *is* alive, their sick fascination with him is a bit too coincidental."

She swallowed. "I believe he's there. Because if he were anywhere else, I'd know."

Ranger leaned over and grabbed a pair of headphones hanging on the wall and handed them to her. Then eyed her clothes before veering around to the room. "Anyone wanna switch outfits with Sofi so she can go do anarchy?" After getting affirmative responses, he dropped his voice. "Rumor has it you personally keep a running hack list on most of the political guys. So you know who to ask, no?" He rubbed his jawline. "Cuz if you don't? Half of them are—"

"Nasty as heck, I know."

He nodded slowly. "Okay, good. Cuz I like you and your work, Sofi. And I'd hate for you to run into anything you couldn't handle. I'd also hate for you to get creamed by the Corps for this—whether you did it or not." He pursed his lips. "But something tells me you didn't.

"So in that case, if you want my advice for the only way I see it happening." He nodded his chin at the tele where an advertisement was playing of Miguel holding out a health drug to the viewer as he lay in swim trunks on top of two live elephants in a pool full of water. His poetry-tattooed body only enhanced the illusion of health. White teeth sparkled against his naturally brown skin and blue hair.

Ranger pointed at the daft smile on Miguel's face. "Get him to take you."

16

MIGUEL

THE HOUSE WAS STILL DARK WHEN THEY CAME FOR HIM.

To speak to him. Threaten him. Hurt him maybe. Probably.

He'd only just walked in, set his coat down from the UW meeting, and strode out onto his bedroom deck for air when a man moved out from the shadows behind him. A knife touched his right flank, just where an elaborate tattoo of a rooster clutching in its beak a ribbon inscribed with the names of his family covered the soft spot of kidneys and other organs.

"Ambassador Miguel," the man breathed against his ear in the cool night breeze. "All they've asked for is your help, and you continue to flout them with your parties and tomfoolery."

Miguel placed his hands on the railing in front of him and kept his voice casual. Wondering how in *diablos* the man got there without every alarm and camera on the block sounding. "Forgive me if I'm not familiar with your use of 'they.' Nor with your use of 'tomfoolery.' Do I know you?"

The man laughed. Cold. Stiff. Like tequila poured on ice. "The question you should be asking is how we obtained your secret and what we're going to do with it." The man pressed the blade harder against Miguel's shirt.

Miguel's knuckles turned white on the railing. "How'd you get the photos?"

"That's the beauty of this day and age—cameras are everywhere. Even in the darker places you play." He leaned in. "Should've been more careful, mate."

Miguel darted his gaze around the street below them. The cameras must've been shut off along with his alarm system. "And why Corp 24? Why blame them?"

The knife slid through a section of his shirt and cut into his skin. Like giving a paper cut with a razor. Miguel stiffened but refused to groan. Instead, he focused on the voice.

"Our reasons don't concern you beyond your personal interest to keep your side hobbies out of the limelight. All we ask is for you to sway opinion and make Corp 24 take the fall for today."

"If you watched the Fights, you'd know they succeeded at incriminating themselves just fine."

"Ah, but that's not what you heard at tonight's UW meeting, is it?"

Miguel's mind raced. At this moment the meeting was likely wrapping up, which meant the man had been listening in as *un primo bobo* of someone he knew.

"Just imagine what such exposure could do," the guy continued. "Ruin you? Definitely. Damage the others in on it? Most assuredly. But even worse—it'll expose everything you've been planning. And that—" The man chuckled. "That my employer is betting you'll not risk. Not after all your pretty-boy effort."

"And what about the girl—Sofi? What if she's truly at fault?"

He laughed. "We both know she's not, but we thought that'd only sweeten the deal for you." The man's tone pitched harsher. "Or maybe sour it."

Miguel didn't flinch. Just eyed the street again and the four stories the man would fall if he were to reach back, grab the arm holding the blade, and use his body weight to flip him over the rail. Except he needed more answers. He needed to understand the game better before he could finish it.

He swallowed as if to feign nervousness. "And why me? Surely you have dirt on others."

The man snorted. "Says the golden boy of both Earth and Delon societies. Too bad the public tires so quickly of their playthings—especially once it's revealed who those playthings *really* are and what you're up to with them, eh? Just imagine how fast they'll tire of you. Guess that'd be something you of all people would know, considering how quickly you grow bored of yours. Women. Companions."

"*Piérdete*," Miguel muttered.

"Oh, not until we're done." The man laughed again. "Now do what you're told. Convince the world, or we will blow your little fun town sky-high. It's that simple, amigo."

Miguel felt the blade pull away and waited a beat before turning to get a look at the guy, but the deck was already empty. The ghost evaporated.

17

SOFI

SOFI WAS LYING ON THE MED COT—STIFF, SCRATCHY, like a bug on a pad of chloroform. A butterfly pinned beneath a magnifying glass for people to look over and analyze and dissect—deciding whether or not she was okay. Was she okay? It felt like she'd been asking that her entire life.

She wiggled and strained to break free from the straps—like trying to escape a chrysalis. Her wings beat, beat, beating in time to the music in her head.

"Sofi, leave. Fly! Fly!" she could hear Shilo say.

"Fly! Fly!" she whispered to her frozen limbs. All the while knowing her butterfly wings were too tattered.

The microscope moved nearer. The faces peered harder. Their bodies closing in as their hive minds pondered.

Just before they pulled out their knives.

Sofi sat up with a gasp and grabbed for her necklace to ward off one of her many recurring dreams that had plagued her through the years. And screamed for Shilo.

18

MIGUEL

THE CITY LOOMED LIKE A JEWEL, A DIAMOND CUT AND CAST IN pink- and gold-flecked ribbons of sunset that reflected off numerous glass towers spread throughout the metropolitan area. The sight glimmered even lovelier from Miguel's rooftop thanks to the eerie blue tint of the roof's electric field set three feet off each railing to create a sheer ten-foot-tall protective wall. Something no one would notice unless they'd been aware. Something he'd had enhanced since last night's "visit."

Miguel turned from the view to the chefs cooking in the patio's center, surrounded by tables piled high with sparkling colored drinks. So much drink. "To untie the tongues," he'd told the waiters. "Pass them out like dates. Especially along the garden paths and fireplace area." Where a sense of privacy might evoke loose-lipped confessions.

He glanced down at his appearance—a pair of elegant gray pressed pants and a white button-up shirt with the sleeves rolled and collar opened. And bare, pedicured feet. Casual but careful. Reserved but relaxed. He pulled the gray-and-black masquerade swan mask over his eyes, slid a hand through his freshly dyed lavender hair, and tightened his jaw. Then strode over to flip on the evening's music.

"You do realize wasps sting, don't you?"

"Already experienced one, if last night was any indication." Miguel turned to see Claudius strolling over from the elevator, dressed in a blazer and bell-bottoms that his great-great-granddad had probably sequined by hand.

Claudius grabbed a glass of sparkling pink and tipped it at Miguel. "You, my friend, look ravishing. And I'm not just saying that because this glass is a hundred currency. I'm saying it because if you're going to die in wasp venom, I'm proud you'll do so in style. Good man."

Miguel smiled and refrained from commenting on his friend's sequined man-suit. "The question is, *which* wasps will bite? Hopefully we'll get more than the chatty thugs—"

"Handing you your guts on a platter."

Miguel smoothed Claudius's wide collar, then patted his cheek. "My dear boy, do I sense fear already?"

"Not fear. Just hoping to keep my body parts intact. Yours too, for that matter."

"Very funny," Miguel growled. "How was your day?"

"Productive, actually." Claudius looked at him meaningfully. "Seems the rumors about another batch going out might be accurate." He held his glass up to let the fading sun filter through the liquid as he swirled it. "And it might coincide with yesterday's explosion."

Miguel raised a brow. *Interesante.*

"You?"

"Productive as well." He and Ambassador Danya had spent the morning with the UW committee regarding the team's Delonese talking points, followed by lunch with Delon's senior ambassador. But the rest of the afternoon Miguel had spent with Vicero reviewing the stress scans and lie detections from last night's UW meeting. What they'd discovered, aside from the fact that everybody was lying about something, was that a few power players had more stress than warranted. And the VP from Corp 24 was, for all intents and purposes, not one of them. Miguel really had no clue what was going on. But Ms. Gaines, on the other hand . . .

He looked out over the city as shadows stretched out lengthy fingers where moments before the pink and golden rays had been. A soft picture had begun emerging of what they were dealing with. He just had nowhere to go with it. Yet. But he would. Before long, he hoped.

The elevator dinged and slid open, and he turned with Claudius to smile at the first batch of guests to alight. "*Hola*, Ambassador Alis, Nadine, and CEO Hart. Welcome to my humble home."

19

SOFI

SOFI CUT THE TRACKING TAG FROM THE BAG SHE'D JUST PURchased and crushed it beneath her boot before she tossed it in the sky-mall's bathroom trash. Setting the pack on the ground, she checked the door lock again and stretched the kink from her neck. Then shoved the tech and two of Shilo's skin suits she'd kept stashed at Mom's Basement into the bag. Her Corp would've killed her if they'd known.

"Sofi." A sharp knock on the bathroom door. "We need to hurry."

She cleared her throat. "Out in three," she said to Heller and peered at her handheld again to recheck tonight's schedule of Miguel's party.

She'd ask him politely. She'd employ her charm—request him to take her to Delon. If he said no, she'd take it in stride. And find another.

"Did I mention I hate this idea?" Heller's grumble was followed by a *thunk* and scrape against the door, as if he'd slid down and plopped on the tile floor.

"At least fifteen times. Doesn't mean it won't work." She shoved a thin blanket, headphones, and the clothes she'd just bought into the bag. "For goodness' sake, have some faith."

They'd planned it perfectly—which routes and cameras to crack and edit, the up-to-date info she'd gone back and altered. As far as all accessible data was concerned, she was about to travel to her former home in Old North Carolina instead of Miguel's party they'd hacked her into. Heller would monitor from a block away. And Ranger would attempt a rescue if they encountered anything either of them couldn't handle.

She zipped the bag shut and inhaled. Then stripped off the T-shirt and pants she'd borrowed last night and allowed her skin to soak in the brisk air as a news alert mentioning her name suddenly chimed on her handheld.

She glanced up and clicked on the bathroom's tele to the i-reality news station and found drama practically dripping off the star, Nadine's, pastel blue lips. "Did you hear? Sources close to the family are saying Sofi Snow sold out her Corp."

Sofi rolled her eyes and ran a brush through her hair.

How quickly humans could turn on each other when fed suspicion. Like smoke tossed out as solid evidence, whispered into the frightened ears of those needing someone to blame in order to feel safe again. "They are currently tracking down her location in cooperation with the UW's attorney general."

She snorted and imagined her mother's face when it became known her daughter had run off with an ambassador of questionable morals.

The next moment Nadine's coiffed red hair was billowing as she hurried to a doorway—which Sofi recognized as on the south side of Corp 30's building—where a host of staff were exiting from the ground floor.

"Ms. Gaines! Ms. Gaines! A word, please! My employer over at Corp 24 would like me to ask a few questions."

Sofi's mom emerged behind both women, shaking hands with the staff. Sofi narrowed her gaze.

"Were Sofi and her brother at odds?" Nadine asked.

"Well, of course, all siblings are at odds," came Ms. Gaines's reply.

Nadine nodded. "And now evidence suggests she could've been behind the FanFight attack. Can you comment on that?"

"Well, I don't like to assume anything. Particularly when it's, in fact, *your* company, Nadine, that's the perpetrating party. Honestly, I strongly suggest you investigate a little closer to home for your show. Now, if you'll excuse me . . ."

Barking up the wrong tree, Nadine. You should be investigating Gaines. Sofi studied her mom as Nadine moved in to try to question her.

Sofi chewed her cheek a full fifteen seconds. Then cursed. *What all does Mom know?* She picked up the untraceable black-market phone she'd bought off Ranger's crew and, after a glance both ways down the empty hallway, linked to her famed CEO mother.

She watched the tele through three cycles of phone clicks before it beeped on the other end.

"This is Inola."

"Mom?"

Pause. "Hello?"

"It's Sofi."

On the tele, Sofi watched the woman freeze in place, handheld to her ear—staring at the noisy group without seeming to see them. A moment later her mother pushed away from Nadine and strode away until she was off camera. "Is this a joke? If it is—"

"It's not a joke, so listen for a dang minute." Sofi tried to keep her voice down despite the immediate annoyance the woman's tone provoked. "Because I'm alive, and I think Shilo is too."

Hesitation. "What? Where are you? Sofi—"

"Mom, what's going on? Because someone's setting it up to look like Corp 24's explosion was my idea. I saw the files. But you know I'd *never* hurt Shilo."

On the tele Ms. Gaines was strolling from the dwindling group toward where her mother had disappeared. A half second longer and Sofi could hear the woman's voice through the phonecom. "Inola? Everything all right?"

"Yes, Gaines. Thank you. I'll be done in a moment."

"I told them to screen your calls, so if you'd like me—"

Sofi's mom's voice took on a tone she knew all too well as her mother walked back on camera. Ms. Gaines followed. "I'm fine, Gaines. I'd appreciate privacy. You're excused."

"Mom, I know the Delonese have been closely monitoring Shilo for years. And I know that *you* allowed it."

Silence.

Sofi gulped. "I don't know why or what happened yesterday, but I think Shilo's with them now."

More silence.

"Mom, please. Help me understand what's going on and what the Delonese want."

"Sofi, I don't know what you're playing at," her mother whispered, "but there are people looking for you and asking questions. Where are you? And why didn't you come straight to me? Why are you even looking into the Delonese?"

Sofi's throat hardened as she peered in the bathroom mirror at herself, her backbone rippling with childhood anger and hurt and disgust for this woman.

"Come to my office so we can get this whole tragedy figured out, okay?" her mom said. "And anything to do with the Delonese . . . you need to drop right now. Do you hear me?"

"You're joking, right? I'm trying to find your son and you're asking me to come in under investigation?"

"Oh, don't be ridiculous. I'm just saying you need to be here with us and let me handle this. Let me protect you."

"I saw him, Mom. I saw Shilo."

"Wait—what? When? *Where?*"

"When they were loading us on the med beds. He was with a Delonese. And if you don't believe me, then ask Ms. Gaines where he is. Ask her where I was—on floor fourteen in Corp 30's med wing. Ask her where Shilo's tech suit is, and why every bit of info on him has been erased from all the FanFight and Corp 30 databases as of 4:00 p.m. yesterday."

For a second, Sofi thought she caught the slightest inhale. Then, in the background, she heard Gaines again. On the telescreen, the woman spoke into a phone of her own. "What do you mean, you lost her? Trace the phone, check the vids, everything you've been doing the past hour but harder."

Sofi's mom stared at Ms. Gaines with a frown as the woman covered her handset and leaned into Inola. "It's a necessary decision I'm making for all of us," she whispered. "To ensure your and your daughter's safety."

"Mom—"

Her mother got an odd look in her eye, then her voice turned harsh. "I'm sorry. I have to go. Turn yourself in before we come find you ourselves," she said so low Sofi could hardly hear her. "And as far as your other ridiculous assumptions—stop it. You're making up clues far above your level of understanding. I strongly urge you to ignore whatever you think you've found and let us figure this out as a company."

She hung up the call.

Sofi stared at the screen in shock. She couldn't move, couldn't unclench the phone, couldn't do anything other than swallow the rage as her head tried to make sense of it. Her mom wasn't even glad she was alive, let alone attempting to listen to her.

Sofi shook her head. Unbelievable.

On the tele, security had formed around her mother and Gaines and was ushering them away. Nadine smiled into the camera just before it went to an advertisement for her company's Altered.

Sofi blinked away the warmth from her eyes. If her mother had learned anything about her daughter by now, it should've been that if she really wanted her to come around, she could at least fake being warm and open. But to maintain the callous distance and then dish insults? Sofi would respond the way she always did—by doing the exact opposite of what the woman told her to.

She sniffed. It just proved again the woman knew nothing of her children.

With a harsh laugh, she slipped on the short, flirty red dress hanging on the door, which in the bathroom mirror slid over her like blood and wine over brown silk skin. She paused. She liked it. She looked wild. She looked fierce.

She looked like herself.

Another knock from Heller came just as she picked up her bag and pulled on a golden-red *Day of the Dead* half mask she'd 3-D printed.

"Coming." With one final peek in the mirror, she plastered a smirk over the hurt and smoothed her long wavy hair. When she showed up at Miguel's tonight, it would be her last public appearance for a while. She just hoped her mother wouldn't throw in a curveball and show up.

And as far as Miguel . . . Fingers crossed he'd go for it. Otherwise, perhaps Ambassador Lee. Either way, she'd get to Delon and find her brother.

And after that, she and Shilo would evaporate.

20

MIGUEL

DRINKS CLINKED, VOICES CHATTERED, LAUGHTER RIPPLED across the midnight air to ascend and flirt with the moon. A beautiful skyline only added to the glitz of the fire dancers and music. The scene was one Miguel had lived a thousand times over in the past two years, and absolutely planned on living a thousand times more in the future.

He eyed the current who's who of UW, celebrity, and humanitarian guests, all dressed in their finest with masks or costumes or filmy dresses. All getting in on photos like the tabloids were going out of style.

"They're our greatest hope for the future!" a voice rose in excitement.

"What are?" came a reply. "The fashion designers or fusion injections?" Which prompted a hearty laugh from those gathered around the buffet tables.

Miguel took a bite of his hot dog.

"Old skool, eh?" Nadine brushed her hand against the low of his back. He stiffened despite the wound having healed within minutes of last night's intruder disappearing, thanks to Corp 7's med-kit invention.

He pointed to the vendor a few feet away. "Get you one?"

She laughed, sliding her hand from the injury to his bicep, where she left it. "Miguel, you have a caviar and oyster bar, and you're choosing to eat hot dogs with habaneros. Thanks but no thanks. I think I'll stick with my wine."

"You certain?" He winked and pretended to welcome her touch on his skin. "Your loss."

Leaning close, she batted her lashes in the same way she did on her reality shows. "It wouldn't be if you'd tell me what you're up to. I know you think Corp 24's guilty. And Corp 30 clearly wants justice. But you . . ." She bobbed a finger along his arm and gazed up at him. "You've got something you're not saying. So of course I'm dying to know."

He widened his grin and peered around as if looking for cameras. "Oh, my dear, I'm thinking 'secrets of the sordid politicians' has quite the ring for your next episode."

Her giggle bubbled out. So rich and full it almost distracted from the scrutiny of her gaze. She was searching.

Searching for what?

"Ah, there you are."

Miguel turned just as the Icelandic ambassador slipped up. "Typical, he's near the food."

Alis nodded at Nadine. "Mind if I steal him? He promised to chat yesterday's game bets with me."

Miguel tossed his food away and winked at Nadine in drama. "Apparently priorities call. Careful now," he added in an overly loud voice as he followed Alis toward the garden. "I can't promise I'm completely sober."

"All the better," Alis quipped in a tone tinkling with atmosphere. Quietly she added, "Claudius made mention a new cargo shipment was taken."

Miguel nodded. "We'll be able to find out more once we arrive. What of your situation?"

"I've taken care of Delon. I'll be replacing Ambassador Lee on tomorrow's trip after the unfortunate illness he's about to come down with. I'll be traveling with Danya."

Miguel nodded again. "Perfect. On a side note . . ." He eyed her. "Is there any reason your name would've come up along with Corp 24's and the Delonese? Vic found some type of coded connection."

"Funny, I was going to ask you the same thing." Alis pulled a handscreen from her pocket and swiped it. And held up a photo of the explosion. "Tell me truthfully, do you think yesterday's explosion had anything to do with our project? Because why would my name or the Delonese be anywhere near this drama?"

Miguel hesitated. What could he say without uncovering himself or the note? After a moment—"I think it had something to do with the Corporations and Delonese."

She bit her cheek. "So maybe they're just trying to connect anyone at this point—including me."

He agreed as she flipped to another photo.

"And what about her? Will she be a problem?"

Miguel raised his brow. The pic was of Sofi from the hover vid last night. He kept his tone light. "I think she's searching for answers just like the rest of us, but she has nothing to do with it. Although clearly someone's interested in framing her."

Alis studied him a moment. Absorbing, calculating, deciding. Then finally gave a short nod just as a footstep sounded behind them.

"Ah, there he is. The man of the hour!"

Miguel presented a smile before he spun around to find

Corp 13's CEO Hart walking over with a plate of raw oysters on genetically engineered cornmeal in hand—a spin on soul fusion that was one of the big foodie trends. He bowed. "CEO Hart. Enjoying your time, I hope."

"Best event in weeks. In weeks, I tell you." The man was scooping the oysters with his fingers and taking bites. "Wanted to ask before you head to Delon in the a.m.—what do *you* think about this whole terrorist thing?" he said around a mouthful. "You expect it's really an Earth attack? Or maybe the aliens are involved in this one."

His voice was like a magnet. Alis and Miguel had the garden to themselves seconds ago—but the place was now an instant swarm of party attendees. All smiling and chattering and ready to weigh in their opinions in an open conversation.

Miguel steadied his expression and said casually, "I think nothing is ever what it seems."

Hart slapped him on the back and laughed. "Spoken like the true swindler of secrets! I like that. But really, give us a peek. Who is it? Who had something to gain and everything to lose?"

The image of standing on his own balcony being threatened with secrets last night—secrets he could never afford to have revealed—blasted Miguel's mind. *"Make sure the blame sits on Corp 24." In other words, convince them. Turn the elites against them.* He ground his teeth and hesitated as CEO Hart waited for his answer, and the ghost of last night's knife wound pricked again. Why not just say it was Corp 24? Use persuasion to convince every power person here?

He caught Claudius's eye across the lawn.

Because he was an arrogant *imbécil*, that's why.

He could practically hear Claudius begging him, *Don't jeopardize the bigger picture just for your pride, Miguel.*

"Well, if you ask me," Alis piped up, "when the answer's blaring you in the face, it's usually the correct one. Corp 24 did it."

Miguel raised a brow. She was apparently still passionate on that point.

"For the sake of being controversial then," Nadine said, sauntering over, "why don't we say the complete opposite and blame the Delonese?"

Miguel took a water from a waiter's tray. "Gracias." He sipped it. And stayed silent.

"Been here for ten years and they still haven't tried to colonize us yet," Corp 4's female VP said. "That alone is weird."

"I'm voting the girl did it," came a comment from the back.

CEO Hart wiped his hands on a napkin. "I'm personally inclined to agree that it's 24 or the girl. But either way, if it's not Sofi, she'll certainly be out for blood." He looked around as if to ensure CEO Inola had stuck with her decision not to attend tonight. "And the mom too."

"Oooh," a few people purred. "Harsh blow," someone added.

Hart lifted his hand. "Now, now, I'm not saying Inola doesn't have a right to. Heck knows I'd do the same in her shoes. I'm just saying that whoever it was better come clean quick before that woman starts World War Five. We Corps take such things seriously. Heck knows we certainly don't convert taxes into infrastructure and security for nothing. But man, I'd hate to see Inola misuse corporate monies and harm the broader community on a personal witch hunt."

The disgruntled boos turned to chuckles of agreement as Miguel's frown deepened. The guy almost sounded like he was subterfuging.

"I don't know," Nadine's voice slipped in. "From what I hear, the woman wasn't even there yesterday. I think CEO Inola cares more for how it'll make the company look than for the loss of life."

Miguel swerved to eye her just as Aris added, "The daughter, on the other hand . . . You ever seen her fight? She's not just a game hacker. She's got some skills. And if they find traces between her tech access and Corp 24, well . . ."

CEO Hart began nodding along with a few others as Miguel caught Claudius's gaze again from beyond the archway. His friend inclined his head carefully in the direction of the garden entrance. Miguel frowned. What was he indicating?

Tipping his glass to the gathering, Miguel cleared his throat and excused himself.

He'd just passed through the exit facing the patio when everything within him stalled.

He swerved—searching the guests' faces, body heights, and attitudes as the aroma of sun-parched earth and greenthread flora wafted over him. The same smell that had tugged at his lungs and lips for weeks after their first encounter—taunting his dreams and burning his insides to ashes until the central focus in his messed-up life had been seducing her.

He flipped around—and found her standing by the garden wall. Alive. Breathing.

Sofi.

A bit older, a bit wiser, and, from what he'd heard, *mucho más* broken—but still standing nonetheless. Dressed in a slip of a dress that set off her skin like the color of earth and sunset, and her hair like midnight skies, wearing a *Day of the Dead* mask to hide her soul. How Claudius had identified her Miguel wasn't sure—perhaps the same way Miguel did now, by the small threaded owl at her throat.

She'd not seen him yet. He could still get away before his mind took a dive.

Except . . .

He chuckled. She was speaking to a guard and looking as pissed off as ever while trying not to show it. Playing coy beneath the stars and soft lights.

He studied her hair. Her posture. Her little hands that clasped and unclasped when she was irritated. The way she lifted one of them to rub Shilo's necklace against her creamy brown skin as her soft-lipped smile broadened like a moonbeam.

Miguel let a chuckle slip from his mouth. She'd learned to flirt.

He took a sip of his drink and leaned against the garden wall, ignoring three nearby ladies trying to snag his eye. He evaluated her pose, the measure of her distance leaning in to the poor guard she was chatting up—and the just-as-quick leaning back once the man's breath caught audibly and his shoulders softened. Ah, she had him. She was good, he'd give her that. Better than good.

He should know. He frowned as the water went sour in his stomach. He'd taught her.

He pushed his mask up onto his head and strode over. "*Está bien*, Jose, she's with me." And peered down at her.

"Yes, sir." The guard moved on as Sofi's thick lashes fluttered, and then her gaze swung up to lock onto his.

A second later she smiled and slipped close, leaving inches between her barely dressed body and his. Leaning up, she placed her hand on his chest and whispered, "Hello, Miguel."

21

SOFI

SOFI ROCKED BACK IN HER BLACK LACE-UP BOOTS BUT KEPT her fingers on his chest. A song crooned gently behind them, rippling on the air like the autumn leaves swirling beneath the terrace lights in the background.

Miguel's mouth curved with curiousity. "Long time no see."

Sofi chuckled. "I believe that was your decision, not mine."

He paused and his Adam's apple bobbed as if he were wetting a suddenly dry throat. A moment later he leaned over, careful not to brush against her, and set his glass on top of the stone garden wall behind her. She waited. What was he thinking? How long did she have before he kicked her out or asked her to leave? How much should she impress his interest before voicing her need?

"Is there something I can help you with?" he said against her hair before he slowly pulled back.

"May we speak privately?"

"Should I ask what it's regarding?"

"Your past. My brother. Your career's future."

A quiet laugh trickled from his lips as he watched her, his gaze drifting over her face, her neck, her shoulders, as if he could unwrap her thoughts with his mind. "Well, that doesn't sound familiar at all."

She smiled and looked away—to Claudius at the fireplace surrounded by a host of partygoers.

It was, in fact, a bit eerily similar to the first time they'd met. "Sofi, Miguel. Miguel, Sofi," her mother had said the night before the official opening of the first FanFight Games. "If you can ignore Miguel's past, you two could be very good for your brother's future, dear."

Her mom had then leaned close to Sofi and murmured, "Now play polite and don't let your brother eat all the pastries before the game tomorrow. And next time wear something a bit more becoming." As if she knew anything about how many outfits Sofi'd insecurely tried on or the fact that her brother had never eaten pastries, because they were just "bread surrounding the good parts."

But she'd soon forgotten that in the glow of Miguel.

And it wasn't hard to see why. Even now, his soft twinge of a smile, nice nose, and a jawline set above a physique as broad and strong as it was comfortably thick in its own skin. And the voice that hinted at laughter and secrets and a darkly simpering soul hidden beneath impeccable style . . .

Good gad. Seriously?

Sofi blinked and swallowed, then expanded her chest as she straightened her collarbone and chin. *Pull yourself together.*

His eyes stayed locked on hers.

She cleared her throat before reaching up to let her mouth brush his ear. "Well, in that case, it would appear we've come full circle. So how about you take me to your room now?"

22

MIGUEL

HER LIPS WERE A BOLT OF LIGHTNING ON HIS SKIN, IGNITING HIS blood as she let her cool breath mingle with his suddenly warm inhale. Until she dropped off her tiptoes to stand a good bit lower than his shoulders and quirked a smile he knew far better than he should.

Coolness. Rage. Disgust, he'd expected, sí.

But this . . .

This Miguel was not prepared for.

He stayed rigid, refusing to let his mind acknowledge the feeling of her tiny hand still resting against his chest. He swallowed and kept his jaw tight. And frowned. "What are you playing at, Sofi?"

Her brow shot up. "So asks the player," she murmured and swept her gaze out over the patio where the nightlife had taken things to a new high. The fire dancers had emerged on stilts and the brass bands had struck up a slew of old-skool tunes—ones from what had affectionately been dubbed the Gatsby era after some book he doubted anyone under eighty had ever read. At the moment Morton's "Wolverine Blues" was being followed by Berlin's "Always."

He waited as the lyrics trickled over them—"*Everything went wrong . . . Then I met you*"—and tried not to notice her tan skin stretching along her night-lit shoulder or her black makeupless lashes scattering shadows on her high cheekbones beneath the mask.

"The truth is, I need a favor, Miguel."

Her words were so soft he almost missed them, and so simple he almost lost the note of self-annoyance. *Ah, there it is.*

He smirked. It must be a good one if she hated having to ask that much.

"Now, are we going to stand here awkwardly until you kick me out, or are you going to be a decent human and take me someplace to hear what I have to ask? If nothing else, for old time's sake."

He gnawed his lip. Amused. Curious. Fascinated by this turn of events. With a short nod he placed his hand on her back and steered her through the scattered crowds, attempting to shield her from the cast of curious eyes.

"I'm assuming you shut down my cameras and security system," he said when they reached the side door near the elevator.

"Only the parts pertaining to me."

Of course she did. He kept back a grin, scanned his wrist against the lock, and slipped Sofi inside before anyone could suspect more than romance was in the air.

They descended a delicate flight of stairs that opened straight into his carefully ordered room.

She coughed. "Nice space, by the way." She turned to face him. "Although I expected a bit more drama—maybe some girls, silk sheets, a few mirrors."

His jaw flinched at the acknowledgment. "*Lo siento* to disappoint you," he said quietly. Then frowned. His glass doors stood wide open.

She waved a hand at them, then slipped off her mask. "Sorry. Had to leave them that way in case your guards didn't buy my ID."

He took a quick scan of the rest of the room. His bed. Bookcases. Empty bathroom. All clear from what he could see. Then folded both arms across his chest and veered his attention back to her, far more aware of her presence than he should be. And what it was doing to him. "So what kind of favor are you asking?"

"I need you to take me to Delon."

He brain tripped as he practically laughed. *"Perdón?"*

"I need to get to Delon. And I'd like you to take me in"—she checked the time—"two hours when you leave for the hangar."

Miguel rubbed his jaw and stared at her. Trying like heck to figure out why she was really there and what she honestly wanted from him. When she didn't flinch, he took a step back and stared. "Wait, you're serious."

She nodded.

"Okay, and you want me to do this why?"

Her voice firmed. "They have Shilo."

Miguel tried to keep his expression neutral. *Was she joking? The kid was dead. He'd seen the explosion.* "And what gives you that impression?" Miguel flicked another glance at the open doors. Even with his emotions wrapped around her every move, the exposure was making him uneasy.

"I saw him after the explosion. Alive on a med cot, and a Delonese was moving him out."

Miguel went still. *A Delonese medic? Was with him?* He swallowed. *Claudius's discovery about the second flight.*

"I know it sounds crazy." Sofi shook her head. "But . . ." She gave a nervous laugh.

Miguel was at a complete loss. She was bracing for him to

answer no. He could see it in her eyes, the tilt of her chin, the clench of her fist.

And yet she truly believed what she was stating. He sucked in his cheeks. She'd have to if she was desperate enough to come to him. And he could see why if she really did witness a Delonese with Shilo. In fact, Miguel would've thought the same. It was beyond abnormal.

He tipped his head. "Okay. And if I don't?"

"Then you don't," she said so quickly a glimpse of her soul showed through. Cracked. Wounded. Courageous for even coming here during the storm surrounding her brother and mother and accusations flying. "It's just a request."

Guilt stabbed his gut even as he relaxed and recrossed his arms and tried to keep his head clear enough of her to think. "Okay. So, saying I did take you, what do you expect to find? And how do you expect me to do so? The Delonese aren't exactly—"

"I've taken care of that. I'd be a stowaway so you could claim no knowledge. Your records, your ship, their tracking systems—everything would be wiped clean. I've already begun, in fact."

He supposed he shouldn't be surprised, but he was. Of course she could do all that. He turned and strode to the open doors to glare at the deck beyond.

"You know I'm perfectly capable of it, Miguel," she said from behind him. "And if you take me—once we're on the planet I'll escape and take off on my own. Shilo would be my responsibility, and you'd be above reproach. I just need the transit."

Right. Except even she couldn't keep them off the Delonese's radar once they hit the atmospheric shield. He'd have to explain their presence to the aliens, and gad knows that'd be an impossible task.

He shook his head and eyed Planet Delon lit up like a hot-air balloon just past the night's waning moon. And filled his lungs with something other than her perfume. "Except they'll know you're on board before we land. And what are you planning to do—just ask permission to wander through their capital, hunting for your brother? Because as the other ambassadors and I are requesting their assistance, you'll be—what—accusing them of stealing your brother? Marvelous. Everything you'd do there—just you being there at all—*directly* affects me. And not just me, but *them*. The Delonese . . . Earth . . . Sofi, you could start a war, for gad's sake."

"Then help me. Hide me. Convince them I forced you to let me come or that you didn't know I was on board until we'd almost arrived, and I'll return with you when you're done. Whether we find Shilo or not. I just need the chance. I know he's *with* them."

"You've got to be kidding." He shoved a hand through his hair and pulled off his mask, tossing it on the bed behind him. "Not to be rude, but you honestly have no idea what you're asking. Nor of the consequences such a thing could create."

This was *de locos*. Taking her would jeopardize not just one mission but two . . .

Claudius would be furious.

"Actually, I know exactly what I'm asking. These people—this *race*—have spent the past eleven years monitoring my brother. They've been *studying* him."

Miguel stared at her. An image of that second hovercraft leaving the games yesterday passed through his mind.

"And Corp 30 allowed them. And our VP tried to have me questioned and killed yesterday to keep this all quiet."

Miguel frowned. Was she joking?

Clearly not. Which only made him despise the Gaines woman all the more.

He swallowed. The other delegates would be furious. The freaking UW would be livid if they found out. *Híjole*, he couldn't believe he was even considering it.

And yet . . .

"I'm asking for your help."

23

SOFI

SOFI WATCHED MIGUEL PACE IN FRONT OF THE OPEN DOORS against the sparkling city lights. The fact he was actually considering her request made her more nervous than if he'd just laughed in her face. Because, good grief, she was perfectly aware how feeble she sounded. And what if it actually worked? She grimaced. Why wasn't he asking for proof? *Why aren't you pushing back more, Miguel?*

"Sofi, I don't like this." Heller's voice blasted her eardrum.

She jumped, then hissed, "Heller, you're yelling," before tapping her earcom for Miguel's benefit as he turned to see who she was talking to.

"Yeah, well, something strange is up," Heller said quieter. "I think you might be about to have company."

She looked past Miguel through the open doors. "What? From where—the deck?"

"What do you mean 'from the deck'?" Heller said. "Wait. Are you in his room, Sofi?"

Miguel was frowning. "Is that Heller?"

"Sofi, *are you in his room*?"

She stalled. "How'd you—?"

Miguel shook his head. "Vic mentioned Heller'd survived. Congrats to him. What did you mean 'from the deck'?" He turned and examined the area before he pressed his palm to the wall to initialize the glass doors sliding shut.

Heller's voice was loud again. "Okay, *what* are you doing in there? He's not—you guys aren't—"

"Heller, I said I'm fine. Holy heck, are you joking? Do you even know me at all?"

His voice went flat. "That's exactly why I'm asking."

Her face flooded with heat. She refused to justify that with a response and instead clicked the earcom off on her end and glanced at Miguel. "Time's up. What's the decis—?"

It happened so fast. One second Miguel was standing in front of the closing doors as a strain of elegant mariachi music floated down from the roof. The next, three men in black had dropped behind him with face masks melted over their skin.

Miguel stepped back to block her just as the men slid through the narrowing glass slit.

"Sorry, mate. Slight change of plans," said the taller one. "We're taking gamer girl, and you can continue with what you were told. You now have twenty-four hours to comply or—"

"Whoa, amigo. No need to rush." Miguel put up his hands, then slowly moved them behind his back. "Let's talk about what you want with her."

"Miguel—"

"That's our employer's business, *amigo.*"

Miguel's tone went light. "See, I'm thinking it's my business considering you're in my bedroom just as she and I were about to—well, you know." The tip of a knife glinted against his back as he pulled it from beneath his shirt.

The man stepped forward, lifting his gun straight at Miguel's stomach, while the other two moved to each side of him, their face masks blank of emotion. "Cute. But your charm only works in public, Ambassador. You forget who's holding the photos."

"About that." Miguel twitched the knife. "I'd love to know how you got those."

Sofi's skin pricked—her chest tightening with rage at this man who slid his gun against Miguel's left side.

"Same way you got these love handles. *Laziness.* Now, do we have an understanding?"

She stiffened and glanced around the room for something to use. *Dangit, Miguel, why don't you have more weapons?*

"So, you take the girl, and I do my thing. And then I'm clear, correct?" Miguel turned his head toward Sofi and caught her eye. She frowned until she realized he was lying.

The man with the gun relaxed. "Ah, now see, mate. You're getting it." He lifted the weapon to pat Miguel's face just as Sofi dove forward. She kicked out the legs of the guy on the left just as Miguel brought his blade around and shoved it into the gunman's chest.

Sofi's guy went down and she brought her foot to his crotch. Then looked over at the knifed thug already slumped on the ground, blood oozing from his wound. Miguel had the gun in hand and was holding the third gentleman in place with it. Two seconds later he brought it over the guy's head and sent him to the floor, knocked out cold.

"Griffin, we've got a 132—"

Miguel turned and did the same to the man using his earcom to alert whomever. Then repeated it with the knifed dude before he tucked the gun into his pants.

Sofi lifted a brow.

Miguel pulled out his handscreen and tapped a button. "Hey, Claudius, something came up. I need you to meet me at the shuttle bay as quick as possible." He glanced up. "Mind if I ask what they want you for?"

Sofi shook her head. "I don't know."

"Not good enough. Especially if I'm about to risk my life and a whole lot more. So, care to guess?" He strode to his closet.

"Could've been Corp 30. They think I have information they want about the bomb or my brother. Or both."

Miguel stopped. Turned. "Are these Corp 30's guys?"

She eyed the three splayed out on the floor. "I don't know. I don't recognize them, but that doesn't mean much. From the way the news played today, they could honestly be from anyone." She knelt beside the taller one and sifted through his pockets, then followed suit with the other two. Nothing. *Of course.* "Guess we could've asked, if you hadn't knocked them out."

He sniffed. "Fair point."

"But if we wait until they come to—"

"We'll be in deeper crud. I think it's a safe bet we're about to have more." He pulled a bag from the closet and nodded. "Let's go."

Sofi stared. Then blinked and scowled. "So then you're taking me?"

He scanned his palm against the elevator safe-lock. "Blame it on the fact that for whatever reason I might actually believe you. That and . . ." He turned and let his gaze drift over her until her breath caught. His jaw clenched and he swerved back to the door. "Never mind. *Ándele.*"

"What about them?" Sofi waved at the three men on the

floor before ducking by the bed to retrieve a bag she'd apparently stashed there.

Miguel stalled. Chewed his lip. "Right."

He tapped his phone again as the elevator door opened. "And, Claudius, I'd suggest you avoid my bedroom."

24

MIGUEL

"YOU'RE KIDDING, RIGHT?" CLAUDIUS WAS STANDING IN HIS granddaddy sequin-suit glaring at Miguel through the dim outdoor hoverlights. "We're taking a fugitive—scratch that—*taking anyone* to Delon?" he hissed. "Are you bloody insane?"

Miguel firmed his jaw. *Okay, so he's a bit more than pissed.* "Not a fugitive. And it's risky, sí, but—"

Claudius slapped his hand on the outer wall of the shuttle warehouse looming above them. "It's not risky, it's stupidity! Miguel, if you—" He glanced around—probably to check if Sofi was listening from where she was hiding in the dark—before leaning in. "If you thought that note and the pics were a threat, can you *imagine* what this will do? You'll blow the whole thing to hell."

"Or give us what we need."

Claudius shook his head. "No, no, no. This is a bad idea. I don't care what affection you have regarding her, this is not how you do things. You are smarter than this."

"This is exactly how we do things. We take risks."

"Not like this. For heck's sake, Miguel—what if they've *already* exposed you? Exposed *us*? You beat down three of their men and stole someone they wanted. You think they're going to take that lightly?" Claudius plowed a hand through his hair.

"They won't while I have her." Miguel stepped closer. "Think about it. If they already had what they needed without me, they would've leaked those pics by now. The fact they keep threatening means they're desperate. It means there's something else going on—someone in the picture who's breathing down their necks and helping pull the strings. And for whatever reason they need my influence to ensure they're in the clear—meaning something's not as certain as they need it to be in the public eye. And now"—he tipped his head in the direction of Sofi—"I've got the other thing they want. So I'm willing to bet they require me now more than ever. And besides"—he rubbed his neck—"their threats only make it more imperative we figure things out as soon as possible. And she's our way of doing so."

Miguel watched Claudius go still. His words sinking in.

So he continued. "Think about what we've just been offered. Not only do they need us, we have the top hackers in the world using their skills to find her brother. It's closer than we've ever come politically or physically. If Shilo's not there, we can let her fend for herself. But if the whole thing's about to blow up anyway, better we utilize our options sooner than later. Because there's no guarantee that the moment I comply, they won't ruin us."

"But the Delonese—"

"The Delonese will be fine. I'll see to that. The minute they pick up her life-sign, I'll explain we had no choice. If anything, they have a thing for underdogs, and I'll work it to our advantage. You know me, Claudius. You know what I can do."

Claudius's mouth pursed tight. "Don't misjudge your value to them, friend."

"Right." Miguel sighed. "But what good is our value if we don't use it for something? Besides, they came after her with a gun at *mi casa*. Meaning they'd managed to tag her via one of the few cams she didn't disable." His gaze flickered again to where Sofi was hiding. "With that high level of interest, she knows something—or someone thinks she does. And in that case, you and I both know what'll happen if she stays."

"She can keep off the grid just fine."

"Probably. But if not?"

"Then even worse—because that means she can't keep us off it either."

Miguel bit his tongue. He knew what his friend meant, but what if this was their best shot? It made sense. He knew it made sense. And he could see it already working through Claudius's mind, offering promise and presenting the possibilities. "We need her skills, *primo*."

Miguel waited, one eye on Sofi's barely visible figure in his peripheral, one lung still inhaling her perfume, while she sat in her soft dress, headphones on, cross-legged on the ground against the warehouse hangar, tapping on her comp-screen in the dark, from what he could make out. "If it helps, I already had Vic run the numbers."

"And?"

"The outcomes were inconclusive. But there wasn't a sure chance of death."

Claudius barked out a laugh. "Nice. And what of security cams monitoring the entire in-flight shuttle?"

Miguel smirked. "She apparently pulled a vid from two trips ago and looped it into the system."

Claudius paused long enough to look duly impressed. Then after a moment he cursed and turned for the hangar opening.

"Dangit, dude, you better be right." He tapped his earcom. "Security, we're ready to depart. Prepare the pad."

"Hey, wait!" a voice whispered harshly.

Miguel spun to see a kid—Heller, he presumed, due to the geek shirt and skinny jeans—strolling up through the midnight dim as if all security and cameras had simply ceased to exist.

Claudius shot Miguel a look. "You've got to be kidding me."

"Heller?" Sofi jumped up. "What—?"

"No offense, Sof, but if you think I'm going to trust you with these guys on your own, you're freaking wrong." He dropped his bag next to her, then strode past to Miguel. "I'm coming or I'm alerting the UW. Which is it?"

Claudius scoffed. "Don't lump me in with the golden boy." He cleared his throat. "At least not until I'm done being pissed."

Sofi grabbed her friend's arm. "Heller, I don't think—"

"It's not your choice, it's his." Heller stared at Miguel.

Miguel kept his tone cool, calculated, firm. "You'll only make this harder, *cuate*."

"Look, dude. You do your thing, we'll do ours. We only need you for the ride. I've fixed us as stowaways, and I've already taken care of the cams getting here."

Miguel's mouth flattened. "Clearly."

"You'll be at no fault in anyone's eyes. Unless"—he glanced at Sofi—"the Delonese really are telepathic."

Miguel caught Sofi's frown. He lifted a brow. *Telepathic?* He let the hint of a smile edge his lips. "That's an old *mito*. They're advanced, not omnipotent."

"Thank heck," Claudius grumbled from the door. "Or we'd be dead men already. And for the record . . ." He turned back, his sequins shimmering in the overhead light. "This is a terrible idea and I'm against it. But considering Miguel may have a point . . ."

"With Delon's tech, they'll know you're on board as soon as we enter their space." Miguel focused on Sofi and switched into instruction mode. "The key is to get you on the ship here as stowaways so we can cover ourselves regarding Earth. Once we hit Delon's shield, though, it's up to me to do some fancy explaining. At which point they'll either shoot us, turn us around, or allow you entry as asylum-seekers with plenty to offer." His gaze softened at Sofi. "So we'd better have something to offer."

Claudius turned to Heller. "And not just for the Delonese, but for us. We get you in and you're not getting off with just 'hitching a ride.' Because we're not your bleeding nannies. You come—you two are going to put those nerd skills to use on what *we* need. No issues. No questions. Meaning we own you for the duration of Delon. Got it?" He waited for Heller to nod. "Good. Now, are we leaving? Because you're on your own with figuring out how to board." Claudius stepped through the door.

"By the way, nice suit, dude," Heller called after him as the ambassador began speaking over his earcom to their captain.

Miguel turned. "You may have limited the cameras, but I still have to deal with security personnel."

"Right, so what do you need from us?" Sofi asked.

"Hang back until I can clear the space. And then run like heck to get on. And don't get caught."

25

SOFI

MIGUEL WAS SPEAKING IN LOW TONES WITH AN UNSEEN STAFF member when Sofi boarded in front of Heller. The ambassador was standing in a three-foot hall across the main cabin peering through one of four doorways, and whoever he spoke to, they didn't sound happy.

"The security officers and waitstaff," Claudius mouthed at her. He motioned to Heller to move, and as soon as the tech obeyed, pushed past to shut the door. A moment later he turned and beckoned them across the ten-foot space and into a "room" consisting of a thin bunk bed in a rectangle area barely larger than a closet.

Claudius shoved them into it, murmuring, "Did you load up a vid for their monitor?"

She waved a hand at the room's tiny window. "I pulled it from the UW's private server while on the hoverpad." She smirked. "It's all good, dude."

He looked like he didn't know whether to respect her or roll his eyes, so he closed the door instead, shutting them in, just as voices emerged from the next room—the one Miguel had been speaking into. Footsteps began moving around the main cabin.

She glanced at Heller as a voice said, "This is ridiculous, Ambassador. We're here to serve you."

"And I'm simply saying gracias, but this time we won't be needing service. Ambassador Claudius and I have much to get done and prefer the privacy."

Whatever argument continued, Sofi missed it as the speakers moved away.

Heller set his bag on the top bunk and stowed a backpack of tech stuff under the tiniest pillow Sofi had ever seen. After that, they waited.

The shuttle began to vibrate. A door from the room beside them was shut and, from the sound of it, locked.

A minute later theirs opened and Miguel was standing there. "*Lo siento* there's not more privacy." He directed them out to the small main area.

Sofi eyed the windows on one side, two giant teles, and four white faux-leather seats with an uncomfortable knot in her lungs. The ship was like a larger version of a bubble-looking jet she'd once sat in with her dad and Shilo at a rebuilt amusement park. Round and round it'd gone until Shilo had gotten sick, and then as soon as he'd thrown up he'd begged to go again.

She glanced at Miguel. *Good heck, don't vomit, Sofi.*

It wasn't just that, though. Nor was it the homesickness that single memory triggered. There was something else. Something she couldn't yet place. Something about being in this small space near Miguel made her feel she was losing the ability to breathe.

"What about Ambassadors Lee and Danya?" Heller muttered to Miguel. His tone matched the expression he'd had ever since they boarded, like he was suspicious or irritable. Or both. She stiffened. And yet he'd wanted to come.

"The UW prefers we take separate ships in case of emergency. In the long run it saves face and inconvenience. Although . . ."

Miguel glanced at Claudius. "I believe Ambassador Alis is replacing Lee due to an illness.

"That said"—Miguel indicated the room—"the main area is here, the door there is locked to the cockpit, the bathroom is straight back beside the security station, and you've seen the room. There's another just like it by the bathroom. We'll need to stay as quiet as possible. And if for some reason any personnel come out, stay silent and let me talk. Any questions, ask Claudius," Miguel joked, then bent over Heller's chair to show how the full-body belts worked.

When he turned to assist Sofi with hers, she just said coolly, "Thanks, I got it," and adjusted the straps herself.

Something flickered in his gaze, and he paused. She frowned, and the next moment he merely nodded and sat down to lock himself in beside Claudius's seat facing theirs as she bit her lip and peered at the ceiling above his head. That was how she preferred it. Cool distance. Back at his house, in his garden, it had been one thing—she needed to convince him. But now that she had, she didn't want Miguel that close again.

It messed with her head. She clasped and unclasped her fingers together.

The main engines started, and Sofi's stomach did an abrupt flip. She clamped her lips shut and breathed through her nose just as Heller's skin went yellow. *Okay, you seriously are not allowed to throw up, Sofi Snow.*

"How long's this flight again?" Heller growled through clenched teeth.

"Twelve hours."

"You'll get used to it," Claudius said with a wink before he pulled out his handheld and swiped it open.

The shuttle taxied off the pad and onto the barely lit 2:00 a.m. runway that, while tucked into the city, felt all at once a thousand miles away. Sofi could see the lights in the distance, like the stars hanging above and the planet perched in the sky. Waiting breathless by the moon for them to visit in their rocket ship.

Five seconds later the lights dinged and the captain's voice came on. "This is your captain speaking. Please ensure your harnesses are buckled and your chairs are comfy. We'll be taking off in ten, nine, eight . . ."

Sofi counted down in her head. When the man's voice hit number one, the craft shuddered and roared and shot straight into the night air, then tilted and turned its nose upward toward Earth's outermost layer of atmosphere.

"Here goes, kids," Claudius said, not taking his gaze off his screen.

The shuttle took off with a subdued rattle and a whole lot of muffled sound. Sofi watched them climb above the city, the blended lights, the Earth she knew. She tried not to think about how high up they were without parachutes to catch them—instead, just shut her eyes and yanked on her headphones to settle her body and nerves with metronic beats.

At some point she realized her shoulders hurt and glanced down to see Heller gripping his arm around her with his face too close. She shook him off before folding her arms around her stomach and staring out the window at the blackness.

After a bit, Miguel adjusted his seat, but she continued her refusal to even peek at him—to acknowledge him any more than necessary. Being around him wasn't just messing with her mind. It made her chest ache. Like it was doing something to her. Chipping away at her insides, like carving off pieces of ice.

The anger and ache flared beneath her ribs—triggering images of things they'd done together. Places they'd seen and the scent of his hair, his skin—eliciting a longing she wanted nothing to do with.

She frowned. She'd not been prepared for this. For the fact that it infuriated and thrilled her, and reminded her of what had been. Or, more accurately, of what had never truly existed. And she couldn't control that history no matter how much she'd tried.

She watched the haze of sun on the other side of Earth begin to glow just above the horizon until it gradually became a halo. And ignored the fact that she could sense Miguel's gaze flick periodically back to her. Caring. Careful. Grating on her nerves. *What the heck does he want?* She focused instead on the uncomfortable knot still nudging her with the warning that something was off. As it took shape, so did a question: Why had he so willingly brought her?

Eventually she pulled out her handscreen and went to work tearing apart and sorting through more of the code belonging to Corp 30 in an attempt to find the hacker behind it. Only to jump when Claudius suddenly exclaimed, "These guys are ridiculous!" at the tele on the wall in front of them.

"They're really digging with this thing," Claudius said, waving at Ms. Gaines's face filling the screen. "They literally just spent a whole segment talking about the possible terrorist motivations of the actual kid players. Now they've brought the Gaines chick on again."

"I've been staying silent on it out of respect, but at this point I can't deny there's been a rift between Sofi Snow and her mother," Gaines stated.

Heller snickered. "You think?" Then shot Sofi a sheepish look.

She frowned.

Ms. Gaines put on her sympathetic face, but all Sofi mainly noticed was Corp 13's CEO Hart behind her. What was he doing there? "I mean, what parent wouldn't be concerned when her daughter sleeps with half the employees and FanFight gamers. It's been a growing issue with Sofi, and we've struggled with how to support her."

"Whoa." Claudius froze.

"What the heck?" Heller balked at the tele.

Sofi's mouth went dry.

"In fact, multiple of our own employees here have come forward to . . ."

Ms. Gaines kept talking, but Sofi stopped listening. She didn't care. She stared at the screen and tried to find the air that had just left the room. *Crack, crack, crack*—she could practically feel her insides fracture at the anger and mortification warming her suddenly icy skin beneath the awareness of Miguel's gaze. Her throat squeezed.

She blinked and lifted her chin, and refused to take her eyes from the screen. Refused to look at him. To see his expression. To see any of their expressions.

Yes, she'd had relations with two employees in her mother's Corp last year—though it'd been just another way to spite the woman who years ago, long before Sofi had ever even kissed a boy, had suggested privately that Sofi's excessive flirting was undermining her CEO image.

"You need to think of how your behavior reflects on me with the company," Inola had whispered. "Over-friendliness can be misconstrued and your excessiveness seen as weakness on my part. What will they think if I can't even lead my own daughter?"

Sofi had been fourteen at the time and had no clue what over-friendliness even looked like, let alone how it was different from basic friendliness. She still didn't know.

But her retort of "perhaps I'd know how to behave better if you'd been there to tuck me and Shilo in at night" had earned her a week in "therapy" and launched Sofi's mission to prove her mother right. To prove that CEO Inola's daughter wasn't the perfect example of whatever the power woman needed her children to be. She was her own. She was Sofi.

Even if sometimes she couldn't remember who that was anymore.

"That's not right," Heller said. "What is she doing?"

"Sacrificing me for the Corp."

"Why?" Heller's gaze was confused. Infuriated. "That's not what—"

"Because they need to distance themselves in case I really did blow up the Colinade." Could he really be that ignorant after all this time working for them?

Miguel looked over. His face emotionless. Unreadable. "Did you?"

She almost laughed and, for the slightest second, wished she could say yes just to see the shock on his face. Instead, she shook her head. "But I'm currently hunting down who did. And I'm guessing it's *not* Corp 24."

"Same." He offered an apologetic smile.

She nodded and lifted her gaze. To hide the sting that was still burning as, in the background, the tele had moved off of Ms. Gaines. She put her headphones back on and watched Miguel's and Claudius's mouths move as they talked together. From what she could read of their lips, it had to do with one of the individuals replacing another at the Delonese meeting they were headed to.

When she glanced back up at the tele, the news was back to showing pics of the before-wreckage and then those of the construction already begun to rebuild the stadium, which, from the number of workers and around-the-clock shifts, would be done within days. As if this drama warranted all the emergency attention—like it was the only thing going on in the world.

As if impoverished families and black-market babies weren't suffering far worse.

As if families weren't grieving the loss of the players and gamers.

As if her survival wasn't cause for hope but rather a threat to someone's image—and a convenient target for blame.

Was it her mom's perspective as well or just Gaines's? Something told her it was the latter.

She watched the screen a few more minutes, then returned her gaze to Miguel, who was just logging back in to his handscreen. Moments later her eyes drooped heavy—the events finally catching up with her as the rocket ship rocked and the ice-planet waited. She let her mind wander as she drifted in and out, and the heavy bass of her music slowly lulled her into blackness.

26

MIGUEL

MIGUEL SHUFFLED AROUND THE NOTES ON HIS HOLOSCREEN and went back to ignoring Sofi. Ignoring her eyes, her humiliation at Gaines's accusation, her dimple on that one cheek that showed when she was furious, and those giant headphones that were too far out of style to possibly come back in. He cleared his throat and kept right on flipping through data.

As his guilt ate him alive for his part in pushing her into that world.

The first time he'd seen Sofi, she'd been just another girl, albeit slightly more interesting with the whole gamer thing going for her. Another head of rich brown hair and beautiful eyes, attached to silky brown limbs beneath a blue slip of a dress that floated around her like sky around Earth.

What he soon discovered was her brilliant mind could read a room like a coded cipher, and he'd watched her twirl a flyaway piece of that punk hair in its punk ponytail while speaking to a Corp 9 donor, sharing her idealistic thoughts about the world and her absolute disdain for the Delonese. As if they weren't standing right in the same dang room.

He'd liked her spunk. He'd liked the whole package. Even those headphones she wore alongside the owl necklace at her throat. "To cut out the noise and nightmares," she'd eventually told him.

But if her weirdness had caught him, it was her innocence that stole him—and all too quickly he found himself fascinated by something he couldn't dismiss.

And that had been the game. That was always the game—using them as much as they used him before the women could gain leverage or secrets to sell, always under the guise of trying to tame him or own him or be in any way enough for him.

When the truth all along was—they were all enough. More than enough.

He wasn't.

He gave a caustic laugh.

To his *madre* he'd been everything as a child—her *mi cielito*. And to his *padre* and extended family he'd been exactly what was expected—*el mano*. Until they'd been killed at a family fiesta when he was nine, in a terrorist attack during the Fourth War. They'd only lived in Old Colorado for a year.

He'd been out running the streets with his new friends and came home to a hole in the ground where his estate used to be, and the knowledge that he'd shirked his duty to his family—to be there, to have done something to defend them. And he'd lived with that shaming voice ever since—that he hadn't been enough. Until, over time, it became a driving force. Like an empty stomach always starving for approval and needing others' attention to feel full. To feel real. To feel valuable.

To be the man he'd failed at for his family.

And thus had begun another round—but with Sofi.

"Ambassadors, this is your captain speaking. Please feel free to now move about the cabin, and enjoy the rest of the flight."

Miguel looked up from his handscreen and stretched out his neck. Then his arms. Claudius had turned off the news in exchange for a vid game he and Heller were playing. Or rather, Heller was destroying him at. Miguel smirked, then dropped his gaze to Sofi.

It had taken a month—his longest time ever. Pursuing her during the FanFights and then after, as her initial rejection transformed into interest of her own. Until one sun-drenched late afternoon when he saw the look in her eyes. The look of innocence offered, if he wanted to take it.

He almost did take it.

If it hadn't been for the hope in her smile that hit him at the core, and with it, the dawning slowly erupted that whatever she offered, for the first time in his life, he could give nothing but passion and a few good intentions in return. Because with Sofi . . . She'd somehow managed to make him think he was exactly enough.

It had scared the *vida* out of him. So bad that he'd risen from the couch and walked out, and had never spoken to her again.

It wasn't until the next morning, though, that he'd woken with the realization of what Sofi had truly done.

She'd ruined him for what he'd been.

And he'd broken her at a soul level.

Miguel shifted in his seat and cleared his throat. And continued with his notes.

That had been a year and a half ago, and no one but Claudius knew he'd never slept with another person since the week before he met Sofi. That he'd spent every day striving to be the person she had believed he was and that he slowly learned to believe in too. Because she truly had been different.

He narrowed his gaze at his handscreen in front of him and

tried to dismiss the fact that now here she sat across from him. Back in the center of his thoughts and in a controversy worse than she could imagine. Looking like everything he'd tried the past eighteen months to forget.

He switched back and forth between a few files—negotiations to start with the Delonese as well as a plausible explanation for Sofi's and Heller's presence.

And chose to pretend he didn't care whatsoever, as over the next six hours the girl who'd changed everything about his internal world slept.

Until, eventually, he glanced up and caught the look on Sofi's face.

27

SOFI

SHILO WOKE TO AN EERIE STILLNESS THAT SUGGESTED the cargo ship had landed. The kids around him were stirring and starting to whisper.

"We've stopped."

"Where are we?"

"Ouch, you're pushing me."

He blinked and rubbed the sleep away and then scrubbed his hands over his arms to warm up. Where had the ship landed? And how long would it take to find out?

He promptly scrunched up against the metal wall to make himself as small as possible and waited—for someone to come, for a door to open, for any freaking explanation of what was about to happen next.

Half a minute went by and the ship shifted beneath them with a *clunk*. Then a huge bay door shot open with a *swish*, letting in a draft of muggy air and dim light. He shielded his eyes.

Voices. People were speaking in a foreign language that was at once eloquent and terrifying. The boy closest to Shilo suddenly nuzzled against his side with a whimper. *Poor kid.* He slipped his arm around the boy's shoulders as gradually Shilo's eyes adjusted enough to see the others in the ship. Maybe thirty of them from what he could guess. He squinted and peered out the bay door just as the speakers strode into view.

Humans. But not humans. They were too tall, too perfect.

Delonese.

They stepped in and began rounding up the kids. And prodding them out the door.

"Shilo, no!" Sofi's seat shuddered with the ship's tilting as her eyes flew open. Her stomach lurched and she yanked against her chair straps—to get to him before it was too late—to rescue him—

A soft hand slipped her headphones off while another gripped her arm. She shoved it away because she had to try, even if she couldn't stop him or save him from what was coming.

"Sof, it's a dream," a voice said.

She trembled and blinked. *What?*

The fingers clutched her hand as she yanked up to touch the necklace at her throat. *Oh.* She swallowed and blinked harder until her vision cleared and the room came into focus, as did the eyes in front of her. Miguel. He was holding her arm steady, as if willing her panic to fade into his fingers. She took in the ship's cabin, the white chairs and dark windows—and inhaled.

"You all right?" Miguel's hand felt her forehead before cupping her cheek and tipping her face up to examine her eyes.

She nodded and pulled away. "Bad dream."

He cocked a brow. "Like the nightmares you used to have?"

"Yes. No." She paused. "I don't know."

He rubbed his neck and awkwardly quirked his mouth, as if unsure how to proceed. "Want to talk about it?"

She pressed her fingers against her thighs. The images were stronger this time. So intense she was drenched in sweat. "It's fine. I'm fine."

"Clearly."

Something in his tone, in its light teasing, eased her tension. She relaxed. "For reals it's fine."

"Right. And yet here we are with a few hours to spare. So good gad, please, do share."

Oh. She smirked. *He's bored.* "Let's just say they're getting more realistic than the medical-type dreams I had when you knew me."

He waited quietly.

Fine. She wet her throat. "It's like I'm tracking with Shilo, experiencing everything he's experiencing over the past two days." She glanced out the window at the planet looming so close. "And what I'm seeing isn't comforting."

"Not comforting how?"

"As in, I'm seeing what he's seeing, as if in real time. And it's of the Delonese."

"Have you had these with him before? Like, in the past?"

She frowned. "Not that I remember. Not like this." She squinted at the planet. As if . . .

She glanced at Miguel and abruptly realized she was leaning toward him. She pulled away. "Could something about the Delonese or their atmosphere possibly project or magnify a mental connection?" The idea actually freaked her out. To have them influencing her head . . .

Miguel settled back. "*Es posible.* But it'd be strictly an external influence. As I said, they can't get in your head." He rubbed his neck. "What are the images of, exactly?"

"Shilo on a cargo ship with a bunch of other kids. Thirty maybe, all Shi's age or younger. This last dream—they'd just landed and the Delonese boarded and surrounded them."

"Do you recognize any of the kids?"

What? She frowned, then shook her head. "It was too dim."

His gaze turned thoughtful. "What did the area outside the ship look like?"

She tried to concentrate—to think back. "A metal-type warehouse with shiny white walls and floor. I don't know—everything felt hot and stuffy and overly bright. And they were dressed like guards and more medics." She shook her head and gave a self-deprecating smile. "Sorry, it's weird. *I* don't even know what to think of the dreams."

"Weird maybe, but that doesn't mean invalid."

She caught his eye. What was that supposed to mean? That he believed they were real? That he trusted her? She looked away, only to realize Claudius wasn't in the room. Neither was Heller. She frowned again.

"Heller's in the bathroom," Miguel said. Great, now he was reading her mind. "And Claudius went to bed." He shrugged. "Like I said before, I believe you."

His honesty struck like a gut-punch. She almost let out a sardonic laugh. She recognized that lilt—that tone—from a year and a half ago, and yet it still evoked emotion as if it were yesterday. She went to pull her gaze away but stalled at the look in his eyes.

As if for an instant he was exposing his soul—past all the exterior flirtations and women and drama. She bristled. How many times had she thought that before?

Remember what he did. What he does to every woman he meets.

With that thought came the ache. The gut-cleaving hatred of a fifteen-year-old girl whose mother had suffocated and shamed her in firm attempts to shape her. And in her wide-eyed innocence she'd fallen for her first crush—and believed his words and promises that she was different. Only to realize a month later that the only thing different was his changed phone number and the way he never looked at her again. The following evening he'd appeared on the tele with a new sports car and girl. His smile just as adoring and promising and intoxicating for the public as it had been with her.

And Sofi spent a week crumpled up on the floor. Barely eating. Barely speaking. Until her mom stopped by to inform her she'd assigned Sofi and Shilo to the next set of games and training started now.

And that was the end of her ignorance of ever being used again for someone's gain.

She opened her mouth, then shut it as Miguel's expression shifted to concern. Ha. He probably thought she was crazy after all. She rolled her eyes.

He didn't react. Just studied her. "So, tell me. Why would Corp 30 want their CEO's daughter and lead gamer?"

"I told you—to distance themselves."

He was shaking his head. "I mean back at my house. You said the thugs could've been Corp 30 and Gaines has an interest in making you disappear for . . . good."

Oh. She let a smile tweak her lips. "That I'm actually not sure of. My gut says it's to do with Shilo and the explosion, but perhaps it's to hide something of her own. Either way, I'd prefer my freedom," she added dryly.

"Seems fair."

"Although I'll ask you the same. Because from what I heard, they were blackmailing you." She curved an ironic smile. "You have twenty-four hours," she said in the gunman's accent. "So what do they want *you* for?"

Miguel's entire body went still. As if—what? As if he'd expected her not to notice they spoke only to him and not her? That they clearly had an agreement with him? A handful of snarky comments entered her head, but she just waited.

He inhaled. "Someone has decided I should help sway public opinion against Corp 24. Seeing as I know nothing of the situation, I've obviously been hesitant to do so."

"Hasn't stopped you before," she almost quipped. Instead— "You don't know who?"

He shook his head. "No idea."

"Well, what are they using against you?"

It was his turn to open his mouth, then close it and remain silent.

"I see." Back to his inability to be trustworthy—because if he was that averse to saying it, it must not be good. "Still haven't learned to trust, I see. Or is it that the vulnerability will kill you?"

"Vulnerability will pretty much always kill you. Give anyone a peek at your weakness and they'll latch on and use it against you for the rest of your life. It's just more knowing who it's worth being indebted to."

"Right. Because real relationships are a death trap. Hence, you keep them shallow." She knew it was a low blow, but she couldn't help it. The ache simmered beneath the surface. This space was getting too close. Too suffocating.

"Real relationships are a death trap only because they force you to die *daily* to shallowness. To care about the person more than your pride. So, yes, they're a death trap. But anyone who complains has never truly understood that."

She almost laughed. "And you've been in love?"

He froze. His expression going sterile even as his eyes flamed up with a thousand replies. But whatever the answer, he wouldn't admit it.

"Have you?" His voice was lower.

Her gaze faltered and dropped.

And suddenly the gravity of Earth was seeping into the shuttle, increasing the weight between them. The distance. The loss. She opened her mouth, then shut it. And shoved down the ache and hunger for—what? Something that no longer existed. Something that wasn't even real. That was *never* real. She uttered a curse in her head. Then leaned forward, until nearly touching him, and—

"Am I interrupting something?"

She flipped around to see Heller standing in the hall staring at them.

She choked. "Not a chance. Please." Then pulled back, beckoning a hand toward his seat. "How you feeling?"

"Fine." Except he clearly wasn't. He was eyeing them both with a host of irritation.

When she glanced at Miguel, he'd casually leaned back in his seat and let a polite, "*Me alegro por ti*," speak for his suddenly unreadable expression.

"How about you?" Heller growled, taking a chair. "Everything okay, Sof?"

She nodded. "Of course." Then pointed at the planet.

The next moment she promptly forgot all awkwardness at the sight of Delon looming in front of the small windows. She gasped.

"Beautiful, isn't it?" Miguel said.

Sofi couldn't speak. It was more than beautiful, it was phenomenal. Just like the Delonese's appearances, for that matter. Picture perfect—even down to its perfect placement beyond the moon, which had resulted in reversing Earth's global warming. She watched the snow and ice and environment begin to take forms of mountains and shallow valleys. Each swirl of atmosphere and cloud like an artistic brushstroke over the entire globe. All sparkling whites and grays and evoking a homesickness for such a raw, simple, untouched work of glory.

Suddenly her chest began shivering again. As if her veins were simultaneously burning and flooding anxiety into every inch of her body. *What the—?*

Something was wrong. She frowned and looked down at her hands as another image flashed into her mind—this one through Shilo's eyes of walking into a medical holding room.

She looked at Heller, then Miguel.

"How long until we get there?" she whispered.

28

MIGUEL

THE PLANET GREW LARGER IN THE WINDOW FRAMES, WITH ITS white hills and shallow valleys taking shape amid ice ponds and massive areas of green forests dotting the surface.

Miguel kept an eye on Heller, whose mood had finally switched from annoyance to fascination as he sat by the pane and fogged it up with his breath. The guy was typing fast on his handscreen.

Which would concern Miguel if he actually thought the kid could uncover anything not already allowed by the Delonese themselves. At least from this distance. Once they got close, everything would be contained by Delon's tech-shield—even so far as wiping out any data or memory collected or recorded while there. Meaning info could get through to them but never get out. They were the consummate players at allowing one to see only what they wanted.

A degree of control that had initially impressed Miguel. Now it struck him on the level of creepy, like in old sci-fi movies.

Miguel caught Sofi's gasp and turned to see her gaze flash with fear and wonder. Her skin paled, but she kept her jaw firm.

He furrowed his brow. Perhaps he'd ask the Delonese to run a scan on her once they arrived to ensure something else wasn't going on. She'd have to keep the dreams to herself, but if they could rule out physical illness . . .

He frowned. Because everything within him knew it wasn't illness.

Her visions. The images. The information.

It was too similar. His mouth soured and he turned to Heller, abruptly aware the guy had been asking a question for the past minute. "Hmm?"

"How's it stay in place?" He was on his handscreen now, sliding graph after graph to examine Earth's scientific theories regarding Delon.

"Same way the moon does. A perfect alignment in Earth's gravitational pull."

"Yeah, I've read that. But it should be messing up our weather insanely."

Miguel shrugged. "If they don't kill you first, you'll have the opportunity to ask the visitors this evening. I'm sure they can explain far better than I. If they're willing." He smiled. He wasn't trying to dismiss him—it's just that Miguel had asked the same thing and never received an adequate answer. Some things they preferred to keep to themselves. Or perhaps they just assumed the details were too far advanced for human understanding.

He sniffed. They were probably right.

He returned to his handscreen notes—

"Good afternoon, crew. This is your captain speaking. We're about an hour out and heading into Delon's atmosphere. You might want to brace yourselves, as it can get a bit bumpy. Ambassadors Miguel and Claudius, you may want to alert our hosts as to any preferences—"

The ship jostled and hit the planet's atmosphere, and Sofi and Heller gripped their seats as Miguel steadied himself.

"There's my cue." He picked up his handscreen and

unbuckled. "If you'll both excuse me, it's time to work some magic on our hosts before they fry us. I'll be back."

He crossed to the bedroom door and, once he'd shut it behind him, nudged Claudius before hopping onto the upper bunk. "We're on, *primo*."

Claudius rolled over to glare at his friend. He rubbed his eyes and barely reacted in time to catch the handscreen Miguel dropped down at him. Then heaved himself up beside Miguel. "How they doing?" He tipped his head toward the door.

"She thinks she's telepathically connecting to her brother and experiencing everything he sees. It's all surrounding the Delonese taking children." He kept his voice steady. "He seems to think I'm putting the moves on Sofi and is apparently pissed and jealous."

"Are you?"

"No."

Claudius faked amusement as he eyed Miguel.

"I'm not. I was simply checking on her because of her *extraña* vision thing."

Claudius licked his lips. "Whatever, dude. Lie to yourself, but just don't expect me to believe it." He swiped his screen. "Do you think she's actually connecting with him?"

Miguel shrugged. "I'd say no chance, except according to her, the visions are chronological. And so far her brother's been in a cargo ship with a bunch of other kids." He peered at Claudius. "Apparently they just landed in a hot, giant metal warehouse with white interior and were met by Delonese medical personnel."

The look on Claudius's face said exactly what Miguel expected. "Ah. Okay, so, super weird, but too detailed and coincidental to be written off."

Miguel nodded.

"Meaning maybe this wasn't such a bad idea."

"*¿Qué?* Say that again?"

"Very funny."

Miguel grinned and smoothed a hand through his hair, then pressed his thumb over his screen. "You ready for this?" A moment later he set up a holo-call and put it through to Delon's ambassador general.

"Ethos!" he said when the Delonese's face blinked and became a hologram extending a foot off the screen pad.

The man tipped his head at them as the handscreen translated, "Ambassador Claudius, Ambassador Miguel. We greet you."

"And we you."

"I was about to contact you. My individuals just informed me that once you passed our shield they picked up extra life-forms on your ship. I thought perhaps Ambassadors Danya and Lee had decided to join you rather than take their own shuttle."

His words were polite but his tone suspicion laced. He was offering the benefit of doubt. To which Miguel pasted on his most brilliant smile.

"Ambassador, my deepest apologies. I couldn't contact you from Earth before we departed. We barely made it out in time, due to some personal circumstances, which I was, frankly, unsure how to handle. The two people aboard this shuttle are Heller—" He looked at Claudius. *Crud.* He couldn't remember the kid's last name.

Claudius just shook his head and leaned in. "We have a tech and a head gamer—both from Corp 30. The first a gentleman by the name of Heller and Corp 30 CEO's daughter, Sofi Snow."

They both paused as the ambassador stared without expression. Something Miguel had gotten used to over the past two years. They never blinked. "May we continue to explain, sir?" Miguel added after a moment.

The Delonese nodded.

"I understand that when the delegates and I meet with the council tomorrow, we will be discussing the Corp situations on Earth as well as the explosion. However, on a note of personal confession to you, I have been contacted three times now by unknown individuals pressuring me to blame Corp 24 for the explosion."

Claudius nudged him as if he was giving away too much info. But that was exactly the point. Give enough of the truth to entrust him with a bigger request.

"Sir, as you know, I have no connection with either Corp 30 or 24," Miguel continued. "I have no understanding of what's at play there, but the last time they contacted me was yesterday evening in my home. The girl Sofi Snow was there, and the assailants attempted to attack us and kidnap her. She barely survived, and only did due to action on the part of her and myself. At that point, I thought it wise to bring her to you. Seeing as, not only would you be able to provide far better protection than any of the Corps or security could give, but if she is such an asset to the terrorist who perpetrated this crime, perhaps you might assist me in questioning her. Either way, I felt that whatever she is to them, she would be better used in your care than in the tense environment my people are currently sorting out."

Claudius nudged Miguel's arm and whispered, "Nice."

"This is completely against our policy."

"We know that, sir."

"Not only that, it's dishonoring to our relationship—both with Earth and particularly with you, Miguel. I personally consider this a massive breach of trust and friendship, as will the entire Delonese council."

"I understand, sir. As you should."

"I will contact you again." With as blank a face as ever, the ambassador's holohead disappeared.

The room fell so silent Miguel could hear Claudius breathing. "Well . . . ," his friend uttered after several seconds passed. "That went well."

Miguel nodded. "Far better than I expected." He grinned at Claudius.

"Nice job. Great play on their honor."

"Gracias."

Except they both knew it wasn't merely a play. It was, for the most part, true. Miguel reached down and grabbed a water from the room's wall dispenser and took a long gulp to ease his nerves. Then set it down and waited.

It didn't take long.

The handscreen blipped and the holo of Ethos's head appeared. "Miguel, Claudius. I have discussed the predicament you have put upon us with my immediate advisors, and they would like me to convey again our sincere offense and insult we take at your disrespect and lack of honor. That said, we agree that this may be the best place at this time for both the girl and tech who survived the explosion. We will permit their attendance with you. However, we are forced to take extra measures in screening them along with severely limiting their activities and whereabouts."

"Of course," said Claudius. "We would insist on it had you not."

"In that case, we will see you shortly."

The holo once again clicked off, and Miguel and Claudius both let out deep breaths. Claudius slapped Miguel's back. "Good work. Guess we can break the news they're not getting incinerated yet."

Miguel followed as Claudius hopped off the bed in a considerably more cheerful mood and opened the door. "Oh look," Claudius deadpanned as he stepped into the shuttle's main area. "You're both still here. Goody."

Sofi ignored him.

"What's the news?" Heller asked.

Miguel ran a hand through his lavender hair. "You'll need to go through more vetting than we will, but . . ." He eyed Claudius. "For whatever reason they've chosen to accept your presence." "Much easier than they should've," he didn't add.

"And that's not what you expected?" Heller said.

"I always expect, *ese*," Miguel growled. "Doesn't mean I always win. But you're welcome, all the same." He turned back to the room to change his clothes into something more starched for their landing and introduction to the Delonese meet-and-greet crew. And ignored the hesitation in the back of his mind. That it hadn't just been easy—it'd been way too easy. Ethos's response had been a mere formality, as if for political show, but without any bite. He frowned as a question about Sofi hedged to mind.

The next second he grabbed the wall just as the ship's vibrations picked up—their descent garnering speed. The captain's voice came on. "Just alerting you we are preparing for landing. Please find your seats and strap in."

Well . . . guess he was about to find out.

29

SOFI

"LET'S BE HONEST," RANGER HAD ONCE SAID TO SOFI. "THAT whole not-blinking thing the Delonese do is bizarre. I mean, who doesn't blink?"

"All of them apparently." Sofi had eyed the visitors from across the room.

They'd been at a FanFight dinner, watching the Delonese with the Ns, just like Sofi'd habitually watched the visitors either in person or on the news every day since they'd arrived. And it was true, they never blinked. They just stared, as if peering into a person's mind or soul to gauge what was inside, and it was freaking unnerving.

"I'd be more worried at their emotional health," one of the Ns murmured, prompting Ranger to agree around a bite of tofu. One minute the visitors were the essence of life and energy, and the next they were an expressionless void. Heller suggested maybe they were wired that way—to simply feel all or feel nothing.

But usually it was nothing.

Why the heck Sofi was remembering that convo right now, she had no idea. Except for the fact that she was standing once again watching them not blink, as twenty unemotional peacekeepers and Delon's lead ambassador, Ethos, stared down at her from their insanely tall height. With those perfect humanlike faces and perfect dark hair and perfect human features that had never seen a wrinkle. She squirmed.

The ambassador handed them earcoms to put in, and Sofi could promptly understand what his unblinking face was saying. "Welcome, Ambassador Claudius, Ambassador Miguel, boy Heller, and girl Sofi. We are privileged to host you for the next three days." Knowing his words didn't help.

In fact, it made her shoulder blades itch.

Sofi took in the docking station they'd landed in, which was for receiving high-class guests, obviously, with its bright, smooth silver walls and clear glass ceilings that looked straight up into the planet's golden afternoon atmosphere.

Was she more relieved or disappointed it looked nothing like her dream? During the flight's descent, she'd noted it was attached to a larger main docking station. What she wouldn't give for a window to peer out at the actual structures and world they were in.

She clenched her teeth and tried to eye what sat beyond the two opaque doors in the otherwise blank room.

"You will find we have provided rooms for you in our limited space," the ambassador continued. "And we invite you to attend the gathering we have created this evening. As of now . . ." Ethos looked over Sofi and Heller. The politeness in his tone made Sofi uneasy. "We will proceed with processing you per our protocol and then put this unpleasant intrusion behind us in order to make the most of your time here."

"Thanks for having us," Heller blurted out, grin blazing.

Sofi ignored him and glanced at the peacekeepers, more specifically at the tech-bots attached to their wrists that could stun for a minute or incapacitate for life. She'd often been envious to own one. She smirked and winked at the security team. Then realized the ambassador's silence had become awkwardly long and swerved to find him watching her.

She raised her chin.

Without pause he turned. "Follow me." And they were suddenly all striding after a seven-foot-tall human-looking alien whose green cloak and pants flowed with every movement.

He led them through a sliding door to a med room, where Sofi almost choked up yesterday's coffee right then and there.

The blank white room was full of Delonese medics wearing the same coats she'd seen on the visitor who took Shilo. She shut her eyes and reopened them, her spine feeling like it would shake loose from her bones and collapse on the ground in front of them.

"Do we have to undress?" Heller asked.

"Absolutely not." Claudius swagged a hand down his slacks and button-up shirt. "You think I look this fabulous just to strip?"

"We have wondered," Miguel murmured, bumping Sofi's arm. When she peered up he wrinkled his brow as if to ask if she was okay.

She licked her lips. Nodded. Looked away.

"Our technology does not require that." Ethos stopped and put out a hand without turning. "Ambassador and Ambassador, this way. Boy Heller and girl Sofi, you'll step through there."

Sofi stiffened, and somehow Miguel must've caught it, because he put his hand on her back briefly—long enough for Sofi to pull from his strength. And even if it *was* his habit, she appreciated it this once.

She inhaled. *Come on, Sofi, what's wrong with you? Stop spinning apart. If the aliens have Shilo, this is where your research begins. So get on it.*

She followed Heller through the door Ethos indicated and entered a private room of more white walls and flooring, full of Delonese medics who were apparently required to keep blank expressions and stay mute to every question she put to them. Even though Sofi knew they could hear—her testing of dropping random, inappropriate exclamations garnered widened eyes and frowns from a few.

At least Heller was amused. He snickered as they watched the visitors prod and poke and run full-body scans over every inch of her and Heller. At one point, visions of Shilo in similar med rooms filled Sofi's head and her panic about flared. Until she realized these tests were familiar. Like the scans they went through before stepping into the game stadium. In fact, it was the same tech for the most part.

She spent the rest of the time taking in every detail of the Delonese faces and minimal equipment, noting how the comp-screen on the wall appeared to have a similar layout to the ones at the Games as well.

Huh. Their tech offerings in the Games might make this a tad easier.

A half hour of mouth probes and saliva swabs and more bone and muscle scans, and they were suddenly through and being ushered into the waiting area. Heller nodded as if to say it wasn't so bad. But when Miguel looked at her she ignored him.

"Come, I'll show you to your room," Ambassador Ethos said.

"Room?" Heller coughed in her ear. "As in singular? Well, this oughta be interesting," he whispered as the ambassador led them through a private hall that was a longer version of the space they'd just been in. And yet still no windows or glimpses of the planet or city they were settled on. They passed small pockets of Delonese visitors who paused and observed them walking by.

"Why do they keep staring at her?" Heller mumbled to the ambassador.

"They're wondering if the rumors are true—if she set off the explosion," Ethos said.

Sofi snorted. "If they really believed that, they wouldn't let me be here in the first place," she said quietly to Miguel.

He nodded. "Agreed." And casually slipped back to walk behind her.

Ethos stopped at a single door, which promptly slid up when he stepped in front of it.

"I've put you together as usual," he said. "Girl Sofi will have the room on the left. You three will have the room to the right." He spread his hands out to welcome them into a long suite, set up like a hotel from Earth, with couches, a tele, table and chairs, and bedroom doors on either end of the room. "The restroom, as you call it, is there." He indicated a door beside the guys' bedroom. "Please refresh yourselves and we will call for you shortly."

Then he was gone.

"You'll find your bags with your tech supplies and clothes already on your beds," Miguel said the instant the door skimmed shut. "We have about two hours, so if you're willing . . ." He glanced at Claudius. Then handed them each a tiny earcom. "For your other ear—just in case we need them. I'd like to start in on getting results from this trip."

"And what exactly are those results?" Heller asked, slipping his com in.

Sofi nodded. "And what does achieving them require?"

Claudius glanced at Miguel. "We need you to hack into their system so we can access Earth links from here."

Sofi's brow went up. "So nothing too hard, huh?" To which Heller snickered.

"We need an internal layout of the planet and . . . *certain rooms* on it." Claudius patted Heller's shoulder. "Think you two can manage that?"

Sofi let a grin pucker around her mouth. They'd just asked them to break about fifty different international laws and done it without a flinch.

This she could live with.

On the way to her room, she ran a hand along the lengthy white wall facing the door they'd walked through—the one without any teles or refreshment dispensers or anything at all. Then paused to press harder when the wall's strange surface rippled. Without so much as a rumble, the white coating began to fade and dissipate until it'd turned into a floor-to-ceiling clear glass window looking out directly across the ice-planet.

Sofi gasped and stepped back.

She'd assumed they'd been at ground level, but . . .

Heller let out a whistle. "Nice."

Sofi turned. "Where are we?"

"This is their Main Station," Claudius said, strolling over. "Sits three stories off the ground and holds about thirty rooms—some for meetings, others for council members and people like ourselves."

She placed her hand in front of her eyes to hide the buildings and took in just the view beyond them. The hills and divots and sparsely set forests. All freckled with snow. A picturesque scene of unfiltered, unfettered beauty. It was easy to see why they'd found a way to bring their entire planet with them into the Milky Way rather than just invade Earth on a spaceship. Who'd want to leave this behind? Even with their assistance in Earth's environmental restoration, using massive fusion-fueled filters and reseeding, her home planet would never look anything like this.

"The rest you're seeing around us with those buildings is the majority of their capital."

Capital? She peered at him. She wasn't sure what it was, but there was no way in any imagination it was a main city. "You're joking, right?"

He shook his head. "They prefer simple."

She wrinkled her brow and stared back at it. "Simple, yes, but this . . ." This wasn't a capital. This was a baby industrial town.

"Where's the rest of it?" Heller asked.

Claudius smiled. "Sorry to disappoint you, kids. But not all that glitters is gold."

Sofi studied the low, snow-covered metal buildings that were laid out in patterns akin to a military base. Few windows, few doors. Just row upon row of warehouses that looked eerily like barracks.

The sense of panic came back, cascading through her veins. She swallowed and held herself in place just as Miguel nudged her arm and pointed. "There. Watch it."

She followed his gaze to the low foothills in the distance where a wave of fog was building above the outer tree line. Like a storm of smoke and ice. The next instant it came crashing in like the tide, pouring so fast and harsh that Heller jumped back and swore. It hit the window in front of them and cut off their vision in a sea of white.

Sofi looked at Miguel. *What the—?*

He nodded.

"Soooo, I'm no genius, kids," Claudius muttered. "But I'm gonna say it might be a good time to start with some hacking."

30

MIGUEL

MIGUEL SAT ON THE TABLE'S EDGE WATCHING SOFI AND HELLER type like fiends on their comp-screens while he fiddled with his handheld. "How's it looking?" he finally asked. "Even remotely *posible*?"

Heller tipped his head to Sofi. "We've managed to set up a minimal privacy shield for this room—meaning we can talk and work without them listening in. Other than that, there's not much either of us can do that won't alert their attention. I mean, my pride is wilting here, but most of this is impossible simply cuz it's so far beyond our brain level. It's like another plane entirely."

Sofi tugged down her headphones and rolled her eyes at him. "That said, using the translation code from the earcoms that Ambassador Ethos gave us, I've managed to patch together a similar translation idea. So, if I can find a program comparable to ones they've loaned for the FanFights, at least I'd have something to run it against. Because right now, I can read about half of what's going on—and only understand a quarter of it."

"Although"—she swung around to face Miguel directly—"the good news is, Earth is using far more of their tech than we realized."

Miguel took a sip of water. "Meaning?"

"Meaning the Delonese are beyond my brain capacity, but

Heller and I know far more of these codes than we probably should."

"Yeah, that's not creepy."

She glanced at him. "You have no idea. If the gamers and citizens knew . . ." She bit her lip. "I'm starting to wonder what else their reach extends to."

"Then what would you need to get more complete access?"

Sofi looked at Heller. When the tech nodded, she shrugged at Miguel. "Honestly? We'd need a Delonese."

Miguel tapped his earcom—like the one he'd given the group when they'd walked in—then spoke again. "And if that could be acquired? What would you need from them?"

Sofi studied her comp. Then, slowly, "I'd need security clearance and a program to layer over it, so I could be certain everything translated correctly."

Miguel nodded and tapped his earcom again. "I'll see what I can do. In the meantime—"

"All right, you guys. Speak honestly."

Miguel turned to see Claudius strutting out of the changing room. "Too much? Too little?" He was wearing a suit that mirrored a character from the latest, all-the-rage K-anime. Black hat. Black cloak. Bright-red jumpsuit that V-necked down his bare chest all the way to his belly button.

"Dude, I like it," Heller said.

"*Extraño*, but it works." Claudius's smile broadened until Miguel added, "I guess."

"Sofi. Come on, girl. You've gotta admit this is a lady-killer."

"I'm . . ." Sofi just stared, the look on her face saying exactly what she thought. "There are truly no words," she finally admitted.

Miguel laughed.

"It's the chest hair." She logged off her comp. "And on that note, maybe I should change as well. Ahem."

"Safe plan," Heller whispered. He turned toward the changing room as Claudius plopped on the couch, loudly complaining, "Don't mind me—I'll just be watching Earth news with my amazing chest hair while you all get on with your boring clothes." He flipped on the tele.

Miguel coughed and went to strip down in the bathroom before putting on an all-black suit with lavender bow tie to match his hair. Simple. Suave. It worked.

It wasn't until walking out to slide his shoes on that he realized Nadine was being highlighted on the large telescreen.

"I'll be right here tomorrow for another shot at our unveiling!" She looked at the camera. "We'll be presenting Altered live as the players and gamers prepare their comeback. Then stay tuned for Sunday's FanFight return!"

Miguel straightened. "Wait, what?"

Claudius was staring at the tele. "She's saying they're restarting the Games."

Miguel scowled. "Nada. Not until they've gotten the drama cleared up. There's a reason this went down, and until they know what it is, they'd be fools to restart."

Claudius shrugged. "Yeah, you'd think—"

"Corp teams of all races and preferences," a female robotic voice announced on the tele, as the vid flickered to the nearly rebuilt Colinade, "I'm pleased to inform you the FanFight Games are scheduled to resume on Sunday. We'll be showing the new replacements . . ."

Miguel heard Sofi's door open.

He turned.

"They've got to be kidding." She shook her head. "Why would they restart them right now? How? With who?"

Miguel's entire body stalled. He didn't answer—couldn't answer. Sofi was dressed in a black slim-suit like Shilo wore at the FanFights—one that fit every curve of her body. Her long brown hair had been plaited into an updo, setting off her cheekbones and eyes, making her look more like her mother's heritage than ever. His breath caught. He hadn't meant to notice. Hadn't even thought to notice. Now he couldn't look away.

"Well?"

He blinked, his brain blank.

She stood waiting, glaring as if working out a problem—or waiting for him to figure out what his was. Then swept a hand down her waist. "Does this work for the thing tonight?"

Oh. Right. He looked away and cleared his throat. "Sí, I, uh, I believe it'll be fine."

"Fine? Claudius, thoughts?"

"Sofi, don't hate me when I tell you that the only person more gorgeous than you tonight is me. Cuz, girl, you look hawt."

"Thanks. I think." She glanced toward the changing room. "Is Heller ready?"

Miguel inhaled and peeled his gaze from Sofi just as Heller walked out and the door to the entire suite slid open.

Ambassador Ethos stood outside, characteristically expressionless until he saw Claudius's outfit of awesome. Miguel watched the man's unblinking eyes widen before his perfect face broke into a collage of emotion and admiration. "Ambassador, you honor us with your creativity."

Claudius turned and winked at them all. "And that's how it's done."

Miguel held back a chuckle and inhaled before shifting into his most elaborate personality. *Here goes, amigos . . .*

They exited the room and followed Ethos down the short hall to an open lift made entirely of metal. Inside, the ambassador scanned his palm and the five of them shot up five stories.

The lift spun the opposite direction and suddenly opened into a glass-domed room turning in a slow circle beneath the massive midnight sky, with the moon filling a third of the view. The pock-marked globe of beauty lit up the glass ceiling and, beyond them, the white, snow-tipped landscape far below.

Miguel smiled and glanced over to inspect Sofi's expression as her eyes widened in awe. The moon-filled ceiling was only one aspect. The room itself was a technological wonder—a virtual reality of stars and planets and suns floating through atmospheric swirls of colors and sparkling lights, in a replication of solar systems no human had ever seen, let alone knew existed.

As if that wasn't enough, the moment they stepped from the lift, the most perfect, operatic voice in the Milky Way broke into song and washed an aria over them.

Even Ethos paused at the beauty of it.

"This is rare," Claudius whispered to Heller. "Only the second time they've allowed us to listen in."

"She's well known and beloved in Delon," Ethos agreed. "One of our few treasures we refuse to share with our Earth comrades."

Heller looked less than impressed as they made their way into the sea of Delonese. He was inspecting the room filled with the tall, gorgeous creatures and their perfect penchant for artistic expression. Like an opera house without seating, the room had layers of balconies and stages for the artists, musicians, dancers, and singer to perform all at once.

Miguel caught Sofi's expression again and felt his shoulders tighten. Dressed in black, with hair set off by colored galaxies, she stood soaking it in as if no one else existed.

His chest softened and skipped a beat.

For as many events as he had attended, he'd never seen anyone react with quite as much unjaded wonder as she was prone to. He chuckled. Though, in all fairness, in this case, no one could throw a party like the Delonese. The music, painting, sculpting, and elaborate floral trees made entirely of food all lent to the harmonious blend of communing spirit. It didn't matter that the dishes were the blandest flavors he'd ever come in contact with in his life.

"It almost takes your mind off their faults, doesn't it?" he said, leaning into Sofi.

She grinned. "Is it always like this?"

"It is on welcoming night."

He held her gaze, releasing it only as one of their Delonese friends strolled up.

"Claudius, once again your clothing choices are the envy of the room."

"Sofi, Heller, this is Lex," Miguel said. "And he clearly has the worst taste here."

The guy tipped his head back and laughed dramatically while turning his unblinking eyes to Sofi. "You know, he might be right," he said once he'd caught his breath. He held out his hand. "But come, girl Sofi, let me show you around."

Two females joined them and put their arms around Miguel and Claudius. "We were wondering when you would show up."

"Ladies," Claudius crooned. "We were just telling our guests about your many enjoyments here."

Miguel chuckled even as he casually disconnected from their arms. "And by that, he means your food."

They both laughed loudly, and Miguel kept his smile on, aware that Sofi was observing.

"Ooh, our new guests must try it," Lex agreed, hurrying them all to one of the food trees.

Sofi peeked back at Miguel and lifted a brow.

He grinned and leaned in, lips brushing her ear as he murmured, "Apparently the Delonese figured out a way to streamline meals long ago—making them the most nutritious for the smallest portions. But it's the worst stuff you'll ever taste. Pretend to chuckle, and then pretend to like it."

When he pulled back, she giggled as if he'd told her a joke. "And of course, you'd care." She winked.

Ha. *Bien*. He winked back. Dang right he cared. No matter how many times he'd tried to convince them, the Delonese saw no use for human food. They ate. They consumed cubed portions. But it was necessity, not enjoyment. Which, he'd informed them repeatedly, was an abomination.

That had only made them laugh even more.

He glanced down at his stomach as Sofi leaned back over. "Is that what the stash of chocolate and organic butter are for in the room?"

He glared at her very seriously. "It's for survival." To which she only snickered louder. He studied her as it struck him that this time her amusement was genuine. And it was beautiful.

Claudius's sudden exclamation drew his attention to whomever Lex and the ladies were now speaking to.

"Miguel. Claudius," Ambassador Alis said.

Miguel took her hand and then embraced Ambassador

Danya who was standing over the ambassador. "You two made it."

Their huge smiles barely covered the blatant questioning in their eyes. Alis turned tight-lipped to Heller and Sofi while still eyeing Miguel. "I see you brought guests."

Danya slid in front of her and extended her own hand to Sofi. "Ambassador Danya from the South Middle East region. And you are CEO Inola's daughter and one of our most brilliant gamers, I'm told. I'm grateful to finally meet you."

Miguel saw the polite niceties mixed with mistrust flash across Sofi's eyes as she shook Danya's hand. "And you as well, Ambassador. I've always thought you one of the saner voices on the news clips."

Danya chuckled and glanced over at Miguel. "Oh, I quite like this one. You should keep her."

Sofi's reaction was an immediate snort of disdain.

"Pretty certain she keeps herself just fine," Miguel said. "And allow me to introduce Heller Torn, Sofi's gaming tech and friend."

Alis nodded and drilled her gaze into the boy. "How on earth did you get the Delonese to allow them?" she whispered. Then glanced at Claudius. "And why?"

Claudius tipped his glass. "Miguel had a run-in with special enforcers at his house who tried to take him and the girl out. They ran for it. I followed. Here we are. The Delonese were willing to oblige."

Beside him, Lex and the ladies let out gasps. "Appalling," said one. "Disgusting," said the other.

"Which I'd struggle to believe the Delonese allowed." Danya peered around at the room. "Except they certainly seem fascinated by her. They can barely keep their eyes off her."

Miguel gave her a short nod just as Lex breathed, "Ooh, look, they're about to begin."

A second later the operatic aria broke off and the Delonese froze in place.

31

SOFI

SOFI SHIFTED BENEATH THE ROOM'S DEAFENING SILENCE AS her panic rebloomed. The invisible, untouchable tension a reminder that, for as beautiful as this room and its artisans were during the past half hour, none of that covered up the fact that she still despised them, or that they likely had Shilo.

Maybe that's why they all kept looking at her. If they had him, they'd have to assume it's why she was here.

She squared her shoulders and shoved down the cold and hatred and fear. And clenched her hands into fists. *Just play their game, Sofi. Find out what you can, then get back to your room and finish what you came for.*

She'd just turned to question Claudius as to how much longer they'd be here when the chanting began. It started from the stage and spread out across every inch of the round room. Beautiful. Monotone. Eerie. The Delonese nearest Sofi picked it up after the other hundred individuals as, in the earcom, Sofi noticed she couldn't decipher the words.

She looked around and found Danya smiling softly at her and Heller. "Would you like to know what they are saying?"

"Heck yeah." Heller grinned.

"We are one," Danya translated. "In soul. In beliefs. In harmony. In favor."

Sofi studied the visitors' faces. The words were beautiful, just like them. Ethereal almost. And yet . . .

"We are unified in the richness of life, of sacrifice, of transparency, and of love."

And yet something about them felt so fake.

Sofi swallowed and continued to study the lilt of the words flowing effortlessly off so many tongues. As if they were sharing a part of their souls, their lives, their community—except they'd somehow forgotten the rest of the picture. In a room of passionate individuals who danced and sang and painted and performed, she had the distinct impression this recitation was an act. Like a habit practiced too often, too long, until too much of its meaning died.

She couldn't quite put her finger on it, but Sofi felt that if she were to lean down and scratch a bit of whatever flooring the room was made of, she'd find something far deeper, darker, more revelatory.

And it scared the crud out of her.

Heller bumped her arm. "Incredible, isn't it?" he mouthed.

Sofi nodded and peeked at Claudius and Miguel, only to find similar expressions of discomfort on their faces.

"We are created from technology and born into a product of beauty," Danya continued. "We will rise higher through our own experience, community, and personal power."

Sofi heard Alis clear her throat and watched her shift closer to Miguel. She could only pick up bits of phrases as the woman began whispering in his ear.

"What on earth were you think . . . ?"

". . . wanted by half the Corps . . ."

". . . what if they . . ."

Sofi turned away and watched the rounded glass ceiling and the stars twinkling beyond. She could see Earth—it looked exactly like the photos from old satellite footage. Something moved in her, nudging her like a homesickness she couldn't explain or ignore. Gad, she just wanted to find Shilo and go home—back to their *old* home. And re-create some semblance of a life already gone where they'd danced and made quilted forts and caught fireflies under the same moon beaming at this very moment. Her throat swelled and she tuned back in to Danya.

"And in the end, we will be greater. We will be conquerors of our own truth, our own will, our own death. We will be rulers of destiny."

As quickly as it had begun, the chanting ended, and Sofi didn't know if her heart was more relieved or disturbed. They weren't just rulers of their own destiny and will, but other people's as well, if intuition was to be believed.

She swallowed the flat taste in her mouth. "Well, that was different."

"But kinda cool. I like their philosophy at least," Heller said.

Sofi scoffed and turned, only to catch Alis eyeing her with what appeared to be disapproval. Sofi tossed her a wide smile and watched Miguel and Claudius go back to making the Delonese fawn over them.

Gasping, she suddenly tilted and swerved as the entire room abruptly spun and her head lost all sense of direction. *What in—?*

It was like someone turned off a gravity sensor somewhere and the room's air lightened.

In front of her, Heller frowned as if he, too, was confused. He gave a small jump. Then promptly bounded up four feet and looked over at her, grinning. What in the world? She followed suit, and the floor fell away as she reached out to touch one of the solar systems floating overhead.

Three clicks of a beat and suddenly the music picked up, followed by half the Delonese in the room launching themselves into the air and engaging in a form of dancing.

Sofi raised a brow before pausing to look back at Miguel. He was talking to the tall woman, Danya.

"Tell me you brought her for what I think you did," she overheard the woman saying. "And can she do it?"

He merely nodded and kept his eyes focused on his drink.

"Wait—what?" Sofi wanted to ask, but a crowd of Delonese surrounded her and pulled her up to dance with them. It wasn't the rave style she was used to, nor ballroom like the older generation preferred. This was wild. Free in the same way one moved when tangibly aware of every tissue and bone and electric nerve connecting the body in a blending of grace. And as the music turned up and pumped through the room, for the first time on the planet, Sofi's heart took a breath and let the cold chip off of her a little more.

And in that moment, she shoved the panic and anger aside and melted into the rhythm.

The Delonese swung her around, and between, and upside down until she lost all sense of time and breath. They only set her back down when they decided to show off their acrobatic skills, and Sofi watched as half the room was soon walking and vaulting on the domed ceiling. Even as the food and drinks and tech all stayed rooted in place. "The air is only sensitive to living cells," a visitor said when she asked.

The display reminded her of one of last year's FanFight levels.

She found a spot against the domed side near where Miguel had been speaking with Danya. The female ambassador was exiting the room and Miguel now had a new friend.

"Pretty bit of work there," she heard the Delonese coo. "She got a name?"

Sofi peeked over but didn't recognize him. Not that it meant anything. They all had a strikingly similar appearance. Same hair color, facial features, and those unblinking eyes. The uniformity had stuck out to her more than a few times over the years.

She smirked as Miguel cleared his expression and straightened off the wall he'd been leaning against. "Not one of interest, cuate."

"Truly?" The visitor took a sip of his own sparkling glass—not his first by the swagger in him—and puckered a brow. And turned to stare straight at Sofi. "Not to you perhaps."

Oh.

Oh.

She almost gagged. He was talking about her?

"She's one of the FanFight kids," Miguel said. "Not anyone of interest to you."

"Oh, I know exactly what she is. I saw her at the stadium on the tele introductions. Thought she died in the blast."

Miguel's face shaded with irritation. He refused to look at Sofi, just snorted and said, "Well, good luck with that."

"Challenge accepted," the guy said. But rather than head her direction, he turned and strolled the other way as Miguel became a homing beacon for a gaggle of Delonese men and women.

Huh. Maybe he decided she wasn't that interesting after all.

Good.

She rolled her eyes and went to move on when Miguel lifted

his gaze to her. His eyes swept over her sweaty face and prompt frown, then his expression shifted from strained to amused. She was about to scowl deeper at him, except his countenance just as quickly shifted to something else.

Something that grabbed her and gutted her all in the space of one raw, hungry glance.

She opened her mouth and felt her insides chip away a little more at the thrill of it. Then the guests were flocking to him and blocking his view, and Sofi was left reeling from an emotion she had no idea what to do with.

Stupid boy.

She returned to watching the dancing and pretended he'd never existed. Which came a bit easier once she homed in on Alis and Claudius and Heller carrying on. If she'd ever thought Heller had moves, Claudius put him to shame. The man was a mix-master.

She was about to join them when Danya reentered the room, and Sofi rose to connect with her. To question her. To ask what she'd meant earlier about Sofi being there for what they needed. But just as Sofi was making her way over, the lights dimmed so low she could spot Heller's flashing cheek piercing half the room away.

Suddenly the music stopped. The dancing stopped.

And one by one the hundred Delonese looked up at the moon through the ceiling.

Then, in unison of perfect step, perfect form, perfect stride, they walked toward the giant doors.

And Sofi stopped in her tracks.

32

MIGUEL

BACK IN THE ROOM, MIGUEL TOOK OFF HIS JACKET, THEN PULLED out his handscreen and set it on the chair. When he looked up, Sofi was staring at him through thick eyelashes in a way that made his lungs skip a breath. He raised a brow. "Everything okay?"

"Other than what just happened back there?"

Heller nodded and plopped his elbow on her shoulder. "Yeah, that was some freaky twilight stuff." He glanced at Claudius. "But fantastic. Sweet dance moves, dude."

They knocked knuckles just as Sofi shook her head and ducked from Heller's arm. "I'm not just talking about the chanting or antigravity dancing. I'm talking about the fact the lights shut down and the aliens just walked out in a trance."

Miguel tried not to smile. It had weirded him out the first couple times too until he realized it was nothing more than just an unusual tradition. "Not a trance exactly." He scrunched his forehead. "Genetically altered maybe."

Sofi's face sallowed. "Wait, are they? Genetically enhanced?"

He grinned and chuckled. "Nah, I'm just messin' with you. I actually have no idea. Although I wouldn't doubt it for as perfect as they all look."

"It's the skin," Claudius said, nodding.

"Well, enhanced or tranced or whatever the freak it is—there's something seriously wrong with those people. We will rule our own destiny—while we all stare up at the moon and walk out like robots?"

"Hot tea, anyone?" Claudius said.

Sofi shook her head.

"I'm changing," Heller called, as if anyone cared.

"They have strange customs, sí," Miguel admitted. "But to be fair—so do humans."

"Yeah, well, the sooner we find my brother and leave, the better."

"Tea?" Claudius said louder.

"Yes. No. I don't care. Claudius, I—" Sofi turned and put up her hand. Only to have it brush against Claudius's V-necked chest of man-hair. She yanked back. "Gah, seriously? Okay, fine. Yes. And thanks." She strode to her room and came back a few minutes later wearing purple fluffy unicorn pj's and carrying her handscreen.

Miguel exchanged smiles with Claudius because how could she not know she looked ridiculously adorable? Even when pissed.

Claudius shook his head and pretended to bat fake eyelashes, and Miguel discreetly glared him off.

Sofi set Heller's and her comp-screens across the thin metallic table and opened them. "Sorry," she said after a moment. "This place just gives me the creeps."

"Understandable." Miguel grabbed his handheld and joined her at the table. "So, what do you need help with?"

"You could tell me what you and Ambassador Danya were talking about. What do you want us to do?"

Miguel didn't show surprise at her observation. Of course

she'd been listening. He swiveled his head to indicate his discomfort as to whether the room's security was still intact. Then chose his words carefully. "I'd be able to explain more if we could finish the project from this afternoon." He pulled a comp chip the size of Sofi's pinkie nail out of his breast pocket and handed it to her. "Would this help?"

She eyed it and then him before she took it and slid it into her comp just as Claudius set down three cups of tea and Heller appeared in a pair of "Dead Right" pajamas.

Claudius nodded. "Nice, kid."

"Thanks." Heller glanced at the door. "So where did Alis and Danya go after the dance, by the way?"

"About one hundred feet down the hall. Apparently trying to catch up on Kim's notes before tomorrow's meeting."

Miguel caught the look on Sofi's face.

"Pretty sure Alis isn't too happy with you guys bringing us," Heller said.

"Danya and Alis are good people," Claudius interjected. Then tapped the tea in front of Sofi. "Seriously, drink it. They may have horrid food, but they've become addicted to our version of spiced tea. It's been one of Miguel's greatest—if not only—feats of influence."

"Aside from all the other great feats, you mean." Miguel grinned, then took a sip and kept his gaze on Sofi. "But now let's see if we can accomplish a few more." He tipped his chin to her screen and dropped his voice. "Is that what you were looking for?"

Sofi glanced down and her eyes widened. Two seconds later a hologram emerged from her comp and floated above the table. It was Delon's planet with code scrolling around it.

Heller gave a low whistle. "That's the one. Where'd you get it?"

Miguel shrugged as Heller and Sofi went to work sorting through the words and numbers as if they knew exactly what they were looking at.

Claudius flipped the tele back on—only to growl at it two seconds later. "Aw, come on, Nadine. We want news."

Miguel glanced up.

"Is it true, Corp 30, that you can't find your CEO's daughter?" Nadine looked at the camera. "Or is something bigger going on here? Stay tuned as we continue to give you the truth as it unfolds." She pasted on a wide smile. "And don't forget tomorrow's unveiling of Corp 24's Altered prototype. Is your child an alien? Is your lover a human? Has your brain been secretly altered? Find out how it works when we test it in the morning." She ended with a fan-favorite i-reality wave and then blew a kiss. "Good night from Nadine."

"Think I've got a few people I'd like to try that on," muttered Claudius.

"The kiss or the Altered?" Sofi said.

Claudius looked up as Miguel and Heller snickered. "Very funny."

"Except for the fact it's going to cause a whole lot of drama," she added.

Miguel noted that Heller frowned and kept his mouth shut.

But Claudius flipped around on the couch. "How so, girl Sofi?"

She rolled her eyes. "Anytime you use panic to pitch a product, it creates problems."

Miguel agreed. It'd only increase suspicion rather than peace.

"Except the panic was already there," Claudius argued. "That's the whole reason they developed it."

"What she means," Miguel interrupted, "is that the product is a wise one. The way they're selling it is going to cause mass panic. And shoot their prices through the roof."

"Well, I think it's a crap product anyway." Heller tapped away at his screen. "And I'm betting they're the ones who planted that explosive to keep it from being used."

Sofi scoffed. "You're kidding, right?"

Heller shrugged. "It's most likely a fake—and the bomb drama was just to heighten sales. As you guys said, stir the panic, increase the sales. Just watch, everyone will be clean tomorrow—but Corp 24's shares will go sky high."

Miguel chewed his cheek. "I'd agree with you, except . . ." He glanced at Sofi. "Corp 24 didn't do it."

Heller laughed. "And you know that how?"

"Simple." Sofi turned to the kid. "You and I both know only a few people could have pulled that off—and Corp 24 isn't any of them. They couldn't even manage a stronger firewall, let alone plant something decent behind it." She pursed her lips and peered back at where she'd been typing.

A few seconds later Miguel's handscreen blipped, and Sofi reached over to tap it. He stopped midsip of his tea as Vicero's AI head abruptly popped up in 3-D off the screen. *What the—?*

He looked at Sofi. She did that?

She smirked and shrugged. "Your chip unscrambled enough coding for me to hack a breach through and run tech interference. At least while in this room. For the moment we can only access limited help from your and my data streams. But it's something."

"Um, you're a genius. And I mean that."

"I know," she said dryly.

Vicero's holohead turned to Miguel. "Looks like your girl

here needs some translating and decoding help, yeah?" She suddenly frowned and looked behind Miguel. He turned to see Claudius pulling off his cloak and stretching out across the low couch in his chest-revealing red suit.

"He looks like a hairy cat," Vic said with a not-altogether-unpleasant look on her face.

"Oh. Is that you, Vicero?" Claudius said. "Didn't even see you. And I believe the word you're looking for is *cougar*, my love."

She rolled one of her eyes while the other stayed staring at him. Miguel coughed on a laugh, then glanced away when she glared at him.

"So . . . info? What precise programs does your girl over there need?" Vic tipped her head at Sofi while still trying to see Claudius. She finally gave up and pretended to pop a wad of bubble gum.

"The FanFight BN6, YX9, and Earth's 360 modular of Delon," Sofi answered for him.

Vic pretended to make notes. "Got it, got it, got it. Any preference of order? Cuz I'm gonna send those over in a few."

"Nope." Sofi glanced at Heller, but Heller was just staring at Vic.

"She's kind of awesome," he cooed after a moment. Then peered at Sofi. "I want one."

One of Vic's blue eyes widened to half her face. "Excuse me? I'm not a 'one' to want. I'm a highly functioning AI and—"

"Whoa, buddy. Hands off the hardware," Claudius said from the couch. To which Vicero's holohead blushed electric hot purple.

"Both of you, *basta*." Miguel just shook his head. Then sighed. "Anything else, Vic? What about the rest of the reports you were working on? You said you finished with Corp 24's kid."

"Oh. Right. Yeah, yeah, man—he's clean. Poor family. Poor background. Poor kid with an above-average IQ who got roped into something bigger than he knew, through the offer of power and money." She tapped her finger as she talked, as if to say, "Same ol' story."

Heller shifted in his seat.

"But Corp 24's not your bomber as far as my numbers read."

Sofi peeked over at Heller with a sly grin.

"Did you track down who hired him?"

"It was an off-air account," Sofi interrupted. Vic swerved toward her and nodded. "She's right. Meaning it was likely a Corp rather than an individual. However," she prattled on, "I can tell you that the replacement FanFight players for Sunday's game aren't rigged. They're all the original backups. So in that way, man, things seem to be shifting back to normal."

Sofi and Heller both scoffed.

"Oh, also!" Vicero popped her fake gum. "Miguel, you just made the cover of *Skin-Kiss* mag-stars. And guess who's sharing it with you?" She held up the gossip mag. "You know that chick you did the photo shoot with who tried to suck your face off?"

Miguel heard Sofi's grunt of disgust. "Excuse me. I've started the programs and loaded my own little mix of a virus. I think I'll turn in." She strode to her room and slammed her hand on the wall to slide the door shut.

Vic raised a brow and turned back to Miguel and Heller as Claudius whistled from the couch.

Miguel scowled. "*¿Qué?* Did I do something? Should I go after her?"

"Dude, just leave her alone," Heller growled. "Keep your eyes on the new girls, like from your skin-mag."

Miguel pressed his lips together and assessed him. Then nodded. "Duly noted."

33

SOFI

SHILO.

Sofi could hear him talking. He was weeping and calling out for her . . .

She couldn't put her finger on the words, but whatever was wrong was only getting worse.

He was frightened out of his wits. She could see it in his eyes.

Lying there on a med cot while the Delonese scanned his body. Looking for blood type or organs or stem cells or—what?—she didn't know. She just knew Shilo's heartbeat was growing louder and louder—hammering in her ears, in her teeth, in the dirt beneath his back. The Delonese dirt that was as shallow and fake as their songs of unity and community, while the floor and glass ceilings surrounding her brother bled.

The medics around him were talking now. Their robotic voices blending as her brother's heartbeat pumped down into the bowels of their planet—feeding their roots and trees and becoming the very essence of life to them.

The very breath of life.

The beginning of life.

The machine he was hooked up to suddenly *beep, beep, beeped*, and his heartbeat abruptly stopped.

Sofi woke up screaming. She screamed at this place. At the Delonese who had her—or Shilo—she couldn't tell who was who anymore. She just knew something was wrong here, so very wrong, but no one could see it—why couldn't they sense it? They needed to leave before it was too late. She and the kids needed to escape.

She kicked off her med sheets and bucked against the straps as panic tore through her spine. Miguel's scent filled her head. His fingers clutched her hand. Calming her, quieting her. The bed sagged as he dropped down and sat beside her.

But Shilo just kept screaming. Or she kept screaming. *Whoever it is, someone bloody make them stop screaming.*

Miguel told her to breathe but she didn't know how, and it wouldn't make Shilo's heart beat again. He leaned over and slipped off her headphones and flipped on music from his handheld. And remained with her in this daft Delonese bedroom until, eventually, the screams faded to weeping and the imaginary med sheets and straps dissipated.

"*For these bones are made of beauty and blood, fashioned in a hard-fought, hard-won war,*" Miguel's music sang.

Sofi had no idea how long she sat like that. Tucked up beside this boy she despised more than anyone other than her mother while his music overwhelmed her senses and set them all right again. This man who'd used her and hurt her and probably would again, and yet who stayed, soothing her hair and not saying a word.

"Leaving shadows of our former selves and former loves . . ."

Until sooner or later she looked up through the darkness and realized that whatever she was, whatever this was, whatever life she had that was barely her own because it was mostly CEO Inola–owned—she didn't know how to do this.

To breathe. To be near him after getting broken so badly by him. When all she wanted was to care for her brother because that was all she had left to care about in this world. "Miguel," she whispered through the dim.

"Hmm?"

"Could you please leave?"

Hesitation. "You sure?"

"Positive."

A longer hesitation. And this time when he spoke, his voice was thick. "Absolutely. Good night, Sofi."

He left his music playing. *"But what if just for tonight we forget the brutal and be true to ourselves? Souls sharing skin and something bigger in this moment?"* the song continued as he silently slipped out and shut the door behind him. Without saying another word.

She pulled her knees up to her chest and fell back asleep, safely away from the person who had been her first innocent love.

34

MIGUEL

MIGUEL SAT OUTSIDE SOFI'S DOOR FOR THE REST OF THE NIGHT, staring over the moonlit ice-world.

He curled and uncurled his fingers. Having held her hand like that—listening to her breathing and her heart *beat, beat, beating* in panic inches from his own . . .

He inhaled and accidentally pulled in another lungful of her smell that still clung to his shirt. And allowed it to make him perfectly aware of the fact that he was in the midst of watching his entire world awaken and detonate and implode.

As if he didn't even know *qué diablos* he was fully doing anymore.

He just knew there was no turning back from here, from tonight, from the girl he'd spent the last year and a half trying desperately to forget while trying in every way to earn her approval at some soul level. And from the one chance of doing what he, Claudius, Danya, and Alis had worked too long and hard for to walk away from now.

He sighed and pressed his ear against the cool metal in case she woke screaming again. And drifted into a restless sleep.

Until his alarm went off.

At 8:01, he slipped in and grabbed his handheld from her bed, then shut the door behind him.

At 8:28, he and Claudius left the main room.

And at 8:32, Alis and Danya joined them at the door of the Delonese council chambers located in the innermost section of the compound. They looked at each other.

Danya shot Miguel a questioning glance over Alis's and Claudius's heads, to which he tipped his chin.

"May peace be with us then." Danya took a breath and released it softly. They turned, and Miguel slid his hand over the door. And led them in to face possibly the last main meeting he would ever have with the Delonese.

The chambers were similar to Delon's other fancy rooms. Dome-shaped, windowed ceiling and circular glass sides. But where the artisan room of last night had balconies, this one had stadium seating stacked with sterile, white cushy chairs set on staircasing white floors, all encircling a podium floating in the middle of the three-story space.

"The security chip?" Danya said in Miguel's ear.

He gave a slight nod and kept his eyes in front of them as they were led to their assigned seats just as the Delonese house chairman took his place at the podium.

"Will they be able to do it?"

Miguel leaned over and, without looking at her, whispered, "If they can't, then no one else can either. In which case, we'll all be in deep crud, or they'll cover it enough for us to fight another day. But I believe they'll know by the end of today."

In his peripheral he caught her acceptance of this. "We're scheduled to leave tomorrow evening."

He didn't reply. He was fully aware of the time frame. Instead, he checked his handscreen and set it to mute in case Vic decided to make an appearance. In which case he wouldn't need to wait on Sofi and Heller. They'd all be compromised on the spot.

"Distinguished guests and eminent friends, welcome," the chairman said.

"We welcome you," the room chanted back. "In unity, community, and necessity."

The chairman bowed as the two hundred council members fell silent. "We have with us today Earth Ambassadors Claudius and Alis, and Ambassadors Danya and Miguel. It is their request to discuss their discoveries regarding the tragedy that took place during the FanFight Games this week, to which a number of us were witness. It is also their desire to ask our assistance in the matter. Will we hear them?"

"We will hear them," the room chanted in unison. "Welcome, Earth comrades."

"Also"—the chairman bored his gaze into Miguel's skull—"on a delicate matter. Ambassador Miguel has issued his deep apologies for his intrusion of bringing two unsanctioned humans. His doing so was under duress and with the firm assurance they will be of assistance should we choose to aid Earth in their investigation. It is my recommendation we use them as such. With that stated, I now extend the floor to them so we may hear what they have to say. Will we hear them?"

"We will hear them," the assembly chanted again.

Miguel held his breath until the chairman finished and Alis got up to speak. If they'd uncovered any tech breach from his room or Sofi thus far, it would've been addressed in that speech. He exhaled and proceeded to focus his body language on the Icelandic ambassador.

"We are welcomed," Alis said with a tip of her bald head. "And as such, it is my honor to provide you a detailed display of what Earth's Corps are currently looking at." With the tap of her finger on the handscreen she'd set in front of her, a hologram appeared in the room's center, taking up fifty feet of space as it spread out into a giant port-screen.

"As you can see, the Corps have each invested heavily into Earth's FanFights." A vid flashed on the screen to show a brief history of the Games. "Not just for the sake of citizen entertainment, but for something far greater." She paused for effect. "For unity, community, and technological advancement."

Oh, well done. Even Miguel had to smile at her smooth use of their own credo as a hook.

"For unity, we promote fair competition and contribution in equal ownership among the Corporations. For community, we offer a unified engagement and entertainment on equal ground together—for the Corps, but even more so for the members of humanity who access the Fights via teles. And technological advancement by using these Games to fine-tune the tech and med resources we have developed, heavily due to your people's generosity. And for that, we thank you."

The crowd bowed in unison, signaling their approval of her recognition.

With that, Alis took the opportunity just earned to fill the room in on the pics and details of the explosion—most of which they were quite aware, but even Miguel knew no one appreciated fluid, informed facts as much as the Delonese.

Internally, Miguel used the opportunity to settle in for a study of the Delonese's reactions, just as he'd done in Earth's Corp meeting hall. The main difference being difficulty regarding the Delonese's clear eyes and lack of emotion.

It'd be a definite problem if he hadn't been around them enough by now to know they gave physical clues. At a far lesser level, but they were there. In the lips. In the twitch of a finger. In the way their tan skin sallowed or reddened depending on the underlying stressor.

And from what he could tell, at least half the council members were currently scratching their fingers.

35

SOFI

SOFI GOT UP. SHOWERED. DRESSED. AND WALKED OUT INTO THE wide-windowed shared room overlooking the barrack buildings. She made tea and sipped it while studying those buildings. What types of Delonese lived in them? Families? Individuals? Military? She tried to calculate the number of Delonese she'd seen last night with how much housing and storage and work rooms they'd need once you included children and babies.

She frowned.

Even with how few visitors there'd been, and even if she was only seeing half the capital, it wasn't nearly big enough.

Sofi pressed her fingers harder against her mug—warming them to the point they burned—and allowed her scattered, uneasy thoughts to percolate until they took on shape and form and claimed definition enough to place her finger on. With that, she strode over, set down her drink, and scanned the comp she'd left running all night.

"I could seriously go for a Rush right now." Heller stumbled out of the far bedroom.

"Isn't that the truth," Sofi answered.

"Did the AI chick get those programs loaded?" He rubbed his messy head as he shuffled over.

She nodded. "The virus is still assimilating. But no blaring sirens going off so far—hopefully it stays that way." When Miguel had handed her the security chip last night, she'd been uneasy, but clearly it'd been from someone in Delon's security force. *Thank heck.* "Let's take a look." She tapped the running code and layered it over the Delonese planet holo they'd accessed last night. The image popped up in large 3-D form—but rather than scrolling symbols across it this time, the program began to assimilate them into the topographical information they stood for.

Heller whistled.

The next moment the floating globe became a full, clear picture, as if a puzzle had finished coming together to reveal a perfect 360-degree photograph of the ice-planet.

She handed Heller her tea and bent down to study it. Tilting her head, she reached out and slowly began to virtually spin the holo.

"What the—?" Heller almost spit out his gulp of her tea. He set down the cup and peered over it with the same expression Sofi was feeling. "This can't be accurate."

He turned to her screen and typed while she kept examining.

One minute.

Two minutes.

Sofi glanced over to see what was taking him so long. "It's an updated program—so it shouldn't need refreshing. You should have the images live."

"That's the problem." He leaned back and stared at her. "Apparently this *is* the live image of the planet."

Sofi's gaze widened as she swung it back to the planet. "No way." She shook her head. "There's no way. Where are all the cities? Where's the housing and buildings and the planet's populations?"

He didn't answer.

He didn't need to.

They both were looking at the same thing.

Aside from the tiny "capital city" they were currently standing in, the planet swirling in front of them was a beautiful blank patchwork of forests and frozen lakes and foothills. Breathtaking in its purity, but that was just it. The thing was pure. Clean. Empty of any other cities or farms or houses or factories.

In other words . . .

Outside of this capital, there was nothing else.

She dropped her hand and turned back to the comp beside Heller. The screen blipped as she set a search filter on the security program.

Heller cleared his throat. "Uh, what are you doing?"

"Finding a scan for life-forms in their security database." She glanced at him. "They've gotta have it running constantly anyway. I'm actually surprised Earth doesn't use one."

He shook his head. "Too many life-forms. Unless we had a version that could distinguish between species like that Altered tester thing. Speaking of which . . ." He turned around and flipped on the tele to the pre-Game commentaries. They appeared to be showing behind the scenes at the Colinade and the rebuilt areas. Sofi paused. The place looked perfectly new. It gave her an empty feeling in her gut.

She went back to her screen just as the life scan popped up. She clicked and moved it over and set it atop the planet image. Immediately the holoplanet floating over the table lit up with tiny blue lights.

"Nice." Heller nodded. Then poked at it and adjusted the size.

It showed the same as the other scan. The lights were lumped together around the same spot at the capital. The rest of the planet sat empty as a bald man's head.

She looked at Heller.

He snorted and strode to the window, hands locked behind his head as he peered out over the miniature expanse. "You'd think they'd have a lot bigger society."

"You think they've purposely lied about it to Earth to keep us from attacking them?"

He shook his head and flipped back around. "Doubtful. No matter how small their population, they're still eons more advanced than us. We wouldn't have a chance against them."

"Except for me and you, of course." She grinned and peered down at their hack job into their systems. Her stomach doing that uneasy shift again that told her something was off even though she still couldn't place it. Or place how Shilo fit into it.

"So if they're at least a few hundred years ahead of us," she said after a minute, "I'm wondering what happened to them. Where's the rest of their society?"

"FanFight and Corp 24 favorites!" the tele suddenly blared. Sofi jumped and glanced up to see Nadine on it, wearing a UW flag dress. "We're proud to be here today testing out our new product on the players."

Heller turned it up.

"At Corp 24 we are honored to do our part to achieve the safety of every human on our planet. And that starts here." She fluttered a hand at the Colinade stadium seal rising behind her. "At the very place precious lives were so tragically ended only days ago. But today? We promise to change that."

She smiled as she said it. So cheerful. So carefree.

Sofi wanted to vomit.

She knew all those players and gamers. The idea of their being Delonese, or even part Delonese, was ridiculous. What they needed to do was screen the Corp heads and those kids the Delonese had—

Her gaze dropped to her comp again. It was on its third re-scanning of the planet. She chewed her lip as Nadine kept talking in the background. Her voice urging an idea to slowly take root.

A moment later Sofi pulled up an entry code and accessed their server on the Darknet.

"Sof, be careful," Heller said from the couch. "We're already pushing it enough—you're gonna cause a noticeable security breach if you keep going."

She shoved down the temptation to remind him they were here for more than just watching the tele. "I don't think so." She kept working.

The access chip of Miguel's had held up its shield without even wavering, let alone bumping into any other programs. Like it worked by enfolding them rather than running separate. They weren't alerting anyone.

As soon as the net opened enough, she logged in to her team's backdoor chat and tagged Ranger.

A second later his name popped up. Sofi. What's up? Thought you were deep cover.

Running through their security. You know the Altered tester showcasing today? Could you find the DNA codes they're using for it?

From Corp 24?

Yeah.

Already hacked them, actually. The guys here wanted to see if they were lying or not.

Ha. Of course they did. She would've done the same had she been with them.

And? Sofi typed back.

A flood of data transferred into her blacknet box.

TY. You're the best.

You know it.

Sofi copied and opened them into a secure program before shutting down the chat and net. Then transferred them onto the scanner that was running.

A bubble of red lights popped up alongside the blue ones on the hologlobe.

"Oh my gosh."

Like before, the rest of the planet's surface was clear, except for a few dots several rooms over from where she and Heller were currently sitting—where Miguel and the team were meeting, she assumed—and another grouping nearby.

Heller glanced over and she pointed at the holo. To the barrack building that sat maybe five hundred yards from their room.

He got up and strode over.

"See those?"

"Yeah?" He frowned. "What are they?"

She sat speechless. Her mind numb. Her stomach freaking out. Her spine began to shake.

"Sof, what are they?"

"According to the Altered tech, they're . . . unaltered."

"Okay? Meaning?"

She blinked, then swept her gaze up to him. "Meaning they're humans."

36

MIGUEL

"SO WHAT WOULD YOU HAVE US DO?" THE CHAIRMAN SPOKE for the room. "We've seen your tragedy and we sympathize with you, but in all truth, Ambassador Miguel, there are certainly more pressing needs in your world than the loss of a few lives at an entertainment venue."

"Agreed, Lord Chairman, and normally we would treat it as such."

The chairman tipped his head toward the holographic telescreen that was currently blank. "And yet it is on every one of your news vids."

"In this case, the issue is one of integrity at the root of our UW council and Corps. The manner and place it was carried out has created concern. The attack focused on one of the few venues all thirty Corporate Nations engage in. Even you must see the undermining of trust that it's caused between the Corps." Never mind he'd helped that along at the UW meeting by stirring the pot.

"As I told a few of you privately yesterday," Miguel continued, "I personally have been approached to accuse a certain corporation, which leads one to believe this is an internal issue. Making it all the more detrimental if not handled with immediacy."

Beside him, Miguel felt Claudius nudge his leg. "Well done."

Unblinking, the chairman stared at him. "Ambassador, we agree it would be a grievance to see your governmental relations break down over a thing so petty." He turned toward the members in the room. "We, too, understand your desire to complete the investigation for the sake of Earth's UW and Corps unity." He stared at Miguel and spread his hands out in a very human gesture. "But what assistance can we offer that you do not already have?"

Miguel stifled a groan. He'd literally just spent a half hour describing in detail what they could lend assistance-wise. This stall of ignorance on the chairman's part was simply to say they weren't interested in investing more.

He smiled. "Chairman and Assembly, if anything, the UW Council would ask you to consider sharing any info that might . . ." He paused to word it as delicately as possible. ". . . shed light on activities we should know about among the Corps."

The assembly was a sea of frozen faces and stone bodies.

"Just as you have lent your assistance in the past," he added carefully, "regarding oversight of some of our lesser-than-legitimate organizations, we ask you to lend us your thoughts and tech serums once again."

"You have lie detector tests. Perhaps consider using them."

Miguel kept his smile stiff. "Alas, we all know it's not as simple as that. The accessibility of memory and heart-steadying chemicals produce false results far too often."

"You would have us share our info gathered through trusted relationships instead?"

"That is the hope, yes."

The audience stirred for the first time since the meeting began.

"I'm sorry, Ambassador, that is something we cannot do. You, of all people, will understand the folly of revealing privacies relayed in trust."

Miguel clenched his jaw. He fully understood. But that didn't change the need.

He sighed. *Déjame en paz.* Then let frustration drip heavy into his tone. "I understand, but frankly, we had hoped you'd be a bit more willing. Especially considering that, should this be a deeper discrepancy within one of the Corps, the lack of safety will affect all of us, including the Delonese—as they continue to enjoy Earth's entertainment."

If the chairman could've widened his eyes, Miguel guessed he would've done so. As it was, he noted multiple of the Delonese members twitching their fingers again.

The chairman just stared at him.

So long, in fact, that Claudius and Alis moved uncomfortably in their chairs.

The chairman eventually turned and nodded toward the vid-screen hologram. It promptly turned on and displayed a live news tube. "Yet we are faced with this."

Nadine was there, chatting up the Games from the looks of it.

The vid panned away from her to a shot of a crowd of protesters outside the Colinade, waving and decrying the inhumanity of the Games. They'd taken photos of the kids who'd been injured during the FanFights or died in the black markets afterward, and enlarged them, blood and all, to paste on signs.

Miguel frowned, until he realized the camera was continuing to pan past them.

Ten seconds later it landed on a group of protesters yelling even louder.

They were screaming obscenities and hate comments—all spewed toward the news vid, demanding the aliens go home. The camera zoomed in on their signs. They pictured drawings of dead aliens and of alien-human hybrids doing unconscionable actions.

Beside him, Danya shifted and Claudius flinched. "Ouch," he whispered.

The chairman turned his gaze to Miguel even as the scenes of anger toward the Delonese continued to play, as if on repeat.

"In that case, perhaps we should speak plainly," Miguel said without emotion.

37

SOFI

SOFI STARED AT THE HOLOGRAM OF DELON FLOATING IN FRONT of her. Watched it spin, filling up the room, her vision, and her heart with hope. This was it.

Shilo was here after all.

She couldn't breathe—could barely blink back the tears of fear and relief and joy that emerged from nowhere and affirmed that what she'd believed hadn't betrayed her.

Please be in those buildings.

Except . . .

Except his heart had stopped in her vision.

Bloody heck.

That part was the dream, Sof. Just the dream. She pulled up the security feed Heller had set to working on as soon as she'd shown him the human dots and traced the distance from their location along the best path to reach him. Trying all the while to bite back her anxiety. He was so close.

She slowed and inhaled, resisting the urge to drop everything and race for that cluster of red dots. *Careful, Sof. Don't let your emotions compromise his safety.*

"So why aren't *we* showing up on here?" Heller tapped his fingers on the table.

"Because of the shield we put around this room."

"Ah. Right." He waited while she continued to study it. "Soooo," he finally said. "That's the security as far as I could access, and I think we can do it. I vote we go."

She opened her mouth and stopped. After a second, she licked her lips. "I think we should wait for Miguel and Claudius."

"Wait, what?" He hesitated. "Sof, I've got it dialed in and figured out—what d'you think I just spent the past twenty minutes doing? Look, I told you from the beginning I'd help you rescue Shilo, and now I am."

"I know." She bit her cheek and forced her mind to stay steady. "I just think they know this place and the Delonese better than we do. If you were worried before about getting flagged by security—" She studied the feed. "This would be the situation."

"Are you saying you don't trust me?"

What? She looked up. "No. I—"

"Then come on. This was our mission. Let's finish it."

"And what then? We could compromise the whole thing. And we need a ship, Heller."

He shrugged. "Let's just see if he's there. If he is, we bring him back to this room and go from there."

She shook her head and studied the snow-crusted buildings. The one with all the humans would be around the farthest corner. She could see the very edge of its steep metallic roof. "I won't chance messing up what's most likely our only opportunity to help Shilo. We wait and see what Miguel can do."

"Unbelievable." He shoved a hand through his hair. "I thought you'd be freaking excited and here you are being—"

"Responsible." She frowned and estimated the depth of snow, determining how high up it'd hit on the slim-suits she'd brought.

"So we just wait until whenever they get back?"

She nodded. As much as it was killing her. She could almost feel Shilo's fading presence from here.

"You know . . . You sure this is about safety, Sof?" Heller tipped his chair on its back legs. "And not about Miguel?"

Her brow furrowed deeper. Where was this going?

"I know he was in your room last night."

"Yeah? So? We weren't doing anything."

He shrugged. "Maybe. Maybe not. But it seems before he came into the picture, you were fine being yourself. Now you're just . . . softer."

Sofi froze. Was he joking?

He let the chair drop onto its front legs. "I just don't want to see you give any more of you away is all."

She didn't respond. She didn't know what to say. She wasn't softer. She needed to think—to assemble their things. If Shilo was there . . . If the kids really are in that building . . .

If.

It wasn't even a question and she knew it. The kids from the Delonese shuttle were here. They were in that building, as blinking little red lights on that screen. She couldn't explain it other than to say she knew it in the same way she knew that she and Shilo would've won the FanFight Games this time around if the attack hadn't happened.

She glanced back at Heller. "Can you help me assimilate the slim-suit program Vic sent over?"

"Yeah. Sure." He rubbed his nose. "You wanna use them?"

"I think we'll need them if we're going to have a chance."

He moved to her comp-screen and worked over their coding, adapting it with the minimal security they'd accessed from the Delonese end.

"I'll get the suits." Sofi strode to her room and pulled them from her bag, trying to keep the butterflies contained at what they were getting ready to do. At what they were about to attempt as soon as the guys returned. She inhaled and turned when her handscreen went off with an incoming message from Ranger.

She frowned. She thought she'd logged out of the Darknet chat room.

She slid it open but nothing appeared. Huh. Must've been a time lag from earlier.

She hoisted the suits and carried them to Heller.

"Perfect." He laid them across the table and clicked the neck linings, then patched the altered security code into their sewn-in pads via Sofi's comp before he linked the whole thing to their handscreens.

Heller eyed her while they waited for it to finish. "You know what you need, Sof? You need to stop going for the wrong dudes." He stretched his hands behind him and tipped his head toward her bedroom. "Or one of these days it's gonna catch up with you."

She snorted and glanced toward Miguel's jacket still strewn over the couch.

"Ah, here we go. Suits are done."

Heller looked down just as her handscreen blinked in front of him. He grabbed it. "Looks like Ranger."

She leaned over him. "Weird, it just said the same thing a minute ago. And I thought I'd logged out of the net."

"Maybe it's a time lag."

She took it as Ranger's words showed up. *Hey, Sof. Something came in my box today. Said it was for you. May not be anything but sending it now.*

The box dinged and she quickly opened it. And promptly choked.

Her world stopped. Her heart stopped.

She flipped through the photos, slowly at first, then faster. "What the—?"

The pics didn't make sense. Or . . . they made too much sense, revealing more to a story that shouldn't exist—that couldn't possibly—

She leaned back, and Heller bent over to swipe through them as her stomach crashed and her heart lit in flames and set her chest on fire in fury and disgust.

Miguel.

Heller looked at her.

She didn't speak.

Something was wrong—not just in her head, but on the screen. As if she'd been played at a game she didn't even know was on the table. And just as she'd become what her mother assumed she was and what Miguel had rejected her for, he had become what she most loathed.

And he'd been on her bed last night. In her head. In her lungs and chest and messing with her emotions.

She shivered and clamped back the revulsion flooding in at the image of him speaking to her the past few days. She'd let him hold her—*touch* her. Let him feed his sick need for attention through her.

Heller growled. "What a perv."

She shook her head. What kind of person could do that? Could *be* that?

She would kill him.

She grabbed one of the slim-suits, began stripping down to her skin-thin thermals, then pulled on the stretch material. When she glanced up, Heller was staring. "Change of plans. We need to go *now.*"

His face was bright red. He cleared his throat. "Right. Yeah, we definitely need to go. Sorry, just not used to girls, you know . . ."

"Wearing a thermal beneath their clothes?"

"Well, just not thin. And not in front of me. Excuse me." He grabbed the other suit and jogged to her bedroom to change. When he emerged a minute later, he looked exhilarated.

"So we go investigate," Sofi said. "And *if* we find Shilo or the others, we make a vid uncovering their operation."

"Agreed. I'll take care of broadcasting it."

"And we bring Shilo back with us."

He nodded.

"We might also reveal how few Delonese there actually are, as added incentive to keep us alive. Other than that . . ." She inhaled and grabbed her handheld. "We play it by ear."

He grinned. "My favorite way. And, Sof, about the Miguel thing . . ."

She tuned him out and leaned down to the comp running the life-form scanning through the FanFight program. She pressed *Yes* and then enabled its password restriction and shut it. The hologram of the planet disappeared from over the table. "Once we reach the hall, let's test the security coding to ensure the suits keep us undetectable to their feeds." She passed Heller his handscreen. Then clenched her lips and slipped to the door.

Sofi didn't look back at her bedroom or Miguel's jacket or the window-reflected room as the hatred and ice retook their place over her soul. She wasn't soft. She was the better woman. The self-powered woman who took rather than bled.

"We good?" Heller breathed beside her.

She swallowed the vomit in her throat.

She nodded. Better than good. Better than ever. Because for the first time since seeing Miguel two evenings ago, she was wholly focused on what she'd come for.

38

MIGUEL

MIGUEL WATCHED THE TELE ALONG WITH THE REST OF THE council members as it continued to show calls for violence against the Delonese.

In some ways it was nothing new. Resistance and fear had always been a part of humanity—and not just toward other species. Mostly toward themselves.

At the same time, this instance stuck out to him. As it had more and more in recent months. As if to remind Miguel he used to believe in what they were doing when he'd first gone for office. The youngest ambassador in Earth's history, running on the belief of today's youth carrying the future with *vitalidad* and *visión*. And flirtations that reminded the older members what it was like to feel young again.

But it was still the same platform—to keep the elite in power. Those with higher vision who could make the best decisions for the masses. He glanced at the people calling for blood, then at this room containing another species of elite, and he wasn't so sure anymore. How was any of it different?

"You'll excuse our blunt talk, Ambassador." The chairman's voice echoed through the round room. "But this is what your people offer us in the same breath as requesting our help. This is the safety issue we face every day from your world."

He pointed at the tele just as the news flipped back to Nadine. She was holding up Corp 24's Altered scanner. "And yet you manipulate us to expose ourselves to more hate by betraying confidences."

Nadine smiled widely and turned as the camera panned up to show the inside of the perfectly reconstructed Colinade. The fact they'd fixed it to look brand new was a feat in itself. That they'd done so in a day and a half was a miracle. The vid zoomed back to Nadine and, behind her, two rows of FanFight gamers and players—eight each—of the Corps still left in the game for tomorrow's restart of the final rounds. Including their replacements in Corp 30.

"We are here to offer our latest services in security. In a moment we will be scanning our Altered invention over each of these young men and women. At least"—she leaned in—"those who've agreed to it."

The vid pulled away to reveal CEO Hart, from Corp 13, and Corp 30's Ms. Gaines standing to the side looking extremely unhappy.

"Let's question them, shall we?" Nadine said in an excitedly chipper tone. "CEO Hart, Ms. Gaines! It's well known you've contended against this pain-free, life-protecting service. Can you share with us once again why? And why you're here today?"

CEO Hart snorted. "Lady—"

"We formally oppose this development on the part of Corp 24," Ms. Gaines injected. "On the simple fact that it's an insulting invasion of privacy. Nothing more. We value our staff, our team, our players, and we—"

"So you're saying you won't allow your people to be tested?" Nadine peeked at the camera.

Gaines and Hart weren't fools. They knew a corner when they saw one. "Oh, you can test them," Gaines said. "But we will adamantly fight this being a common implementation in the future out of respect to our players and their basic genetic rights."

In the background, Corp 24's medical staff had begun to run their scan tester over the players and gamers, one at a time.

"And how about you both?" Nadine leaned toward Gaines and Hart. "Would you both be willing to undergo it?"

Hart sputtered.

"Anyone who thinks that guy's been Delonese altered is an idiot," Claudius murmured beside Miguel.

The vid went suddenly mute and the Delonese chairman turned back to Miguel and his team. "You see? It is some of your Corps themselves, such as Corp 24, who inspire suspicion and violence. Not just against you, but us as well. I believe you'll agree there seems to be one common thread." The vid panned to Nadine's face and, behind her, the giant ad for Corp 24.

"Our suggestion at this council is that you take care of that specific Corporation first. By the roots."

Miguel stiffened his jaw and went to respond. But before he could say anything further, a shrill alarm sounded through the room.

39

SOFI

SOFI FLIPPED THE SUITS ON AND DOUBLE-CHECKED HER screen's connection with them. She turned up the invisibility function and watched Heller slowly fade from view. Not all the way, but enough to convince the eyes of anyone looking around that he was just a trick of light. Perfect. She did the same for hers, then waved the door open.

They waited until the few Delonese down the hall turned a corner before exiting, then followed Heller's screen map to the metal lift. His phantom hand scanned his handheld against it.

Sofi held her breath until the lift bumped and dropped down three stories. She exhaled. The code had worked.

"Told ya," Heller whispered with a ghostly wink.

At the bottom, the lift opened onto another hallway. *Cripe.* She glanced at Heller who swiped his screen and scanned it again. The metal box promptly flipped around and opened onto the outside world of snow and ice and freezing wind.

"Bloody heck!" Heller yanked the slim-suit up over his mouth.

Sofi smirked and sucked in the cold. It felt good. Felt real.

Felt safe.

She scanned the area in front of them. The white, flat expanse was dotted here and there with fifteen-foot-tall metal posts that, from the limited map, acted as sensors that triggered vid interaction. Other than that, the giant yard was a winterland of ice and simplicity beneath a gray cloud-covered sky and a backdrop of those low foothills and perfectly aligned trees and the giant moon taking up a quarter of the horizon. Just ahead of her and Heller sat six rows of three barrack-type houses each. Exactly as they'd seen from the window. According to the dots on the screen, the humans were located four rows down and three back.

"Guess they don't get many guests," Heller purred. "Note the lack of guards. No wonder they were so lively the other night."

Sofi kept her mouth shut. There wasn't just a lack of guards. There was a serious lack of anybody.

The uneasiness flooded back in, growing in her chest, nudging a silent alarm that this was too easy. She tipped her head and they ran a straight, thin line between the two closest sensor poles and rounded the corner of the first barrack.

"Dang tall Delonese."

She glanced over to see Heller trying to inch up to peer inside the high windows. Except they were four feet above him. She ignored him and slid down the side, then waited for him to check the map for the next sensor poles.

She went to move again when a couple Delonese came around the corner. She jerked her hand against Heller to stay back. The visitors were striding slowly across the barracks in front of them and heading toward the far end.

"So what do you think is the issue with their low population?" Heller whispered against her neck after they'd moved far enough away. "They breed but can't make reproduction happen? Or are they monitored to keep their birthing rates low?" His breathing came short behind his mouth mask as his tone took on a creepy inflection. "Or what if they're like worms and can self-propagate?"

She shook her head.

"Maybe I could write a book." He pretended to stream a mini sign in front of his face. "Sex Lives of the Very Few but Beautiful, Bad-Taste-in-Food Aliens Among Us."

Her eyes scowled even as her lips cracked a smile. "Heller," she hissed. "I swear, if you get us caught because you're talking about their breeding abilities—"

"Just saying."

She beckoned him and they passed the second barrack, then a third, and suddenly they were rounding the corner of the one holding the humans. Holding her brother possibly. Hopefully.

She paused at the wall as Heller nodded toward the single tall door down at the end.

She inhaled and suddenly her stomach was butterflies and her spine a bleeding, shaking mess.

What if Shilo wasn't there? What if he was?

Why would they have taken him anyway? Why would they take kids, let alone any humans, against their will? What was their need?

The next second Heller was slipping past her and slinking up to the door. He waited for her to catch up, then scanned his handheld against it.

She heard a slight *click*.

The door slid up.

And they stepped into the silent space.

Sofi's breath stopped.

40

MIGUEL

THE MEETING HALL WAS ALIVE WITH VOICES. AS IF THE BLARing alarm had flipped the switch on the Delonese's emotions and they were instantly wired with intense feelings and opinions. Even with the thing shut off moments after it'd begun, the noise in the room had continued to climb.

It didn't slip past Miguel that none of the visitors were looking at them anymore, nor seeming to acknowledge they were there at all. As if they'd ceased to exist.

He looked back at Claudius, then Alis and Danya. "Do you know what that alarm meant?" he asked the latter.

Danya frowned. "No, but it sure triggered them."

"You think?" Alis looked at her. "These are your people, and you can't tell what's going on?"

Danya shook her head. "Just because I'm Delonese doesn't mean I'm still privy to all their workings. And unfortunately in this case, I'm as lost as you. I can read their expressions and comments, but they're acting as if even I'm not here. I can ask, but they'll not respond."

"What does that mean?" Miguel asked.

"It means that, for whatever reason, they're choosing not to trust me right now."

"Was it a security breach perhaps?" He gave her a piercing look. Had they discovered Heller and Sofi's hacking?

She was watching the room. "No. The chip I gave you for that was flawlessly secure. This has to do with the Corp and Games. I'm guessing with the Altered scanner and Corp 24, specifically."

Miguel froze as Claudius and Alis both stared at Danya.

A second later she nodded toward the chairman who'd raised his hand for silence as he looked right at them.

"Ambassadors and Ambassadors, it seems an issue has come up regarding boy Heller and girl Sofi. As you yourselves made us aware, they are being sought by a number of members on Earth."

He paused. "However, it seems Earth has taken Corp 30's warning regarding girl Sofi and raised the alert to high level. Meaning the UW has classified her as a danger. Due to that, our systems have taken the caution and reclassified them as well."

The chairman peered around the stadium room before he licked his lips and directed his gaze back to Miguel and Claudius. "Considering they have been flagged in Earth's system as being a viable threat, and as you yourself said, we would be best suited to observe them and discover the truth. We will need to detain you and your friends here. Indefinitely. Until this situation is cleared up. And in the meantime, we will take them for questioning and begin running a series of tests on them."

Miguel frowned. *¿Qué?* "And what would that entail exactly? These *tests*?"

"I can assure you our probes are of the utmost delicacy. Designed to cut and extract only the specific information needed. Your friends will remain mostly as they were."

"What?" Miguel said far too loudly.

Danya was shaking her head. "This isn't good. Something's not right. Miguel, they can't—"

"You may leave for your room now. However, we will ask you not to interfere with our med staff when they come shortly to take boy Heller and girl Sofi."

"Like heck they will." Claudius stood up.

41

SOFI

SOFI CHOKED. SHE LOOKED AT THE SCREEN AGAIN. THE BLUE lights were there. The red lights were there. It even showed the two guards still walking outside through the compound. It showed the red lights gathered in this room, right in front of where she was standing.

Except . . .

Except the room was completely empty, barren of furniture, of clothing, of anything.

"I don't understand," Heller said. "Did we miss something?"

She shook her head. "It's got to be a misreading."

"How?"

She was striding around the large room now. Feeling through it to ensure it wasn't a trick of the mind or some kind of tech abilities like the suit she was wearing. She searched harder. Waved her arms around wider—in every corner, along every wall and floor edge.

No, no, no. This is impossible.

Her breath came short. Her throat started burning, as if her chest were catching fire.

This couldn't be. They were supposed to find him. The sensors said they'd find him here.

The burning in her throat reached up to her eyes, and within seconds her gaze was blurring as her hopes dropped from her fingers to dash on the metal flooring beneath her.

"Sof, I'm looking at the map and we're in the right place. Maybe it was an old scan after all. Or maybe you coded it wrong," he added hesitantly.

"I don't know. But it's got to be wrong. Maybe we're seeing residual heat signatures."

"Like maybe they were here and just got moved?" He frowned.

"I don't know," she snapped. "I don't know how, Heller. I don't know the answer. I just know it's got to be wrong."

At least he was wise enough to keep his mouth shut.

She flipped around. "What do the other barracks show?"

"What, you want to go search each one?"

"Yeah, I do."

He put a hand out against her chest. "Okay, that is a bad idea. That's how you're going to get us caught. If we haven't been already and that's why there're no humans here."

"Does it show any other red dots on any of the rest of the map?"

"Just those of Miguel and Claudius and them. They're all blurred together in the main building. And our red dots are missing, but that's cuz of the suits."

She nodded and walked the room again. And tried not to throw up.

"I say we go back—"

"I'm going next door."

"You're what?"

"I'm going to check the two buildings on each side of this. How many Delonese are in them?"

"Four in one. Two in the other. But, Sof—"

She ignored him and slipped out to run the few yards to the next barrack over. She made sure her suit was at max discreetness, then scanned the door with her screen. And slid her head in far enough to peer inside.

Empty. Completely.

She walked the room the same way she had with the previous one, but unless the Delonese could actually vanish and become air, they weren't here.

She repeated it with the third barrack, this time as Heller followed, knowing before she even opened the door that she would find the same.

Sofi stepped out and stared at Heller's vaporous face.

He grimaced. "What now?"

She gritted her teeth and looked back toward the main building and their room three stories up. "We go back to the room and wait for me to kill Miguel."

42

MIGUEL

MIGUEL WAS STANDING IN THE MIDDLE OF THE SUITE WHEN THE door slid up and Sofi and Heller slipped in. All dressed in black. Faces pink from the frozen winterland air.

He crossed his arms and waited for them to speak. To explain. To say anything about where they'd been or why he'd come back to an empty room and thought for five brief seconds they'd already been taken. Except their comps were still there, and the Delonese who'd accompanied him had stopped in the hall to say he'd send an extraction team for the human friends shortly.

"Nice of you to join us," Alis said from behind Miguel.

Heller glanced up, scowled, and turned for the bathroom as Sofi tramped straight to her bedroom without a look or word in their direction.

"What the—? Hey," Alis said. "We're talking to you guys." Her anger practically sizzled through the air while Danya and Claudius sipped tea together and paced.

Miguel ignored the ambassadors and followed Sofi to her room and ducked under the door just as it dropped shut, leaving the two of them alone.

"I'd strongly suggest you not be here right now," Sofi said, not looking at him. She unzipped the upper back portion of her slim-suit with one hand, then her thermal beneath, while tossing her handscreen on the bed with the other.

"I'll leave after you tell me what the heck you were just doing."

"Exactly what we came here for. Or what *I* came here for. Forgive me if that's directly opposed to your plans."

"Me? What plans? You mean the plans to keep you both alive and from starting an interplanetary war while you're out doing gad knows what to piss off Earth?"

"I've no idea what you're talking about." She stripped off both suits and left them on the floor at her feet.

His eyes immediately sought out the ceiling. He swallowed. Trying to keep his gaze above her head—trying to keep his tone steady and the roiling anger in check against the fear weighing on his shoulders. "Sofi, I need to know—where were you and why'd Earth just flag you as a class-one threat?"

"To the first: I was looking for Shilo. To the second: As I said, I've no idea."

He looked at the floor and stepped forward. "For Shilo? Where? And what were you thinking—do you have any idea the kind of security threat you just set off?"

"Me? How about we both just agree that *you* pose a bigger security threat than anything I could've done—here or on Earth."

¿Qué? He squinted as she reached for her leggings. What was she talking about? "Uh, we're on the same team—at least we *were* until you disappeared to heck knows where and triggered some kind of security panic. Now they're coming for you and Heller, and I still don't even know what the freak is going on."

"You're joking, right?" She grabbed her shirt and yanked it on after her leggings, then picked up her handscreen. When she turned back around she was shaking, eyes flashing. The look of hatred clouding her face.

She set the device in his fingers and stepped back. Unblinking.

He frowned and glanced down. "What—?"

Oh.

Oh.

Crud.

He flipped through the first four pics and then tossed the thing on her bed. And met her gaze.

Her hands clenched as if she was about to pounce. Her silent accusation pouring from her skin, her expression, her disdain.

Liar.

Deceiver.

Seller of children to the highest bidder.

"Sofi—"

Her hand flew up. "Don't. Just don't. As far as I'm concerned you are everything I hate."

His jaw tightened and he kept his voice smooth. "I know what those photos look like, but they're not what you think."

She laughed. "Oh really, no?" She grabbed the handscreen and pulled up the first pic. "What's this? A collage of five of the FanFight kids who've gone missing in the past two years. And following that?" She flipped to the next pic. "Oh, a satellite shot of you with the first kid after he'd disappeared. Note the date. Note the minimal clothing. And this one—" She scrolled to the next pic. "That poor girl can hardly remember her name from the looks of it. And you just—what? Happen to have your arm around her to comfort her?"

He shook his head. "That's not it at all. Let me explain—"

"Explain what? That you're one of the political boys who uses the black market for pleasure? I just didn't expect you to stoop that low—and with so many. But then again"—she scowled at him and threw the screen onto the bed—"I should've known better."

He ground his teeth and stared at her, waiting for her to finish. Trying like insanity to figure out how to explain it in a way she'd actually believe.

She let out a laugh again. "Is this what those guys were blackmailing you with? Poor Miguel, what will he do when these hit the presses? Whatever helps you sleep at night, dude." She picked up her slim-suit and shoved it into her bag along with everything else of hers.

He strode over, grabbed her handscreen, and swiped it back to the pic of the first kid. "Look."

She kept packing.

"Please look at him."

She stopped. And glared. He held it up to her face. "That kid was taken. Just like Shilo. He failed out after the second round three FanFights ago and was gone within a day. The only reason I know is because I was walking by protesters a month later and he was there, looking like this. And he mumbled something to me in Delonese. But when I asked him, he couldn't recall anything about where he'd been or even who he'd been with since the first morning of the Games."

"And this girl." He dropped his voice and swiped to the next pic. "Same thing. Claudius, Alis, and I were investigating an anomaly for the UW when we came across her. And just like the boy, she knew a bit of Delonese. But the moment we questioned her, we discovered her memories had been completely erased as well."

He had her full attention now. "The reason I agreed to bring you here is because you were right. They're taking kids and doing something with them—and Claudius, Alis, Danya, and I haven't been able to figure out what or why or how. But I find it incredibly interesting that it's so often kids associated with the FanFights."

Her face had gone from hatred to horror to grief. To belief.

"The people who took these photos have no idea what I've done for those kids. Or maybe they do—and that's why they're upset, I don't know. All I can tell you is that I haven't messed them over. I've been helping them."

Even if her expression claimed belief, her tone stayed suspicious. "No offense, but it's a little hard to trust a person who's made it his life's work seducing others. Or, oh wait, that was just me you tossed away. Cuz apparently I wasn't even good enough for you."

He scoffed. Was she kidding? How did this just go from him not abusing or selling kids but actually saving them to her being offended he didn't sleep with her?

The expression on her face gave the answer without him needing to ask.

His chest clenched. He'd hurt her. So of course, she'd assume he'd hurt others. If he wanted her to believe him—to trust him—he'd have to be honest with her.

After all this time.

He looked away and ran a hand over the back of his neck. Then nodded and peered back at her. "It was *never* that, Sof." His voice thickened. "It's that you were too good. *Santo cielo*, you have no idea." He shoved a hand through his hair as she snorted and glanced away.

But still listened.

"Remember on the shuttle how I said that real relationships are vulnerability and dying to shallowness? Well, I'm going to be more vulnerable with you right now than with any woman I've known. I remember exactly what we had. And what you are. And it is better than I ever could've hoped to have had, or to have been. You were so much more than good enough—so much better than what I'd known—that it broke something in me I have never recovered from."

She actually chuckled. "So I was too good. Which perfectly explains why you left and pursued other lovers."

"I didn't. I left for myself."

"Right."

He opened his lips. Shut them. Inhaled. "Sofi, I have never slept with another person since the day I met you looking all pissed and bored at that FanFight party."

Whatever reaction she had faded into an arched brow. "You're lying."

"Ask Claudius. It's the truth."

She stared at him, her eyes boring into him as if she could read the truth there.

"You left," she said after a minute. "Without a call, a text, anything. I spent two weeks crumpled up on the floor of my apartment trying to find the air you'd stolen. To find myself. My focus." She laughed caustically. "And you're saying I helped you find yourself?"

A second later her voice cracked and the venom came. "In that case, perhaps I should thank you. Because I, too, eventually found myself. Or some variation. But that doesn't justify the fact that you always want more—even when it's not yours."

Her voice softened along with her expression. "You have everything, yet you don't even know who you are inside. It's the worst form of self-loathing, because you use it to rob from others. Until we become a freaking shell of who we were." She looked away, but he'd seen the pain in her eyes. "Until, between you and my mom, I became a shell."

He leaned in and carefully brushed a hair from her cheek. "And the guilt for that has killed me every day for the past eighteen months."

She frowned and pulled back slightly.

"You don't think I've seen? That I've not watched you? That I haven't known where you've been the past eighteen months or didn't care?" He let his gaze carve into hers, as if he could speak healing into the cuts and wounds and icy edges with his words.

She stalled and stared. And swallowed.

He tightened his jaw. "Well, you're wrong."

Sofi's eyes said more than words ever could. But all she uttered was, "Then why didn't you come back?" And then blinked back the hot mess of tears he watched rising to her eyes.

His lungs broke. His voice broke. His words broke and fell to shatter on the floor.

He didn't have an answer—didn't even know how to answer.

But one rose in him anyway. "Because I didn't think you'd want me."

A knock hit the door.

"What, Heller?" Sofi whispered.

"Um, guys, you need to see this."

"Not right now, *ese*," Miguel said louder for the both of them.

"Actually, this is one of those yes-you-come-right-now things," Claudius cut in. "Get out here."

Sofi glared at the door. Then licked her lips and, with a single glance at Miguel, walked over and hit the door lock.

Miguel followed.

"You know that program you were running, Sof?" Heller said as soon as the door slid up. "Well, it finished, and when I opened your comp-screen, this popped out."

He was pointing at the two-foot-wide hologram floating over the table.

Miguel frowned. "What is that?"

Sofi moved to the holo of the planet and touched it.

"Right. So, um, can someone explain to me what exactly we're looking at?" Alis said. "You know, now that your lovers' spat is done and the Delonese are about to come eat these two alive?"

Sofi stepped back and pursed her lips as Heller pointed to the planet core, then enlarged it.

Miguel moved closer. "This is Delon?"

"Wait, is that the planet?" Alis looked around. "I don't get it—what are we saying here?"

"We're saying it isn't a planet at all." Sofi stared at it. "Delon is a space station."

43

SOFI

SOFI STUDIED THE HOLOGRAM. IT WAS THE SAME SURFACE OF trees and snowy hills and capital city they'd seen before. But the virus she'd used from this week's FanFights had worked better than she could've imagined. It had wormed its way in—not just to reveal hidden passageways or architectural features. It had revealed *all* of them. The entire planet looked like a hive catacomb, with octagons and massive generators and rooms and wires and things beyond like anything she'd ever seen.

Alis dropped a string of swear words.

"My thoughts exactly," Claudius muttered.

"Is there anyone who knows about this—like, anyone on Earth?" Alis glanced up. "Miguel? Danya?"

Miguel shook his head. "Not that I'm aware of." He looked at Danya while tapping something into his handscreen.

Danya was shaking her head as well. "I've lived here most of my life and don't even remember this."

"Okay, great," Claudius said. "We've just stumbled upon the biggest and possibly most dangerous secret of the past decade. Lovely. But also, we need to get Sofi and Heller out of here before they become wards of the crazy-state happening here." He waved a hand at the hologram.

"What, you think they're only going to come for them?" Alis snorted. "Don't you think they're going to realize we've accessed this? You guys, they're going to come for all of us. We all need to get out of here."

"And blow our cover?" Danya said.

"Unless it's already blown." Miguel looked at Sofi. "What do you think?"

"We need to know what we're looking at first, and what the heck this thing is," Heller interrupted. "Also—" He flipped around to Danya. "Back up. Did you just say you've lived here your whole life?"

"Yes. And I've never seen this."

"Um, okay. And *how* is that possible?" He swerved to the others. "The Delonese don't allow—" He stalled. Peered back up at the ambassador and abruptly leaned away. "Oh." Then, "Does Earth know about you being—you know? Cuz I'm pretty certain—"

"An alien? A few do, yes. Only the ambassador and Corp CEOs. They voted me in, as both sides saw the benefit of having someone who'd experienced both cultures and ways of politicking."

Sofi said nothing. But the high cheekbones with slight excess of makeup, the height, the slow-blinking eyes—as if practiced—and the chip Miguel produced last night, the familiarity with which Danya carried herself here, the ability to translate their ancient language with ease . . . It clicked.

"But you don't remember any of this?"

Sofi watched Danya swallow. Then hesitate. "I may have been subject to a repressive-memory scan before I took the Earth position. For my people's safety. The seventy years I spent with them before residing on Earth would've been too risky in the wrong hands."

Heller looked like he didn't know whether to be fascinated or distraught. "Wow, you look good," was all he said.

Sofi didn't care. She snapped her fingers at him. "Hey, I need your help." She glanced up at Miguel. "You said the Delonese are coming for us. So what do we do?"

He looked at Danya.

"I love my people, but, just like humans, I think it unwise to give them access to your body at this point, at least if you want it back. And I'd agree it doesn't look good for the rest of you in this case."

Sofi smiled. At least she was honest. "What do we do?"

"I promise to never agree with Heller again, but in this case, I think he's right," Claudius said. "We make a run for it."

When they all looked at him, he added, "I mean, let's talk options. If we do what we came here for and attempt to find the kids, the Delonese are going to know we know they have a giant magical death-star hive. If we let them take Sofi and Heller, they'll use their brain stuff to get the truth out of them, in which case they'll also know we know they have a giant death-star hive. So—I'm going to go with we all just run for it and grab one of our ships."

"I agree," a voice said from the table. Sofi turned to discover Vic listening in. So that's who Miguel had been typing to a minute ago. "I've run the calculations," Vic added. "And that's the one with the best outcome. If you can pull it off."

"Wait—the running? Or Shilo and the kids?" Sofi pointed to the red dots on the planet. They were still there—now just showing *beneath* the building she'd been standing in less than an hour ago, rather than inside of it.

"Wait, why didn't *all* of the lights show up with our original scan?" Heller pointed to the hive-like interior where masses of them were crammed deep inside like a ball pit. "How come just these few near the surface lit up?"

"They're closest to the top, just like the humans," Vic answered for Sofi. "The other Delonese lights are beneath a deeper shield."

"Look at all of them," Alis said softly. "There must be thousands."

"But again, the question comes down to where do we go from here?" Miguel glanced at his watch. "We have limited time—are we thinking we're making a run to the shuttles? And if so, are we able to get to them and then get past their atmospheric shield? Or better yet, not get bombed by this giant honeycomb?"

Sofi chewed her cheek and peered at Vicero's floating head. "Do you think you could use my virus to interface with the space station itself? Like, could you get me access to run a program off of it?"

Vic nodded. "If you can turn off the feedback loop so it doesn't trigger once I ease through the firewall."

Sofi glanced at Danya. The visitor nodded. "I believe they've wiped that part of my memory, but my brain processes fast. I think I can assimilate it. I don't know how far my clearance will get you, but I'll give what I have." She leaned over and began typing on Miguel's handscreen.

Heller made a sound and frowned at Danya. "Doesn't it weird you out at all that you're betraying your own kind?"

She kept typing. "I've spent the past ten years on Earth as a human. So while my allegiances lie here, they lie with humanity and my adopted family there as well. Which was the whole point, I believe. So I follow my conscience, and in this case I believe the misleading of your people, and the taking of your children, is not something I can support."

"How do you know they've taken them?" Heller's frown deepened. He looked around.

"It's what we've been working on for the past year and a half, among other things," Danya replied as she continued with Vic.

Sofi looked at the group. "I know you won't be comfortable with this. But I still want to get my brother and—"

"You're joking," Alis scoffed. "You want to go into the death-star where there's more of a chance of getting caught?" She glanced around at them as if Sofi was crazy. "We're—"

"Actually, I agree with her," Claudius said.

"So do I." Miguel rubbed the back of his neck. "It's what we came for. And after this, we'll be lucky if we get back to Earth in one piece, let alone with any believable explanation." He shot Sofi a slight smile. "Like I said, if we've got one shot, might as well go all the way."

Danya straightened. "There, I think that should give you access."

"Yep, on it," Vic said.

Sofi turned and logged in to the Darknet and accessed Ranger. She opened portals to both him and Vic on her handheld.

What's up, Sof?

If I sent you a security file with access via my virus, could you help maneuver and monitor us through it? Sofi typed.

If you get me through the firewall yeah. Why? What're we doing?

She tapped her screen. We're playing a FanFight Game. Basically. But on Delon.

"Wait, are you really?" Claudius looked at her. "How?"

She smiled. "You forget who we are. We know their system, and so far we have enough access to their security that we can hide behind it." She leaned over. "Vic, can you get me access to our shuttles?"

"Sure thing, man."

Sofi looked up at the group. "I suggest you grab what you need and get ready to run. Because in this case, speed will be the deciding factor."

Heller tapped his handscreen. "Okay, I'm in with Vic and Ranger. What do we need?"

"To use the IC program we used for this week's Games."

His gaze widened. "Are we creating a totally alternate reality? We don't have time."

Alis frowned. "You guys can do that?"

"Considering it's a giant electrofusion comp—technically we should be able to run it like one. If we have the right access. Be right back." She ran to her room and changed back into her slim-suit. When she returned, Heller had read her mind—he was wearing his as well. And Miguel and Claudius had their bags over their shoulders.

"Everyone have the earcoms Miguel gave us?" When they nodded and clicked them on, Sofi pulled on a pair of gloves and slammed her comp closed. She handed it to Heller, who put it in his bag with his own.

She voiced her text. "Ranger, how's that going on your end?"

"Perfect. I'm in thanks to whoever Vic is," Sofi read out loud.

"Vic's my lady AI," Claudius said. "Hands off." He leaned

in. "And, Vic, what say when I get back, you and I do a proper date?"

Vic paused and blinked. Then batted both eyes and blew him a kiss.

Sofi could only imagine him seated across from her holo-head at a pricey restaurant. Eating enough for both of them. She smirked and decided she rather liked the idea, before she grabbed her handscreen and turned up Heller's and her suits until they were ghosts again.

"Whoa," Alis said.

"Bien," Miguel added.

Sofi lifted the planet diagram off her screen and pulled it into a holo. And began turning it with her hands. "Okay, Ranger, try running the Delonese code filter over the FanFight data. And, Vic, can you use the suit data to match the shuttles on a larger scale?"

Vic spoke up. "Already done. When do you want me to ghost them?"

"As soon as we've accessed the kids. Then pull both out and bring them to the coordinates I'm sending you now.

"Heller," she added. "Can you see enough to code in a few distractions without flagging security?"

"I'm on it." He glanced up with a grin. "Creating replicas of you all as we speak. I'll leave them in this room for the time being and have another set light up down a back hall once these get found."

She turned to Danya. "How about your people? What should we know?"

"They won't all be after us. Only the peacekeepers specifically assigned at given times. In that way, they are comfortable keeping to themselves and allowing the protectors to do the dirty work."

Sofi nodded to her. "I'd normally take issue with that, but today it works in our favor."

Miguel's hand touched her back. "Sof, we need to go."

Right. She inhaled. And tipped her head to the group. "Ready?"

Then touched her screen and turned a scrapp song on low in their earcoms.

Miguel looked amused and opened the door just as the bass dropped.

44

MIGUEL

THE AFTERNOON FOG CRASHED OVER THE COMPOUND LIKE A wave of perfect timing to cover everything in ice and shadow. So deep that Miguel could barely see his fingers. Or maybe it was that Vic had found a way to thinly stretch the invisible cloaking on Sofi's and Heller's suits to act as an almost-shield for the rest. If they stayed close enough. He reached out with his senses and set his hand against Sofi's as they retraced Heller's and her steps from earlier. Sofi didn't react to his touch. Didn't pull away.

He hoped she knew. Hoped she understood. He'd never been more in awe of her than he was at this moment.

"So far so good," Claudius whispered. "No sirens."

Miguel didn't reply, even though everything in him yelled for them all to shut it. At least until they got someplace with a better visual.

The walk was short and within minutes they were through the door and inside an empty barrack. Sofi dropped Miguel's hand and looked at her handscreen. Then pointed toward the wall. "It's saying there's a door here." Miguel could barely see her near-invisible self as she strode over and felt around until her hand found the smooth edges of what was a scanner.

"Nice," Claudius breathed.

"Bizarre," Alis said.

"This way." Sofi's ghostly arm waved them into the metal elevator that looked identical to the one back at the Main Station.

Miguel peered at the security monitor in Heller's hand. So far Vic seemed to be holding everything pieced together. He'd have to remember to give her a bonus.

Heller scanned the handheld over the access module and the door promptly shut. The next second the lift dropped so fast Miguel's stomach lurched and Alis's face turned yellow in the dim.

When the thing stopped its drop, it spun around and opened onto a ledge overlooking a giant, dark, complex system that really did look like a massive hive. A collective gasp went through the lift as the group froze. The place was literally buzzing with activity and noise. Thousands upon thousands of Delonese were moving and working and participating in a societal world he hadn't even known existed until half an hour ago.

He peered closer. Fascinated.

Then frowned. The only aliens he saw were adults. No kids. He'd never thought to ask anyone, but he was suddenly curious. How long did they live? And how often did they procreate?

"Um," Claudius breathed.

"Crud. Sorry, guys." Heller scanned the monitor again and the door slid shut before the lift spun around and reopened on the opposite side. "That's better."

"Miguel?" Sofi murmured.

"On it."

"Hey, Vic," he said. "I think we're about ready. Both ships will need to be prepped and waiting to move pronto."

"Got it, man."

"Sof, try your scanner," Heller said. "Something's frozen with this door."

Miguel watched Sofi use her handheld on the door. *Nada*.

"It has tighter security," Danya said.

"Maybe try hitting it." Alis shrugged. "Always works with my hover."

Miguel chuckled and dropped to the ground—and jammed his hand into the scanner. He jumped back as the thing sparked and shorted out with a loud *zap* and smoke. He yanked the casing off and looked through the interior wires, then moved back for Sofi. She peered in and pressed the two farthest back and suddenly the door swished open.

Twenty pairs of very human eyes looked up at them. From twenty very frightened faces.

White gowns.

Shaved heads.

Smooth skin.

They were as clean as the room itself.

And yet the entire atmosphere smelled of urine and fear.

His heart stung. They were all races and sizes, but Miguel doubted any were over the age of seven.

Heller looked around and then peered at Sofi. "Sof, these kids are all too . . ." His voice faded.

"Young," Sofi whispered.

45

SOFI

SOFI WAS FRANTIC. IT COULDN'T BE. HE HAD TO BE HERE. SHILO had to be with them. She dimmed her slim-suit, and she and Heller became visible again so as not to scare the kids. Then Sofi stepped into the room and scanned their faces even as the panic grew. She strode forward to sift through the children with her hands as she hissed Shilo's name over and over.

No answer. Just frets and whimpers from the kids they'd just woken.

She reached the back of the room, having looked over all twenty. He wasn't here.

Oh gad, he wasn't *here*.

"Shilo," she whispered. She forced back the rush of tears in her throat. "Shilo!"

"Maybe he's in another area," Heller said from behind her. He moved beside her and leaned down to one of the older kids staring up at them.

"Are you here to take us home?" the boy asked.

"Yeah, in a minute. But are there any older kids here? Like teenager types?"

The boy shook his head, his eyes like saucers.

"Were any others brought in with you?" Sofi asked sharply. "Like ones who came but the aliens already took away?"

Again, the boy shook his head.

Sofi wanted to shake the kid. This couldn't be happening. "Are you positive?"

"Sofi."

She ignored Heller's hand on her. "Are you certain? These are the only kids you've seen?"

The boy's eyes reddened as he nodded. "No one else is here but us. Can we go home now?"

Oh gad.

Anything left of the ice surrounding Sofi's emotions shattered right on the spot. At her grief. At Shilo not being here. At the expression of the little boy in front of her.

She looked around, suddenly saw the reality on their faces. The fear. The hope. The innocence. Melting everything within her. For him. For the children with him. She bent down and put her arms around the boy. "Yes, we can go home now." And in seconds all twenty of them were whimpering and encircling her and clinging to her legs, her arms, her suit, whispering, "I want to go home too. I want my mum."

Sofi's ribs cracked wide open twenty times in a row to match each new voice—each tearstained cheek—looking lost and scared and believing that she could save them.

Oh heck. This is what Miguel has been seeing. What he's been doing.

And this is why he does it.

She glanced back at him.

"Okay, amigos." He was speaking quietly, in a tone that sounded adorably cheerful. Like a spark of hope and sunshine in the midst of a pee-stained, fear-laced room. He picked up the smallest child and put her on his hip. "What do you say we get out of here, eh? Anyone ready to get home?

"Shhhhh." He handed the child off to Claudius and whispered, "Okay, see this dude here?" He put his hand on Claudius. "And this woman?" He pointed to Danya, who already had one kid on each hip. "These guys are kind of like secret superheroes. And they're going to lead you to a ship that'll take you to your moms and dads. But in order to do that—" He held a hand out to the next closest kid. "I'm going to need you all to hold hands and follow them single file. You got that?"

"Everyone hold hands." Danya moved through the group, pulling them to their feet.

Sofi stared at Miguel as any last crumb of hate or bitterness or grief she felt for him dissolved into the beauty of his soul. As if her very bones called to him, recognizing the reckless, whispered heartbeats of who he was at the core.

He was a completely different person than he portrayed day in and out on the tele.

Miguel glanced up and caught her eye. And cocked a brow.

She smiled.

"Sofi, I think—"

Heller's voice was cut off by a massive alarm that was so loud it shook the walls.

Sofi flipped around as the kids broke into weeping and screeches. She grabbed their hands and began pushing them into the lift along with Claudius and Danya.

She could already see the blue dots moving on her handscreen. They were coming from below, not above. She shoved the last of the kids at Claudius. "Take them to the shuttle." She could also see a number of small red dots. They were on the floor below and to the right. *What the—?*

"Sof," Vic's voice said. "What's going on?"

"The security's been triggered."

"Not on our end or yours."

Sofi stalled. "What do you mean?"

"I mean it's internal. Not us. Meaning someone alerted them. Sofi, you guys need to watch your back."

Sofi looked over. They were all in but the lift was straining under the weight. She looked at Miguel. He glanced down at the screen. He'd seen the red blips too.

"Heller," he said, his gaze locked on hers. "Get us to the surface."

The tech scanned his handheld against the module and the door shut, and the next second the lift rose, stopped, and opened, practically spitting them on the floor. "Let's go," Sofi hissed, grabbing little hands and helping them hurry.

The ghosted shuttle was waiting just outside the barrack, door open, shimmering in the late-afternoon light as if ethereal. The child closest to Sofi gripped her fingers and oohed at it.

The captain was waiting. "Ambassador Danya, I received a note from Delon, as well as you, requesting an immediate departure."

"Thanks, Vic," Sofi murmured.

"Gotcha covered, girl."

"But are you wanting me to take all of you?" The captain eyed the kids. "Because this thing can hold twenty—twenty-two at most."

Miguel stepped forward. "Captain, I'm ordering you to take all the children, Ambassador Claudius, Danya, and Heller."

"Not me," Heller cut in. "Ranger, Vic, and I can monitor the shuttle from here. But I told Sofi I wasn't leaving her alone in this. So I'm staying. We can catch the next shuttle."

The alarm got louder. Heller glanced at Sofi. "And in the meantime, we can hold them off."

She nodded as she helped them load the kids on board. Then Claudius and Danya stepped on.

"Gotta go if we're going to have enough fuel. I'll make sure shuttle two's on its way to pick you up."

"Wait, where's Alis?" Claudius suddenly looked behind them.

A second later the door sealed shut and the ship glimmered like an apparition in the light. Then disappeared.

46

MIGUEL

MIGUEL FLIPPED AROUND TO STARE AT SOFI AND HELLER. ALIS.

Miguel's knuckles went white just as a *click* sounded in his earcom.

"Hello, Miguel."

The group all turned to him. She was in their earcoms as well.

"Where are you?"

"With the Delonese. I'm sorry I had to slip away so quick. It was getting a bit heated in there. And I had to hedge my bets. I think I made the right decision, though."

"Alis, what did you *do*?"

"Exactly what I needed to. What you didn't have the guts to do."

Sofi glanced up at him. Her eyes burning in determination. Sofi pointed to her handscreen where the other red lights were flickering, smaller but there. Just down a floor from where they'd been.

Where was the second shuttle?

"Back in the room, I tried to argue," Alis continued. "I tried to give you and me a fighting chance to get out of here alive, reputations intact. But you sided with her."

Miguel glanced at Sofi.

She raised a brow and snorted. "Dang right, chick." Then was flagged in a message from Vic. Other shuttle is down. Delonese were able to decloak it. Best suggestion is hide until I can regain access to its controls.

What about the kids' shuttle? Sofi typed back.

> Still in control of it. Gave it an extra boost so it should be out of the atmosphere soon. No sign of space station loading weapons.

"They got to you, too, didn't they, Alis?" Miguel looked to Sofi and made a motion at her and Heller that they head back into the metal lift. He pointed to the red blinking dots and mouthed, "Up here we're sitting targets."

They nodded and shut the barrack door. Then hurried for the lift.

"You and me, baby. Days ago. We're the pawns. Except you got the blackmail, I got the money."

Sofi scanned the wall mount and the lift moved down and then to the right, like a vid game.

Miguel frowned. "What'd you offer them, Alis?"

"Whatever they asked for. Wasn't hard. Especially when I saw what was on the line for their way of life and Earth's future."

"What'd they ask for?"

"Same as you. Corp 24 on a platter. And if I threw Sofi in, an extra few years of peace."

He stalled. "Sofi? ¿Qué—?"

"Corp 30 knew you wouldn't go for that part. Apparently your emotions aren't as hidden to some—not that I would've ever guessed. At least until we got here. And Corp 13 didn't care one way or another. So they hired me as the backup. To ensure the job was done."

The lift stopped and Sofi spun it around.

"At the risk of the children's lives we're saving."

"I think you mean at the safety of our children's lives and future. We play our part and contribute, and the Delonese leave us to continue our lives. How could that be too complicated to understand, Miguel?"

Sofi turned and stared at him in the dim light, her brown skin and graceful body stiffening at Alis's insinuations. The lift stopped again, and Heller just kept focusing on his handheld.

Miguel's stomach sank.

"Come on, this way," Sofi whispered just as the door opened into a dark hallway that smelled of formaldehyde and mint. They slipped into it and began walking.

"What CEO Hart and Ms. Gaines did with that explosion was to protect the human race. We should be thanking them. If the world had discovered that some of their players had been altered by the Delonese, they would've had a hissy fit. And for the Delonese—it's more than just experimentation and study, you know. It actually means something—it's worth something."

"You're speaking of the greater good?" Miguel said casually, encouraging Alis to keep talking.

"The lesser of two evils, the greater good—yes, however you want to word it."

Miguel stood quite still as he watched Sofi freeze, then turn toward him. He saw the look in her eyes. His voice went cold. "Who was altered? Which players?"

"That ultimately doesn't matter, does it? What's important

is that the programs will go on and Corp 24 and their Altered invention will go under."

"Bien, it doesn't matter. But who was altered, Alis?"

"Good-bye, Miguel. Take care. And be careful. I'm guessing you have about two minutes before they find you."

47

SOFI

"GUYS, DID YOU HEAR HER?" HELLER CHOKED. "SHE SAID TWO minutes. I say we call it quits and—"

"And what? Our ship is gone." Sofi moved cautiously down the hall as the alarm continued to blare.

Why weren't there any guards or med workers in this section? The place was a ghost town.

"Right. So maybe we just turn ourselves in. Or make a run for it."

Sofi ignored him and turned a corner to discover a lengthy, dimly lit room facing them. According to her handscreen, this was where the other humans were.

A low light flickered on. Then turned brighter to reveal shiny white walls, white flooring, and overhead lamps that rivaled the sun. It was a lab.

Oh.

"Oh gad," Miguel whispered.

Heller slipped a hand over his mouth, his skin yellowing.

Babies. Children. *People.*

Up until the age of ten from the look of them, inside biovats in suspended animation.

Miguel strode over to one of the fifty or so giant-size cylinder tubes each filled with blue fluid and a human—hanging from the ceiling like bulbs. They were giving off heat.

Beside the first ten of them was a small incubator, housing what appeared to be a baby of Delonese-like form.

Sofi almost threw up. Her stomach spun. No wonder she'd never seen or heard of a Delonese baby. Or a pregnant adult, for that matter. Were these test-tube Delonese babies? Made from test-tube humans?

"Did you—?" Sofi turned to Miguel, her tone full of horror.

He was shaking his head. "I had no idea this is what they were using them for." He ran a hand along the side of a tube, disgust and anger emerging on his face. "I honestly suspected they were simply testing and enhancing Earth's kids. Like what Alis said. But this—"

A sound erupted nearby and Sofi turned in time to see Heller vomiting on the floor. After he finished, he turned to Sofi with the faint hint of a smile. "At least that answers my sex question."

Sofi scowled as Miguel strode forward. "C'mon, we need to keep moving. In case . . ."

He didn't finish.

He didn't need to. Sofi knew what he was thinking.

In case Shilo's in one of these.

Sofi tried to follow. Tried to walk. Tried to put one foot in front of the other, but her legs wouldn't budge. What if Shilo *was* in one of these? What if he'd been used for—?

Think, Sofi. Had she seen this in her visions? Had Shilo shown any of this to her? She shut her eyes and sorted through the pictures in her mind that swelled up along with a new wave of nausea.

No. She'd never seen this before. *Oh, Shilo . . .*

Miguel's hand slipped to the low of Sofi's back. Securing her.

Soothing her. Heat rushed up and burned her eyes as she blinked back tears that had no right to be there but somehow insisted. They slid and shuddered and dripped down her cheeks and off her chin to hit *tap, tap, tap* onto her suit.

"You okay?"

She nodded. "We just need to be sure he's not . . ." She swallowed and lifted her chin at Miguel and Heller. "We split up and keep searching. I'll look toward the back-hallway rooms. Miguel, can you take the hall to the left and, Heller, to the right?"

"Yeah, of course." Heller patted her arm and took off—as if the sooner he got out of there, the better.

"Don't get caught," Miguel whispered. "And, Sofi . . ." He turned his gaze to her.

She nodded at him. "I know."

He paused. Studied her. Her eyes. Then tipped his head. "See you in a few."

Sofi moved into the next room. This one had more bulbs hanging from the ceiling, but rather than being giant like the previous ones, these were tiny. Barely bigger than a watermelon.

They hung there like small moons, lighting the room with their bluish glow.

Sofi moved closer, her chest clenching.

Parts.

Body parts.

Hearts and lungs were inside them to be exact.

"You guys finding anything?" Heller's voice sounded nervous in her ear. Tense.

She clicked her com. "Just a room of tiny jars of hearts and lungs hanging from the ceiling. They're putting off heat like the others. How about you?"

"Yeah, uh . . ." There was an odd shuffling in the com, then he cleared his throat. "I think that's the same here."

A sound behind Sofi erupted just as the alarms turned off. "Finally," Heller uttered into her com. She dropped to the ground and scrambled behind one of the tables. Two male Delonese came in. Speaking in their foreign tongue. Sofi tapped her com from them to translate.

"They blocked our systems so we can't get a lock on the shuttle."

"How? That's impossible. And what will happen if they make it back to Earth? The amount of research lost—"

"I'd be more worried about what Earth will say."

"Earth? If we don't finish our research, it won't matter. Their DNA is the only chance we have at rebooting our own and regrowing our population."

Then they left. She breathed. And tried to absorb what she'd just heard without throwing up.

"Hey, Sof, I think I found something," Heller said. "You might want to come down here."

"Me too. You guys—"

"Where?" Miguel replied.

"Next room ov—"

She tapped her com. "Repeat that?"

Nothing.

What the—? She tapped it again and whispered. Still nothing.

It was dead.

Her handscreen suddenly blipped as a message popped up. Ranger.

> Sof. I thought you might want to see this. Your mom sent it in a private message I intercepted.

It was a vid.

She clicked on it. Then frowned. It was recorded from her mom's phone.

A sick feeling emerged in the pit of her stomach as she backed against a corner in the dark. Something told her no matter how hurried she was, she needed to watch it now.

"I had to, Inola," Ms. Gaines said. "CEO Hart made it clear his investment with us was contingent on our continued success. The other Corps were getting too close. What would they have done had they discovered what we were doing with their kids? With *our* kids? That we were jacking the games? Corp 24's Altered would've ruined everything."

"So you had them killed along with my son?"

"They were going to expose us! All that work we've put into this company to help people—to make them better!" Ms. Gaines was practically foaming at the mouth. "It would've been thrown away. As would our relationship with the Delonese, which you and I have worked too hard to build."

"It wouldn't have been thrown away." Sofi couldn't see her mom, but she recognized that determined tone. "It would've been exposed and broader access given for those cures to the public. As far as our relationship with the Delonese, who's to say what they would've done? Found another Corp? I'm sure there are others out there who'd kill for the chance."

Ms. Gaines's eyes were wild. "But if the Delonese knew we'd let their secret escape—with blood on our hands in front of the world—they'd be called into question too. It could rock the entire political system our world has worked too hard to establish, Inola. People would've lost faith in them and us. And there would be riots. And likely war. The only reason I blackmailed Miguel was to stop them from accessing those kids on Delon. If you'd kept your daughter under better control—"

The vid flipped over, and suddenly Sofi's mom was there, shaking her head and blinking back what looked like real tears of frustration.

And for the first time she could ever recall, Sofi felt a twinge of sympathy for the woman.

The rejection. The years of disapproval. Sofi's eyes fought tears of her own.

"Everything I've done has been for this company. Everything," her mom said slowly. As if she were voicing it more to the camera than to Gaines. "I let them test my own children. Let them use them in the games to further our research so we could *help* people. I lost my first child because we couldn't get the cure fast enough—and even after I'd lost her, I left my other kids to pursue that cure for others. But this? This is too much. I wanted a better world for my kids, Gaines. Not a better world at the cost of them."

The vid ended.

She also sent this over. Looks like some coding from Corp 30. Not sure what her purpose was, but there you go.

Sofi opened the file and scanned through it in three seconds. It was some of the deleted items regarding Shilo they'd been searching for that night back at Mom's Basement, along with the stripped code from Corp 24.

She frowned. And then her lungs imploded. She'd recognize that coding style anywhere.

It was Heller's.

48

MIGUEL

MIGUEL STARED AT HIS HANDHELD AS THE VID OF SOFI'S MOM and messages from Ranger that Vic had mirrored to him from Sofi's screen ended.

"Miguel?" Vic said after a sec.

"Yeah. I got it." He clenched his jaw. "Gracias, Vic."

He looked up.

And clicked his earcom. "Hey, Heller, you there?"

A pause. "I'm here. Sofi's not, though. I think her com's broken or something. Why?"

"Where you at, dude? I'm gonna come find you."

49

SOFI

SOFI FOUND HIM IN THE ROOM NEXT TO THE ONE THE DELONESE had walked out of.

She was shaking. Her teeth chattering in fury even as her skin felt like someone had set it on fire. "What have you done, Heller?" She walked up behind him.

"What? Nothing, Sof. I haven't done anything." He glanced behind her. "Where's Miguel?"

She stared at him. Then stepped closer and lifted her screen with Ranger's message. "We have known each other for three years, and I have *never* not trusted you. So tell me again," she whispered. "What've you done?"

"Hey, I swear, whatever you're seeing isn't me. You're reading into things." He raised his hands in the air as if defensive. "You're just upset we've not found Shilo, but don't take it out on me, okay?"

"How'd you get away from the Colinade the day of the explosion?"

"*What?* I told you."

She shook her head. "No. No, you never told me. That night I was heading over to meet you at the Basement—I asked. But you never answered."

His Adam's apple bobbed as she watched him swallow.

"How did you escape the Colinade?" she said softer.

His gaze grew darker. Glassier. As his breath began to stir heavier. "I tried to help you in the Colinade, Sof. I even warned you—I yelled for you to get back from the window." He was growing agitated. His hands and eyes animated as if trying to persuade her to understand. "I yelled it twice and then I grabbed your arm and pulled you just before the explosion. Don't you remember? And I was protecting you from your brother. He'd been infected for years with their genetics."

She stared, unable to answer.

Sofi was choking now, her body wracking with dry, cracking breaths that were breaking into her words. "*What* did they pay you?"

"Nothing. They paid nothing. Don't you see? It's not about me. It's about you. About our future. About Earth's future."

She dropped the handheld, shoved him against the wall, and hissed, "Liar. What'd they promise you, Heller? Because you cannot look me full in the face right now and tell me that you sacrificed me, you sacrificed our team, my *brother*, for this."

"Not you. I saved you. Just before the blast I pulled you away." His hand reached for her hair. To pet it. To comb it. She didn't know what the heck he was trying to do. She shoved him harder and yanked her hair away.

He didn't seem to notice. "It's what I've been trying to show you since the explosion," he said more excitedly. "That you don't need any of that. Your mom. Ms. Gaines. Miguel. I'm the one who will always be there."

Sofi's heart stopped. What was Heller saying?

His lips turned an odd shade of white, making his smile look like the stiff plastic on the dolls she used to play with. "I'd think you'd be thanking me, Sof."

"Thanking you? For what? Hijacking our system and almost killing my brother?" Her stomach began to shake. Like a mini earthquake starting in her gut and spreading out through her veins with the warning that something was about to open up inside her chest. And whatever it was, their friendship would not recover. Heller would not recover. *She* would not recover.

He moved his face closer in the eerie pink light, his expression softening, becoming clearer. More tender. "For saving you."

What the—?

He patted her shoulder. "Don't you see? I protected you. I've always been protecting you. Here—*now.* This whole trip. And before. I helped the Corps, but I didn't let them harm you. I'd never harm you."

She wrenched away from his sweaty palm. What was he talking about? The shaking grew harder, making her lungs ache. She was disgusted by his touch, his breath. The way he was looking at her . . .

"I made them sign off on it in my agreement to assist them. Ms. Gaines, CEO Hart—they needed to protect the evidence."

She shook her head. "Heller." She dropped her voice. Steadied it. Strengthened it. "This isn't you. You are one of *us.* You're the normal one—the good one. You're my *friend.*"

His eyes flashed. "I yanked you away and then dove through the door. I saved you, Sofi!" His voice was getting louder now, evoking fears they'd draw the Delonese's attention. "I saved both of us! That's what matters!"

"Heller, I . . ." She shook her head again and choked on the words. "What have you done?"

He smiled and shrugged.

She stalled. Dangit, why couldn't she stop shaking?

"Sofi." He calmed his breathing and tone. As if speaking to a child or wild animal or butterfly that was likely to flit away in the summer breeze. "We need the Delonese's technology."

"Not at the cost of our children, Heller. Not at the cost of Shilo."

He spread his hands out as if he were opening an imaginary holoscreen to visually explain a game. "I didn't know about the kids here or the body parts. I swear—I didn't know they were taking them for other . . . *experiments*. But a few human lives in trade for the tech and resources and energy the Delonese offer? Compromise is the only way we survive. Maybe choosing to sacrifice a few for the greater good isn't always black and white."

Her throat was quivering now. Apparently so were her hands and arms, and suddenly there was water on her cheeks, leaking from her eyes. "Heller, you sacrificed my brother. Even if he's not dead, you were willing to let him die—to kill him."

"I had to—don't you see that? Our world—the Corps—humanity must protect our future. It's a responsibility we all have."

"Then you should've sacrificed your own life for your cause rather than choose another."

He stopped and frowned, his expression turning thoroughly confused. "But they need me."

She stared at him as the tears kept falling and her legs went weak and her chest began shivering at the horror of not just his words . . . but his absolute elitist belief behind them.

And then she punched him across the jaw hard enough to knock him out.

50

MIGUEL

MIGUEL'S HANDSCREEN BLIPPED AND A MESSAGE POPPED UP. He glanced down as he desperately made his way through the maze of rooms and hallways that had all begun to look the same. White rooms with shiny white floors and rows and rows of med cots. "Sofi," he whispered.

"Sofi!"

Why wasn't her earcom working anymore?

"Miguel, you there?"

He jumped, then swiped the screen. "Vic?"

"Heya, dude. I'm sorry, but I thought you might wanna see this right away." The AI's blue eyes stared up at his. "After hearing Alis and Ms. Gaines, I decided to run a different kind of search—you know, on Corp 30's medical files. And I came across this." She moved her hand and slid a vid from her holodesk onto the screen. Her voice adding quietly, "Please tell Sofi I'm sorry."

The image lit up the dim. It was definitely a Delonese file, newer than any created from Earth tech, but still older than what he usually saw of theirs. It was angled from the ceiling peering down upon a scene. In this same type of room, same flooring, same weird overbright lights he was currently standing under.

The audio was silent, but in the vid he could see Sofi swearing up a storm while strapped down to a hoverbed.

Oh gad.

Miguel began to run faster.

51

SOFI

"SHILO!" SOFI WAS SHOUTING NOW. HE WAS HERE, SOMEWHERE—she knew that as surely as she knew this place. The room she'd stepped into after leaving Heller was all white with bright lights and those doors—endless doors. She recognized it from her dreams as strong as her own reality. Her gaze bounced around frantically while her stomach roiled because *all of this* was too familiar.

Oh, Shi.

There. The door at the end of the hall. White. Sterile, just like the rest of the floor and walls that were lit and bathed in fake sunlight.

Sofi, something in her head cautioned.

She ignored it and began running for the room—even as everything within reeled and bucked and screamed to stop—until it became a heartbeat in her head, chanting, *Don't go in there, don't go in there, oh heck, Sofi, don't go in there.*

Sofi, her head yelled. Except she didn't care. She wasn't listening.

She busted through the door and slammed into a blank space of blackness. She stalled as the sterile scent of her nightmares hit her full in the face. Blinding. Confusing her.

She shoved the door open all the way, and the light flicked on to reveal a medical room unlike the others they'd seen.

She froze.

Something clicked. The smells. The plastic curtains hanging like partitions around the metal cots. The showerheads that she knew—from an experience more real than any dreams she'd had of them over the past years—contained a sanitizer that burned so bad she thought her skin was sloughing off. The needles gleaming in the warm glow that shot her body up with chemicals and cured things like the asthma she'd been miraculously healed of. Before they took a load of her blood.

Sofi leaned down and threw up as other images began flickering in front of her eyes. Faster recollections.

Memories.

As the realization finally dawned that, oh gad, this wasn't just about Shilo.

She had been here before.

Seven years ago.

52

MIGUEL

MIGUEL SLIPPED IN BEHIND SOFI AND TOOK IN THE ROOM, THE vomit, the expressions of grief and horror and dawning on her face as his handscreen continued its display. Revealing a different scene, from years past, that had taken place in this same room. The sound suddenly clicked on the vid, and the entire space echoed with the happenings.

Every hum. Every sob. Every scream.

Sofi blinked and turned around, her hand sliding up to grip the owl at her throat. And looked into his eyes.

As the vid in his hand kept playing . . .

53

SOFI

TEN-YEAR-OLD SOFI CAME TO, LYING FLAT ON HER BACK in some type of white shower stall, with a headache the size of World War III. It took a moment for her eyes to adjust to the blaring light overhead, and when they did, the Delonese medic in a white suit was standing over her smelling like sanitizer. And she was completely and awkwardly naked.

"Where's my brother?" she snarled.

The medic said nothing, just turned and strode out of the stall. Sofi twisted her neck about, jerking against the metal straps, straining to glimpse him. "Where is he?" she screamed. "What's happening? I want—" Her voice squelched off as her asthmatic lungs issued a swift kick to her throat.

Calm down before you can't breathe. Use your brain, Sofi. Look around. What can you see?

Closing her eyes, she forced her mind to cool and focus, and block out the sanitized smell burning her nose. *So what do they want with us? And where's Shilo?*

Sofi turned to assess the plastic curtains surrounding her. She could see through to what looked like rows of more shower stalls matching her own. They were filled with the other kids, all strapped down like her. Her lungs twisted.

Then the little boy to the right looked up and met her gaze. Shilo.

"Sofi?" his small, five-year-old voice asked.

Before she could answer, a buzzer blew so deafening she thought her eardrums might burst. It was followed by a wall of scalding water flooding their bodies—the intensity beyond brutal as it slammed her bones.

Sofi lay there unable to move, whimpering like a baby as her skin bubbled and boiled in the most excruciating pain. Certain the spray was peeling chunks from her flesh as the aliens melted their bodies.

Maybe they've decided we're not worth keeping alive, Sofi thought as from the stall next to her Shilo was screaming.

"Shi, are you okay?" she yelled.

Either way, she was going to kill every last one of them.

Just as quickly as it turned on, the water shut off and the pain evaporated in seconds. "Shilo, answer me!" Sofi demanded in hysterics. Her arms were bruising from fighting the straps keeping her down.

He didn't answer, but after a moment Sofi could see him moving. Gasping like he'd gotten the wind knocked out of him. But alive and his skin appeared whole and unharmed. Tears filled her eyes. *It's okay. He's okay.*

"I'm all right," he finally mumbled, and a million relieved breaths escaped her chest.

"Are you, Sofi?"

"I'm fine," she assured him. She had to be fine when it came to him. But she peered down at her body anyhow cuz she wasn't actually sure she was fine. She scrunched up her fingers and toes—they still existed—and was shocked to find that, like Shilo's, her skin was still magically intact. As brown as ever. "Like good farming soil," as Papa used to say. And weirdly smooth. Shiny.

Hairless.

A rustling from Shilo's section. "Sofi, I'm scared."

Her heart broke and filled with fury all at once. "Oh, buddy. Hold on," she said, and then began yelling for the Delonese man, wherever he was. From outside her stall, he uttered a string of words and the buzzer went off again.

The next shower blast was so cold it brought bone-wrenching coughs up from her chest and throat. As if someone were yanking the tissue from her lungs and slicing out the asthmatic cells. Over her heaving and hacking up of who-knows-what, the sound of the other kids' shrieking carried into her stall, Shilo's the loudest of all. When Sofi's coughing finally subsided, she was still thrashing against the straps, trying to escape and reach Shi.

The water clicked off and another spigot turned on. This one shut out all noise as it pumped forth a whirlwind of dry air. The heat drowned out her shivers, and when it stopped she was completely dry and her body felt more alive than ever before. Like someone breathed inside of her and filled Sofi's lungs to the brim with life and cleanness.

She heard the shower curtain shift behind her, and then the Delonese man loomed his giant forehead over Sofi's face. Suddenly a sharp sting hit her chest, and she realized he'd injected her with something.

Sofi's screech of surprise and anger was met by matching ones down the rows of stalls. She tried to lift her head to butt it against the alien's face, but her neck muscles refused to move.

Her limbs had turned to gummy worms. She couldn't even look over at Shilo.

A shudder of cold enveloped her. Like the winter breezes come too early on the farm. The kind threatening deadly frost for the harvest. Except, this breeze was inside of her.

She stared up at the Delonese, wondering what the heck he'd just done to her.

And then she felt it. The click.

Terrifying. Exhilarating.

Like a button just got pushed.

Slowing her cells. Her blood. Her core.

Freezing.

Her lungs, her asthma, her mind . . . It just shut off.

Like a switch.

MY PLAYLIST OF THANK-YOUS

I'VE NEVER WRITTEN TO MUSIC BEFORE! NO MATTER HOW HARD I've wished to do so, my brain simply found it too distracting. Until this story. This book was inked out with headphones on, melodies blaring—as if the words refused to come unless the bass was dropping them into place. And oh man, I hope you can feel that in these pages, friend. That soul. The artists I love whose chaos of songs helped weave this idea into an adventure.

I hope their subtle refrains drive the beat of this book.

And just like the soundtrack for this story, I firmly believe there's a soundtrack for this life. Songs that exist and breathe in the forms of people—soul harmonies to which our world spins, and without whom none of our writings or life stories would be possible or whole.

So this is for them. The people whose melodic selves ignite the world.

Peter, my husband of nineteen years, you are my cure. And I'm in love with you.

Rilian, Avalon, and Korbin. You sprinkle stardust on everything.

Bex, Daisy, Amanda, Jodi, Paul, and the rest of my Thomas Nelson/HarperCollins family. I'm so grateful to be by your side. Thanks for giving me wings to fly.

Danielle Smith, brilliant agent, precious friend, and one who brings cookies when I'm under pressure.

Jeanette, for always having the final edit. And for reminding me that walking the great unknown only increases faith.

Lee Hough. Still rocking the free world, man.

Mom and Dad, for making this a wonderful world.

Kati, Dave, Jon, Daniel, James, and your families, as well as my in-laws and relatives. For the laughter and conversations that promise, at the soul of it, we aren't ever really getting older.

Lori Barrow. For continually awakening my soul to the reality that I was made to meet my Maker.

Jay Asher, for the family-friendship and unforgettable Thirteen Reasons Why movie adventures. And for keeping the hysteria at bay.

Marissa Meyer, Nadine Brandes, Courtney Stevens, Katie Ganshert, CJ Redwine, Wendy Higgins, Jonathan Maberry, Sara Jo West, Sara Ella, Kristy Cambron, Katherine Reay, Jennie and Manders of FYA, y'all move in mysterious ways that make me better.

Allen Arnold, Jim Rubart, and my Wildly Unbalanced Writers. Innagaddadavida, babies.

My Father's House family, youth, and leaders. Highs and lows, we won't let go.

Every reader, blogger, publicist, bookstagrammer, person who's written or e-mailed or commented or come to signings or conferences or school visits or simply just shared a piece of your soul with me. THANK YOU. You are the world.

Jesus. Because you are all this heart exists for. <3

I love you guys.

~m

DISCUSSION QUESTIONS

WARNING: SPOILERS AHEAD!

1. Sofi and her mom have a complicated relationship. From Sofi's perspective, her mother has put herself and career above Sofi and Shilo. But from her mom's viewpoint, everything she's done has been to help her corporation save her children and others. How would you feel if you were Sofi? How would you feel if you were her mother? What do you think Sofi needs from her mom as they move forward from here—and vice versa?

2. Even though Sofi's mom hasn't handled every decision as a parent should, do you think she tried? Are there things your parents have done (or haven't) that influence the way you see yourself? Are there things that *their* parents did that influenced them? What are some of the positive perspectives you've developed due to a parent in your life? What are some of the negatives that you could turn into a positive?

3. What backgrounds and cultural factors may have influenced the characters' choices and personalities? For instance—Miguel and his family of origin, Inola's feminine strength from her heritage, Sofi's strength from her mom, etc.?
4. Was Sofi really picking up on visions from Shilo, or were they flashbacks of her own past with the Delonese? Either way, where do you think Shilo is (and is he alive)?
5. The idea of life beyond our galaxy has fueled fantastic books, movies, and scientific theories. What do you believe—is there life out there? And if so, will we ever meet it?
6. Sofi's kind heart and innocence unknowingly helped Miguel find himself (by changing the way he viewed himself). Do you think that's possible—that encountering others who believe the best of us can impact our view of ourselves? Do you think Miguel was wise to pull away for a time—to figure himself out? Do you think either of them ultimately needs the other, or can they become whole on their own?
7. In the space shuttle Miguel tells Sofi, "Real relationships are a death trap only because they force you to die daily to shallowness. To care about the person more than your pride." What do you think of that statement? Is true love a daily dying to selfishness? Is dying to selfishness different from giving up yourself (your soul, identity, and self)?
8. One of the book's themes is the evaporation of Sofi. Or rather, what feels like the evaporation of things she thought she knew about herself, her past, and (by the end of the book) her beliefs about others. Have you ever felt like that—as if everything you have is being stripped away? Can this ever be a good thing? What benefit can come from it? Do you think

the person Sofi truly is will rise from the process, or will she disappear completely? Who *is* Sofi ultimately? Who are *you*?

9. Miguel's life has been strongly influenced by the guilt of shirking his duty of protecting his family. How did this belief play out in shaping his opinions about himself? How did that impact his choices and behaviors? How did it impact the way he treated others? Why are our own beliefs about ourselves so important—and what should shape them?
10. If the idea of Miguel or the Delonese harming kids in this book made you uncomfortable, it was for a reason. A large part of this story is centered around human trafficking, which is a very real crisis across our globe today. And while Miguel was in fact rescuing children (yay, Miguel!), we need more heroes like him in real life. At the time of this writing, 27,000 humans are enslaved and oppressed—and they need voices to speak up for them. To learn more about human trafficking and how you can (1) protect yourself, (2) protect others, and (3) help bring freedom to those who desperately need it, visit A21.org/. And if you are currently one of those 27,000—then please know this: This book is for you. It is your voice being raised for the world to hear, because you are not alone. We're here fighting for you. And we will not stop.

STORM
SIREN
MARY WEBER

AN EXCERPT FROM
STORM SIREN BY MARY WEBER

CHAPTER 1

"FOURTEEN CIRCLES FOR FOURTEEN OWNERS."

I shade my eyes to block the sun's reflection off the distant mountains currently doused in snow and smoke and flesh-eating birds. The yellow flags above me snap sharp and loud in the breeze as if to emphasize my owner's words that yes, she's quite aware such a high count is utterly ridiculous.

Waiting for it . . .

"Fourteen?" the sweaty merchant says.

Ha! There it is. Eleven years of repeatedly being sold, and it's sad, really, how familiar I've become with this conversation.

Today, if Brea has her way, I will meet my fifteenth, which I suppose should actually bother me. But it doesn't.

Brea nods. "Fourteen."

I smirk and turn to watch a gimpy minstrel roaming through the marketplace, which is the closest I've ever been to Faelen's High Court. The poor guy is singing so wretchedly off-key, I want to giggle, except he might be newly returned from the war front, so I don't. Besides, his odd version of the old ballad "The Monster and the Sea of Elisedd's Sadness" reminds me of my home up in the Fendres. *Have you been there?* I want to ask him.

Instead, I look over as the enormous merchant grunts his nervousness and retreats from me, giving the ground a superstitious spit. He eyes Brea. "Fourteen owners says either yer lyin' or she's got the dark-death disease. Whichever it is, you best get her out of my way. I got a money business to run." He makes to hurry off toward the selling stand, almost tripping in his fur-trimmed shoes.

I grin. *Yes, run away in your too-little boots.*

"Wait!" Brea grabs his arm. "Nym doesn't have the disease. She's just . . ."

The merchant scowls at her grip on his sleeve.

She releases it, but her roundish face turns stony with determination. "She's just too uppity for the poorer folk, that's all. There's only so much a master can take of a servant who thinks she's made of better than the rest."

What in hulls? Is she off her chump? My laugh bubbles up and I choke it back, waiting for *her* to choke on her lie. He creeps closer and slides a look of dislike down my partially hooded face, my chin, my half-cloaked body. "She don't look uppity. She don't even look decent enough for the favor houses."

Whoa. I bite back a prickly remark about his mum birthing him in one of those dung havens and look away. Neither of them deserves a reaction. Using my practiced haughty pose, I face the lively crowd gathered like giddy children in front of the selling platform. Five, ten, fifty people. They're all smiling as if the circus with its panther monkeys and manic dwarves were performing instead of a fat guy in little boots exploiting children. Seems even decent women are desperate for extra hands while the men are off fighting a war we've no hope of winning.

The merchant chews his puffy lip and studies me, like he

expects me to help coerce him. *Is he jesting?* I raise an eyebrow and glare at him until, finally, he grunts again and pulls up the cuff on my right arm.

I stiffen.

His gloved fingers run over each thread tattooed around my wrist like tiny bracelets. "One. Two. Three . . ." He numbers the circles slowly, fourteen in a row inked into my skin with the juice of the black mugplant. I almost feel like I should clap for him.

Good job, I mouth. *You know how to count.*

The merchant's face twists into a snarl. He gives me a vicious pinch below my elbow and pushes my sleeve higher up my arm onto my shoulder. I shiver and, narrowing my eyes, start to pull away, but Brea leans into me.

"You hold yourself together," she sputters close to my ear. "And for fool's sake, keep your hair covered, or so help me, Nymia, I'll break your fingers again."

I bite my tongue but refuse her the satisfaction of dipping my gaze to my slightly misshapen left hand, which I'm now curling into a fist.

"How old are you?" the dealer growls in my face.

"Seventeen," I growl back.

"When was she first sold?" This question is for Brea, but I feel his bristly glove squeeze my skin as if he expects me to alert him if she's dishonest.

"Age six. Her parents died when she was five and then she lived a short time with a midwife who had no use for her." She says this last part with a slice of disgust in her voice that's directed at me. And as much as I try to force it down, the hateful shame swells up to eat holes in my chest. She's got me on that one. Two parents, one midwife, and fourteen owners I've ruined, the latest being Brea's own husband. And it doesn't matter that I tried to warn every single one of them.

The merchant's eyes constrict. "There somethin' else wrong with her yer not tellin' me?"

"Nothing's wrong with her. She's perfectly fine. Just give me three draghts and she's yours."

"Three draghts?" I murmur. "How generous."

Either she doesn't hear or chooses to ignore me as the merchant rubs his huge, stubbled jowls and considers the offer. Although I can already sense he'll take it. Three is cheap. Beyond cheap. It's pathetic. I consider feeling insulted.

The minstrel limps by, practically giddy as he continues his fabulously bad recount of the Monster and the Sea. "'Twas the night compassion *forsoooooook* us." He's singing, referring to the night an agreement was struck between Faelen's past king and the great, flesh-eating Draewulf. The price of which had been Faelen's children. "And the big sea, she roared and spit up her foam at the shape-shifter's trickery and our *foooooolish* king."

I swallow and feel my amusement over how much he's enjoying himself catch in my throat at what I know comes next. "The ocean, she's begging for our salvation. Begging for blood that will set our children free."

And for a moment I swear I can feel the sea waves calling, begging *my* blood to set us all free.

Except just as with the Draewulf, my blood comes at a price.

"Blast the crippled croaker! Would someone put him out of his misery?" the merchant shouts.

A louder shout and then a cheer interrupt the inharmonious tune. Someone's just been bought for a higher amount than expected. The merchant looks at the stage behind us and smiles.

Then, without glancing at me, he says, "Done," and fishes into his hip bag to drop three draghts into Brea's open palm.

Congratulations, Nym. You're officially the cheapest slave sold in Faelen history.

Brea hands the reins of my collar to the merchant and turns from him, but not so quickly as to confirm his suspicion that there's something else amiss with me. Just before she leaves, she leans into me again, and her black hair brushes against my cheek.

"Pity you weren't born a boy," she whispers. "They would've just killed you outright. Saved us all from what you are." And then she's gone.

And I won't even pretend I'm sorry.

The merchant yanks my leather straps like he's bridling a goat and leads me behind him to the side of the selling platform where twelve other slaves wait, tethered to a lengthy stretch of chain. Before he bends down to tie me in line, he pulls a thin knife from his right bootie and puts it against my chin. "Try to escape, little imp, and this blade'll find you faster than a bolcrane goin' for a baby." He breathes an extra puff of foul air up my nostrils and grins when I squirm in revulsion.

So, of course, I do what any self-respecting, uncooperative person would do. I spit into his annoying face.

"You little . . ." His knife is as fast as his fury, and before I can move he's cut into my skin just beneath my jaw.

I cry out, and then bite my tongue because he doesn't deserve to see my pain.

"I'll sell you off in pieces if I have to," he says, growling.

"Try," I mutter.

Obviously the heat's gotten to me because I'm smiling a bit crazy in spite of the sting—until his arm rises. I barely have time to brace before the back of his hand finds my mouth with a force that nearly knocks me over. Warm blood gushes from my lip to join the trickle on my neck, and suddenly I'm blinking to keep the whirling world in focus. Curse him.

He yells at someone I can't see, "Get her up front and be rid of her. Now!"

The assistant pushes me to the low base of the stand. Hands shove me onto the stage as a small girl with red hair, who can scarcely be older than five, is being led off the other side. My stomach twists at her frightened expression, at the terror-filled memory of my first selling—the brief image of coming home to the midwife after my curse had wiped out her entire herd of sheep. Within hours I was sold to a man who gave a whole new meaning to the word *monster*.

The merchant's assistant is standing beside me. He looms over the buyers and makes up attributes about me, of which he knows nothing and believes none of. *What a sideshow.*

The bidding starts low. Despite the aching slash in my neck, I stare into the faces of the individuals yelling out prices, evaluating them as they freely evaluate me. Their ballooning silk hats and ruff led shawls, I swear, look strikingly similar to a pair of lady's panties I saw in the sale booth last year. These people appear well-off compared to most I've known in our kingdom. Not as fancy as the politicians from the High Court, but clearly living above the poverty of the peasants. Panty shawls and all.

The bidding begins to climb with the same frenzy the onlookers have been possessed by for the past half hour. Suddenly, a male voice clamors above the rest, "Take off the hood and give us a better look at her. Let's see what she's made of."

I scowl and lean forward, jerking on my reins to yell back, "Why aren't you off helping win the war, you wastrel?"

"Right there, let's see her!"

"Yeah! Take off her cloak!"

The assistant grabs my shoulder. I bristle, but his hand is already reaching for my hood.

I shove an elbow into his skinny stomach, hard enough to knock the wind from him. "Don't touch me."

He yelps. Staggers back like the weakling he is.

Then the merchant swears, and before I can blink he climbs onto the stage and lunges for my wrists.

I kick him in his crotch.

He screams but doesn't crumble. A noise erupts behind me and just as I'm turning to check, two men grab my arms and the merchant is up and plows into my side, nearly knocking me over. He grips my cloak and yanks it off in one harsh sweep.

Before I can count to one, the three of them are stumbling back and tripping off the stage.

The crowd falls silent.

The story continues in *Storm Siren* by Mary Weber.

CONNECT WITH ME

Mary loves to connect with readers! Here's where you can find her online:

maryweber.com

Instagram:
MaryWeberAuthor

Facebook:
Mary Weber, Author

Twitter:
@MChristineWeber

School, Skype, or
conference visits:
mary@mchristineweber.com

ABOUT THE AUTHOR

PHOTO BY SARAH KATHLEEN PHOTOGRAPHY

MARY WEBER IS THE AUTHOR OF the Scholastic Pick, Christy, Carol, and INSPY Award winning young adult novel, *Storm Siren*, and the Storm Siren Trilogy. As a conference and avid school speaker, Weber's passion is helping others find their voice amid a too-loud world. In her spare time she sings 80s songs to her three muggle children and ogles her husband who looks strikingly like Wolverine. They live in California, which is perfect for stalking tacos, Joss Whedon, and the ocean.